The Power Of Neighbourhood Planning

...

And How To Make An *Effective* Neighbourhood Plan

Peter Edwards

Published May 2020

ISBN 978-1-9164315-4-6

Bath Publishing Limited
27 Charmouth Road
Bath
BA1 3LJ
Tel: 01225 577810
email: info@bathpublishing.co.uk
www.bathpublishing.co.uk

Bath Publishing is a company registered in England: 5209173

Registered Office: As above

This book is dedicated to my sons,

Harry and Willie

- the neighbourhood planners of the future!

Acknowledgements

The ever-present support and encouragement of my wife, Hannah, is invaluable and has made a very significant contribution to this book.

Also by way of acknowledgement I would like to sincerely thank Helen Lacey and David Chaplin whose friendly, collaborative and professional approach makes Bath Publishing a pleasure to work with.

Contents

Chapter 3: Elements of Development Control   27

Planning conditions   27

Planning obligations   31

Planning enforcement   33

Chapter 5: Making a Neighbourhood Development Plan

The neighbourhood plan in force 146

Chapter 6: Neighbourhood Plans and Housing 155

Table of Cases

Table of Legislation

EU Legislation

Statutes

Statutory Instruments

Chapter 1: Introduction

Why read a book on neighbourhood planning when there's already an abundance of online material, guidance notes, social media comment and other information available in addition to the increasing weight of legislation on the subject?

As well as town and parish councillors and the committed parishioners already involved with, or considering, a neighbourhood plan, the intended readership is far wider and includes the increasing number of professionals with an interest in this growing component of planning law. Ultimately, this book should be read by anyone interested in influencing how the area in which they live is developed in the coming years.

For all the material on how to get involved in neighbourhood planning and how to produce a neighbourhood development plan ("NDP"), there is relatively little guidance on how to achieve particular objectives from this brave new – it is still relatively new and constantly evolving – world of localism. Most of the guidance follows a fairly routine box-ticking approach to producing an NDP without going into the often quite tricky detail or offering much advice on how to ensure your neighbourhood plan does the job intended of it.

A brand new NDP that has attracted glowing praise from an examiner and comfortable majority support at referendum is all well and good, but perhaps not so worthwhile if the first developer to really test the plan rides roughshod over its planning policies! A question that anyone making a neighbourhood plan – or a Neighbourhood Development Order ("NDO") for that matter – should constantly keep in mind is: what will the finished product add to the existing local plan policies or permitted development rights? What will it actually achieve?

As with so many subjects in this information age there are masses of mainstream sources all saying essentially the same thing and all towing the party line but very few offering genuinely critical analysis or detailed guidance on how to accomplish the results that you – the reader, consumer, parish councillor, resident – would like to see.

Neighbourhood planning is one of those subjects that encourages those who endlessly tweet, post, comment and generally promote their thoughts at every opportunity, to do so. But how many of them really understand the background to localism, the place of neighbourhood planning in the wider planning system and the political imperatives it is intended to address?

Many of those who have worked tirelessly to produce a neighbourhood plan seem to think, sometimes with an air of complacency, that their job is done and they can rest safe in the knowledge that their NDP will protect their town or village from unwanted development for the foreseeable future. But is that really the case?

Are the examination and referendum the real tests of a neighbourhood development plan or is it how an NDP affects development control decisions that ultimately determines how successful it is?

Whether or not there is a neighbourhood plan in your area, what other ways are there of influencing local planning decisions?

In recognition of the fact that more and more people want a say in development proposals and development plans, the planning system increasingly provides opportunities for local influence through representations and consultation as well as neighbourhood plans. However, an opportunity to have your say is often a very different thing from genuine influence. Why is that and what, if anything, can be done about it?

This book answers these questions and provides other insights into how neighbourhood planning, in the broadest sense, works (and sometimes doesn't). It explains how best to try to influence the shape and character of the place you live, whether or not you are a local councillor, within the context of the planning system.

There are many planning rules and procedures that are neither well known nor well used. This book also touches on how town and parish councils in particular can invoke some of these lesser known planning mechanisms to achieve particular objectives.

The whole concept of neighbourhood planning and localism is still in its infancy and offers huge potential for people to really organise themselves and directly manage development planning for their communities, to find local solutions to local problems and protect, at least to some extent, the character and culture of an area from centralist control. This, too, is considered in more detail later in the book.

The starting point for any consideration of neighbourhood planning is an overview of the wider planning system; its origins, legislative framework and main functions (*Chapter 2 – The Planning System*). It is important to understand key elements of development control and planning enforcement (*Chapter 3 – Elements of Development Control*).

We then look at neighbourhood planning in more detail, considering the principal statutory provisions and the various elements that comprise 'localism' in planning (*Chapter 4 – Neighbourhood Planning*).

How to go about making a neighbourhood plan and seeing the project through to a successful conclusion is the subject of the next chapter (*Chapter 5 – Making a Neighbourhood Development Plan*).

Neighbourhood plan makers can no longer afford to ignore, even if they might want to, the thorny and increasingly complicated subject of housing and housing supply. 'Housing' is therefore the one substantive planning subject area that warrants its own dedicated chapter (*Chapter 6 – Neighbourhood Plans and Housing*).

The various other ways of influencing local planning decisions are explained (*Chapter 7 – Other Means of Influence*) before concluding by considering the full and as yet undiscovered scope of neighbourhood planning and the future potential for localism in planning (*Chapter 8 –Which way next? ... The Future for Neighbourhood Planning*).

Ultimately, this book is intended to illustrate how town and country planning has a very real, physical and practical effect on all our lives and how, through the nascent neighbourhood planning regime, each and every one of us can have a say in how we shape the environment around us.

This book is not intended to be the last word on planning or neighbourhood planning, rather that within these pages – as well as a factual analysis of the current state of play – are observations and ideas that may stir new ways of thinking about our planning system and encourage those of all ages to become more involved in it.

The premise herein is that, although the legislative framework is essentially sound and has accommodated significant change since its inception, no part of the UK planning system really works as it should. The culture of the planning system is rather tired yet the concept of neighbourhood planning is a radical one that has great potential. That potential is not only largely unrealised but is now in danger of being suppressed by the centralist approach that it was surely intended, originally at least, to counter balance.

It is hoped that this book may act as a catalyst, a forum for discussion and a call to action, and therefore any thoughts, comments and suggestions on what you are about to read will be welcomed.

Chapter 2: The Planning System

History and overview

The planning system as we know it today was introduced in 1947 by the first Town and Country Planning Act, to put in place the legislative framework for the planning and control of development and the creation of authorities to administer those functions. The detail of that system has changed numerous times since then but it was only after 1947, or from 1 July 1948 to be exact, that the basic rule that 'any development requires planning permission' was introduced.

Prior to the Second World War, the regulation of development was not universal and was limited primarily to imposing spatial planning and public health requirements on the mass urban housebuilding taking place in the early twentieth century.

The imperative for a more comprehensive system of planning was essentially twofold; the increasing pace and variety of emerging development and the need to rebuild urban areas after the War. It was envisaged that new towns and garden cities would provide some of the housing that was needed. This line of thinking was, in turn, inspired partly by the utopian vision of well planned, self-contained and essentially self-sufficient settlements providing in one place all the necessities, services and amenities for modern living.

At the heart of the utopian garden city movement was the concept of the 'public good', with development corporations buying up (by compulsory purchase if necessary) the land needed and recycling the development value profits, or betterment, into the project; that was the theory anyway. Several versions of this idea did become reality, perhaps the best example being Letchworth Garden City.

This is not a history book and there is little point here in analysing in any detail even such an important era in the emergence of the UK planning system, though the immediate post-war period is a useful reference point for a number of principles and observations that are worth keeping in mind.

First and foremost, the universal UK-wide coverage of development control established in 1947 under the title of 'town and country planning' means just that; it applies to town *and* country. The UK planning system[1] is universal in its coverage and effect; it doesn't just deal with buildings or towns, it affects every square metre of land in the country. The planning system is informed by and reflects land use of all types and there is nothing more fundamental or important to human existence than how land is used.

Secondly, planning is a legislative system and evolves through common law (case law precedents) to set out how development plans should be made and development control decisions taken. It is a system of public administrative law. Fundamentally, and in its universal application at least, it is a regulatory system. The two primary functions, 'development planning' and 'development control' (though now known as 'development management', the function is essentially one of control) are both regulatory in nature. This is important and is at the heart of many misconceptions about what the planning system should actually do – it also helps explain why 'planning' doesn't accomplish everything that many politicians and their advisors believe it should.

Thirdly, it is fundamental that because planning is a system of public law it was designed and intended to operate for the public good and in the public interest. Such terms are rarely used these days though the courts occasionally uphold these principles, as they have done in some notable planning decisions of recent years (for example in *Cherkley Court*[2] and *Welwyn*[3]). A system of public law requires transparency, fairness, observance of natural justice and impartial, objective decision-making based, where appropriate, on a proper assessment of relevant evidence. Such principles should be applied universally, in favour of individuals as much as, arguably more than, corporate interests.

As well as directing development to the most appropriate locations, planning is also about protecting all parts of the country from inappropriate development. It is very much in the public interest that it should do both effectively. It is therefore also in the public interest that this system of public law should reflect the interests of individuals and communities as

---

[1]   Northern Ireland and Scotland are now disaggregated but have identical regimes and some aspects of the planning system in Wales is devolving. This book concentrates on the law and practice in England, which still to a large extent affects Wales also.

[2]   *R (oao) Cherkley Campaign Ltd v Mole Valley DC* [2013] EWHC 2582 (Admin).

[3]   *SoS for Communities and Local Government & Anor v Welwyn Hatfield BC* [2011] UKSC 15.

much as it facilitates the aspirations of developers.

Fourthly, whilst this is no more a book about politics than it is history, the politics of planning cannot be avoided. There may be relatively few planning topics that cause ideological, party political division but the planning system is inevitably invoked, and chastised, in pursuance of political objectives and to excuse political failures.

In terms of national politics, the main battleground is the number of houses successive governments claim to have built, even though in reality governments stopped building houses many years ago! Maybe it is because they actually have relatively little influence on the supply of new houses that all governments relentlessly claim to pursue rampant housebuilding (via policies that rarely achieve those objectives) and when housing targets are not met, the planning system is inevitably to blame. Few politicians will acknowledge that developers only build houses when it is sufficiently profitable for them to do so and that that is more dependent on various economic factors than it is on the planning system.

So, of course, planning is moulded by national politics, but it is in local decision-making, at district and parish level, that the politics of planning really heats up.

Fifthly, it is important to understand how the planning system, as a function of local government, is constrained by the level of public spending. Whilst local planning authorities ("LPAs") must adhere to national planning guidance in the form of the National Planning Policy Framework ("NPPF") and the Planning Practice Guidance ("PPG") that ministers can change on a whim, it is also significant how certain LPA planning functions are targeted by government incentives, bonuses and other forms of funding ostensibly directed at improving efficiency but really directed at producing certain quite specific development outcomes.

Governments like to make out that it is the inefficiency of the planning system that prevents more development and that the way to break that logjam is to incentivise planning departments to issue more planning permissions. Others would say, with some justification, that an efficient and well-functioning planning system should refuse as well as permit development, and should certainly refuse to permit inappropriate development. Maybe it is the quality of much of the development proposed that needs to improve more than the efficiency of the planning system.

The reality is that the regulatory function has been undermined by public spending cuts whilst grants or bonuses are awarded for selected outcomes; for example, the speed (rather than quality) of planning decisions (via the now outmoded Planning Performance Grants) and the number of planning permissions granted for housing, by way of the New Homes Bonus[4] (though the latter also takes into account empty homes brought back into use). This rather crude central government approach to planning is rather like military training; knock the stuffing out of it (through underfunding), then instil obedience (by only rewarding certain skills or functions).

Yet the wholesale recycling of planning gain or betterment to invest in development for the public good has never been fully resolved. No one wants to pay for the essential infrastructure elements of major new developments, least of all developers. UK governments have proved incapable of finding an efficient and reliable approach to harnessing private planning gain for the public good and many believe this has had, and continues to have, an adverse effect on the quality of resulting development.

The current mechanism for securing essential public infrastructure is the still relatively new Community Infrastructure Levy ("CIL"), payable upon commencement of development pursuant to a planning permission. How effectively the controversial CIL works in practice remains to be seen but there is no doubt that the under-resourcing of LPAs and the demotivating effects of that undermine the efficiency of the planning system and the quality of its output.

However, whilst the administration of the planning regime is all too often chaotic and inefficient, the fundamental legislative framework and legal principles behind it are generally coherent and well resolved.

It is worth considering the main elements and fundamental principles of the two main functions of the planning system, forward planning, or plan-making, and development control or in NPPF-speak 'decision-taking'.

---

4   https://www.gov.uk/government/publications/
    new-homes-bonus-final-allocations-2018-to-2019.

The functions of the planning system

What is "development"?

Operational development or change of use?

In simple terms, the purpose of the planning system is to plan for and to regulate development so it is essential to understand what is meant by "development".

There are very broadly two types of development defined by the Town and Country Planning Act 1990 (as amended) ("TCPA");[5]

- 'building works' – also known as 'operational development' – meaning "building, engineering, mining or other operations in, on, over or under land", and;

- "a material change in the use of buildings or other land".

This is a simplification of the statutory definition but nonetheless provides a starting point for understanding what is within the scope of the planning regime and the parameters within which development control operates.

Operational development includes works normally undertaken by a builder, though not works to the interior of a building or which do not materially affect the external appearance of a building. Demolition is operational development though in many cases it will be permitted development, as are many other types of operational development.

A material change of use is one that involves at least a change from one planning use class to another, so both the existing and the intended planning use class are significant. The various planning use classes and the actual uses they relate to are set out in the Town and Country Planning (Use Classes) Order 1987 (as amended) ("Use Classes Order" or "UCO").

Even from one use class to another, only a *material* change of use constitutes development requiring planning permission. What is material comes down to details individually assessed in each case, such as intensity of occupation, noise levels and traffic movements. An LPA will generally consider any change of use from one use class to another to be material so, although it may be possible to argue otherwise, that is the cautious

---

[5]   At Section 55, TCPA.

line to take. A further consideration is whether the intended change of use is permitted development.

Permitted development

Not all development within the aforementioned definitions requires planning permission as there are many types of operational development and changes of use that are classified as permitted development; these are set out in the Town and Country Planning (General Permitted Development) (England) Order 2015 (as amended) ("GPDO").

Under Schedule 2, GPDO, there are 19 Parts, each one setting out a different category of permitted development rights including development within the curtilage of a dwellinghouse, minor operations, changes of use, temporary buildings and uses, agricultural and forestry, retail and industrial and renewable energy.

The various classes of development permitted under the GPDO are numerous and the detailed rules and conditions relating to a particular class are notoriously complex. Some permitted development may be undertaken with no recourse to the LPA, such as the various classes of development under Part 1 of the GPDO; development within the curtilage of a dwellinghouse.

Others, including agricultural permitted development rights, and some permitted changes of use are subject to a prior notification procedure that requires the applicant to submit specified details of the proposed development to the LPA which may, in certain circumstances, then require further details to be submitted.

The prior notification procedure enables the LPA to scrutinise the proposals and within a specified statutory time period to respond to the applicant in one of several ways. The LPA may either determine that the proposal is not permitted development and a planning permission is needed; or it may require further details before deciding whether the proposal amounts to permitted development; or it can confirm that the proposal is permitted development and may proceed without the need for a planning application.

The general principle behind prior notification is that if the LPA does not respond at all within the prescribed statutory time period, the applicant may consider the proposed development to be permitted development and proceed accordingly. However, if material details that would take the proposal beyond the scope of the GPDO are omitted or misrepresented from the prior notification, then the development in question is not permitted and if undertaken without a planning permission, would constitute unauthorised development that could be subject to planning enforcement action.

Permitted development rights may be withdrawn in certain designated areas, such as a conservation area, by what is known as an Article 4 Direction issued by the LPA.

Suffice to say that a parish council should be well versed in permitted development rights and prior notification procedures if it is to discharge its planning functions and neighbourhood planning powers effectively. There is no point, for example, in preparing NDP planning policies dealing with development that is permitted development because the statutory provisions of the GPDO would prevail to allow the development in question regardless of the NDP policies.

So, although what constitutes development requiring planning permission can be complicated, the concept of 'development' is fundamental to planning; it is what the planning system has jurisdiction over.

Forward planning or plan-making

Forward planning is the making of development plans. A development plan will set out planning policies to guide the type, form, extent, design and sometimes the precise location of development within the plan area. The policies in the development plan will be the basis for development control decisions; that is, decisions on the determination of planning applications.

This, in principle, is all very straightforward yet it is the detailed scheme of forward planning and the length of time typically taken by planning authorities to produce their development plans that often complicate things.

This part of the planning system changes more frequently than any other as every incoming government believes it can usher in a new, more efficient and streamlined forward planning process. In this limited objective, none succeed. That is partly because of the complete mismatch of timeframes for achieving planning objectives and political objectives. Political objectives generally need to be fulfilled far more quickly which is why few politicians really understand, or want to understand, the planning process.

They – the politicians – are under constant pressure to achieve results before the next election which will never be more than five years away, often much less. The current scheme of forward planning is, in terms of the process anyway, probably as straightforward as it has been for many years. Yet generally, from initial evidence gathering through to adoption, it will take at least five years to produce a local plan and often considerably longer!

The reason the making of a development plan takes so long is that every policy in it has to be based on and tested against technical evidence on an ever increasing number of planning issues.

Those issues – affordable housing, flood risk, climate change, green travel plans, contaminated land and others – were barely on the radar of a local plan 20 years ago but now have to be resolved in fine detail before related planning policies can be lawfully adopted. Each of these subject areas is within the remit of an ever larger number of specialist bodies, technical advisors and interest groups who all need to be consulted at every stage of the plan-making process.

This inevitably leads to greater complexity. That is not the 'fault' of the planning system as politicians like to make out, rather the result of the number of issues the planning system has to process, arbitrate on and find solutions to.

That process – the forward planning or plan-making process – has to ensure that planned outcomes are acceptable in principle and workable in practice when scrutinised against all the other planning objectives. There is no point, for example, in allocating a site well served by public transport for much needed affordable housing if it is within a high-risk flood zone.

The detail of all planning policies and their likely consequences must be thoroughly tested with all interested parties before they become part of the development plan. The fact is that most national politicians, who idealise about a speedier planning system, are not interested in the details of the processes involved and therefore fail to understand why speed-ing up those processes is so difficult to achieve. Although efficiencies could certainly be made, the inherent complexities mean that a quicker plan-making process is unlikely to be a better one.

The significance of the "development plan"

The "development plan" is the document or documents (there may be more than one), prepared by the planning authority with the statutory responsibility to do so, and which contains the planning policies for the area.

The term 'statutory development plan' is often used synonymously with the development plan. Where there are a number of documents which may be referred to as the development plan, the statutory development plan refers to the documents containing planning policies which have the force of law behind them. This is best illustrated by examples.

In England and Wales the scheme of forward planning comprises;

National Planning Policy Framework ("NPPF") – the government-produced national policy to guide local planning authorities ("LPAs") on plan-making and, in the absence of an up-to-date local plan, decision-taking. The NPPF is often referred to as part of the development plan but is not part of the statutory development plan. Planning Practice Guidance ("PPG") is the government guidance on how to interpret and apply the various provisions of the NPPF – it is online only (accessed via the www.gov.uk website) which enables it to be readily and frequently updated.

Local plans – prepared by the LPA (whether a district council, a county-wide unitary authority or a city council) for its area are part of the statutory development plan.[6]

Neighbourhood Development Plans to give them their full title – prepared by a town or parish council or a neighbourhood forum and are part of the statutory development plan.

The significance of the development plan (that is the statutory development plan) is imposed by Section 38(6) of the Planning and Compulsory Purchase Act 2004 which states that:

" ... any determination under the planning Acts must be made in accordance with the development plan unless material considerations indicate otherwise."

---

[6] The local plan may be part of a suite of documents known collectively as the Local Development Framework ("LDF") – a legacy of the system introduced under the last Labour government. Whilst all LDF documents are considered part of the development plan, it is generally only the local plan itself that is the statutory development plan.

This provision gives effect to what is called 'the primacy of the development plan', the principle that underpins the plan-led system of planning in the UK. The primacy of the development plan asserts that an up-to-date planning policy is king and should be the first point of reference for anyone – whether planning officer, planning committee or planning inspector – making a determination on a planning application.

Development plan policies

It is often said that there are two main types of planning policy; 'site-specific' and 'generic'.

Some guidance on neighbourhood planning mentions 'criteria-led' policies but this is just a way of describing how a planning policy is set out. Most planning policies are criteria-led, and site-specific and generic planning policies are usually framed in this way.

For neighbourhood planning especially, strategic policies in a local plan have real significance (addressed in more detail below) and may be considered as a particular type of planning policy. Strategic policies too can be either site-specific or generic depending on the subject matter.

A site-specific planning policy is one that applies to a particular site, sites or area. It may be set out in permissive terms – amounting to a site allocation policy – yet may also apply strict criteria for development, and often the redevelopment, of a particular site or area.

A generic planning policy covers anything that is not site-specific. A generic planning policy will not necessarily apply universally to all development across the neighbourhood plan area but will often only apply to a certain type of development or certain types of designated area. It is generic in the sense that it applies generally across the plan area rather than to named sites or areas within the plan area.

For example, a policy stipulating general requirements for residential development will be a generic policy, though if it includes more detailed requirements for named residential sites then, to that extent, it will be site-specific.

A policy containing the restrictions and constraints that apply in conservation areas or Areas of Outstanding Natural Beauty ("AONB") will essentially be a generic policy even though it may be possible to identify the named designations which are subject to it.

The significance of strategic policies in a local plan

For the purpose of neighbourhood plan making, identifying a strategic policy in a local plan is far more significant than the distinction between site-specific and generic policies.

It is the strategic policies in a local plan that a neighbourhood plan must be in 'general conformity' with. The concept of general conformity is fundamental to neighbourhood planning and is one we will return to. For now, we are considering what makes a strategic policy.

The NPPF sets out very clearly what is meant by strategic policies at Paragraph 20:

> *Strategic policies should set out an overall strategy for the pattern, scale and quality of development, and make sufficient provision for:*
>
> *a) housing (including affordable housing), employment, retail, leisure and other commercial development;*
>
> *b) infrastructure for transport, telecommunications, security, waste management, water supply, wastewater, flood risk and coastal change management, and the provision of minerals and energy (including heat);*
>
> *c) community facilities (such as health, education and cultural infrastructure); and*
>
> *d) conservation and enhancement of the natural, built and historic environment, including landscapes and green infrastructure, and planning measures to address climate change mitigation and adaptation.*

Just as significantly for neighbourhood planners, Paragraph 21, NPPF goes on to say that:

> *Plans should make explicit which policies are strategic policies. These should be limited to those necessary to address the strategic priorities of the area (and any relevant cross-boundary issues), to provide a clear starting point for any non-strategic policies that are needed. Strategic policies should not extend to detailed matters that are more appropriately dealt with through neighbourhood plans or other non-strategic policies.*

As the NPPF makes clear[7] a local plan may also contain non-strategic as well as strategic policies though where there is a conflict the (local and therefore non-strategic) policies of a made neighbourhood plan take precedence over non-strategic policies in a local plan.

Whilst the current NPPF guidance on strategic policies is more direct than it used to be in the 2012 version, there is still scope for confusion over what amounts to a strategic policy. Notwithstanding the advice to LPAs at Paragraph 21, NPPF, it is important to note that not every local plan policy labelled as 'strategic' will necessarily be strategic.

LPAs have had a tendency to label most if not all of their local plan policies as 'strategic' whether or not they comply with the NPPF/PPG definition of a strategic policy and this is particularly evident in local plans based on the 2012 NPPF guidance.

Not all LPAs or their officers readily acknowledge the distinction between strategic and non-strategic policies or the significance of that distinction. This is in part because the NPPF clearly intends non-strategic matters to be dealt with not by LPAs but by parish councils in neighbourhood plans. The harsh reality of this for LPAs is that their responsibility for, and control over, non-strategic planning matters is being transferred away from them. That is why some LPA officers remain unenthusiastic about neighbourhood planning.

Strategic policies are those concerned with the location and delivery of certain types of development for which there is a strategic need. It cannot be overemphasised that it is essential for neighbourhood plan makers to be able to identify and distinguish between strategic and non-strategic local plan policies at an early stage of their NDP process.

The presumption in favour of sustainable development

The presumption in favour of sustainable development was introduced in the first version of the NPPF published in March 2012. That document, published by the Conservative-led coalition government was intended to simplify the planning system by replacing the previous quite detailed *Planning Policy Guidance* documents, published on a range of planning policy areas, with a single, less prescriptive document.

At the core of that approach was a supposedly game-changing principle

---

[7] At Paragraphs 20 to 30.

that instead of slavishly following planning policies that took years to come to fruition and were therefore often out-of-date soon after adoption, there should be a presumption in favour of development, the only qualification being that the presumption should operate only in favour of *sustainable* development.

The presumption was updated in the current NPPF as set out below.

Paragraph 11, NPPF 2019

Plans and decisions should apply a presumption in favour of sustainable development.

*For **plan-making** this means that:*

a) plans should positively seek opportunities to meet the development needs of their area, and be sufficiently flexible to adapt to rapid change;

b) strategic policies should, as a minimum, provide for objectively assessed needs for housing and other uses, as well as any needs that cannot be met within neighbouring areas, unless:

> *i. the application of policies in this Framework that protect areas or assets of particular importance provides a strong reason for restricting the overall scale, type or distribution of development in the plan area ; or*

> *ii. any adverse impacts of doing so would significantly and demonstrably outweigh the benefits, when assessed against the policies in this Framework taken as a whole.*

*For **decision-taking** this means:*

c) approving development proposals that accord with an up-to-date development plan without delay; or

d) where there are no relevant development plan policies, or the policies which are most important for determining the application are out-of-date, granting permission unless:

> *i. the application of policies in this Framework that protect areas or assets of particular importance provides a clear reason for refusing the development proposed; or*

ii. any adverse impacts of doing so would significantly and demonstrably outweigh the benefits, when assessed against the policies in this Framework taken as a whole.

It is important to briefly consider what is meant by sustainable development because there is no indication of that in Paragraph 11 itself, yet that is what the presumption hinges on.

The NPPF does recognise, at Paragraph 7, that:

... the purpose of the planning system is to contribute to the achievement of sustainable development. At a very high level, the objective of sustainable development can be summarised as meeting the needs of the present without compromising the ability of future generations to meet their own needs.[8]

What this means in practice is set out at Paragraph 8:

Achieving sustainable development means that the planning system has three overarching objectives, which are interdependent and need to be pursued in mutually supportive ways (so that opportunities can be taken to secure net gains across each of the different objectives):

*a) **an economic objective** – to help build a strong, responsive and competitive economy, by ensuring that sufficient land of the right types is available in the right places and at the right time to support growth, innovation and improved productivity; and by identifying and coordinating the provision of infrastructure;*

*b) **a social objective** – to support strong, vibrant and healthy communities, by ensuring that a sufficient number and range of homes can be provided to meet the needs of present and future generations; and by fostering a well-designed and safe built environment, with accessible services and open spaces that reflect current and future needs and support communities' health, social and cultural well-being; and*

*c) **an environmental objective** – to contribute to protecting and enhancing our natural, built and historic environment; including making effective use of land, helping to improve biodiversity, using natural resources prudently, minimising waste and pollution, and mitigating and*

---

[8]   This definition derives from the 1987 Brundtland Report commissioned by the World Commission on Environment and Development (WCED).

adapting to climate change, including moving to a low carbon economy.

To the extent that the presumption in Paragraph 11 provides any practical guidance for plan-making, it is in very broad terms only. In essence it says plan positively (and allocate sites) for objectively assessed strategic need unless there are significant adverse impacts, and with sufficient flexibility to reflect change. This has always been the stated purpose and intent behind the making of development plans. It is only the last part – flexibility – that has always been difficult to achieve because the plan-making process is so time-consuming. There is nothing in the NPPF that effectively addresses that.

The other difficulty for plan-makers is that the Paragraph 8 sustainable development objectives are really just that; they are rhetorical, and appear quite removed from the process-orientated principle in Paragraph 11. How exactly are the sustainable development objectives to be assessed, weighted and evaluated, particularly when they conflict with one another, as they inevitably do in almost every case?

There is no answer to be found in the NPPF but the simple answer to that question is that any and every development satisfies at least one of the sustainable development objectives because it can always be said to have an economic benefit, even if only from the employment of those engaged in its construction. It is amazing how often that is argued as being the (sometimes only) sustainable element of a development that has no environmental benefit whatsoever. The implications of this in the context of the presumption are dramatic.

Whatever the NPPF should be seeking to achieve – efficient plan-making, better quality development perhaps – the effect of Paragraph 11 on plan-making and decision-taking in practice is clear. Unless there are up-to-date development plan policies, then the presumption applies and if the economic benefits of a proposed development are not outweighed by very obvious and significant adverse impacts, then it should be granted planning permission.

This is particularly so when it comes to the government's main planning related obsession, housing development, in relation to which the convoluted guidance of the NPPF coupled with the increasingly arbitrary approach to assessing need means that all plan-makers will struggle to keep up. This has crucial implications for those making neighbourhood plans and for decision-taking on planning applications (which are considered below in *Chapter 6*).

Forward planning – summary and conclusions

'Planning' implies reliance on a plan and the forward planning function of town and country planning relies on a development plan. The statutory development plan comprises those plans that have statutory force; local plans and neighbourhood plans.

The main part of the development plan is the local plan produced by the LPA which may be a city, district or unitary council.

Every LPA has a statutory duty to produce a local plan, though because this is inevitably a rigorous and time-consuming process involving the testing of evidence for each policy, many parts of the country do not have an up-to-date local plan. LPAs often find that by the time they get to the final stages of producing their local plan, the statutory process has changed and they have to start all over again, or at least go back several stages.

The currency of a local plan – how up-to-date it is – is a crucial consideration that is often controversial. The statutory development plan is comprised of the last adopted local plan for the area but this may be ten or 15 years old, sometimes more. An emerging plan is not part of the statutory development plan until it passes the examination[9] and is formally adopted yet in its final stages prior to that is likely to be far more relevant and current than the old local plan.

Therefore, when deciding what the relevant planning policies are, it may be the 'saved' policies of an old, adopted local plan that comprise the statutory development plan.

However, if those policies are considered out-of-date for NPPF purposes then the presumption in favour of sustainable development at Paragraph 11 NPPF overrides the primacy of the development plan. In this situation the presumption applies and the principles of the NPPF carry more weight than the old local plan policies. The more up-to-date emerging policies of a soon-to-be adopted local plan may be a useful guide to a planning determination but will not have statutory force.

A neighbourhood development plan is also part of the development plan, that fits in beneath and as a lower tier to the local plan. An NDP must be in general conformity with the local plan, although it is possible for an NDP to be 'made' in the absence of an up-to-date local plan. However,

---

[9] At an examination held in public by a government appointed planning inspector.

it may be better to delay making the NDP until after the local plan is adopted if that is imminent. Where there is an NDP and a local plan, both comprise the statutory development plan for the area; the latter providing the strategic framework and objectives with the NDP covering matters of local detail.

The development plan contains planning policies that set out where development of different types should be located. The determination of planning applications must be made in accordance with those planning policies, unless material considerations indicate otherwise. This is the statutory principle of the primacy of the development plan; the essence of the plan-led system of planning in all parts of the UK.

The processes of preparing and adopting the development plan (whether local plan or NDP) are all part of the essential *forward planning* function of the planning system; the plan behind the planning.

So, the development plan should indicate where different types of development may be located. The determination of planning applications – with due regard for the development plan – is the second main function of the planning system.

Development control or development management

This function of the planning system is about controlling or managing development through the administration and determination of planning applications in accordance with the development plan.

The expression 'development management', ushered in as part of a cultural change over recent years to make the planning system more permissive, has made the term 'development control' increasingly obsolete.

However, it is questionable whether development management reflects the various statutory powers and responsibilities of LPAs as meaningfully as development control. For example, when a planning application is refused so that no development occurs, there is no development to manage, and when enforcement powers are invoked to remove unlawful development, again development is being controlled not managed.

In any case, the term development management is here to stay and what it essentially involves is the consideration and determination of planning applications, or in NPPF-speak 'decision-taking'. This is where development management interacts with forward planning; where the development plan is current and up-to-date, the determination of planning applications must have regard to it.

Where a made neighbourhood plan is in place for the area, any relevant policies in it must be considered in the determination of the application. Such policies should influence the decision to be taken on the application, maybe prompting a refusal of planning permission or by supporting an approval or by ensuring that appropriate planning conditions are imposed.

The administrative requirements for planning applications

There are numerous administrative requirements for the submission, consideration and determination of planning applications. Those that all submitted applications must comply with are the responsibility of the applicant. Others relate to the application process and must be observed by the LPA. These various rules are to be found in the Town and Country Planning (Development Management Procedure) (England) Order 2015 (the "DMPO").

A detailed analysis of the DMPO is beyond the scope of this book but it is important to know that it regulates various matters including pre-submission consultation, validation requirements, ownership notices and certificates, publicity for applications, applications for non-material amendments, the various consultations during the determination of an application, applications for discharging planning conditions, the time period for determining applications, reasons for the refusal of applications and reasons for imposing conditions.

At first glance these administrative requirements may appear secondary and peripheral but some of the issues they address are fundamental and a breach of the regulations can have significant effects. A planning permission issued pursuant to a material breach of the DMPO Regulations may be subject to a legal challenge and in fact may provide the only opportunity for a third party to challenge the validity of a planning permission, given that a planning appeal (on the merits of the proposed development) can only be made by the applicant against the refusal of an application.

The procedure for determining planning applications

If the determination of a planning application is taken to be the whole process of its consideration, from receipt of the application by the LPA to a decision being made on it, then the first step in that process is validation; the registration of the application as a valid application.

Every planning application must satisfy the statutory validation requirements that include payment of the correct fee and issuing the correct ownership certificate and notices. The date of validation by the LPA is significant because the statutory consultation, advertisement and determination periods are set by reference to it.

The LPA is only under a duty to determine a valid planning application. Validation by the LPA therefore triggers not only the determination process but the need for the LPA to issue a decision on the application after due consideration of all timely consultation responses.

The statutory determination period for planning applications not involving 'major development'[10] is eight weeks. Applications for major development are subject to a 13 week determination period.

Many applications take longer than the statutory period to be determined. In most cases the applicant will have no reason to object to that and may even be the cause of delays if further information requested by the LPA is not made readily available. If the LPA considers that insufficient supporting information has been submitted with a planning application, it may simply refuse to determine it.

The main significance of the determination period is that, unless the applicant has agreed in writing with the LPA to extend the time period for determination, then once the statutory determination period has expired the applicant may appeal against non-determination in much the same way as an appeal against a refusal.

Any planning appeal removes the application from the LPA's jurisdiction and puts it in the hands of The Planning Inspectorate. It is therefore not necessarily in the applicant's interests to appeal for non-determination, which is why such appeals are uncommon and generally only used as a last resort where the applicant believes the LPA is deliberately or incompetently dragging its feet in failing to issue a permission.

The refusal of a planning application must be accompanied by reasons (at least one) for the refusal that should indicate any relevant policies of

---

[10] As defined under Article 2 of The Town and Country Planning (Development Management Procedure) (England) Order 2015.

the development plan that the proposal fails to comply with.

When a planning application is approved it results in a planning permission, which is always a conditional approval even if the only condition is the standard condition limiting the currency of the permission to three years. That is the time period within which the permission must be implemented. Implementation means making a 'material start' towards the development approved by the permission. If not implemented within the conditioned time period, usually three years, the permission expires.

Usually, and depending on the size, significance and complexity of the development involved, there will be a whole host of other conditions controlling everything from drainage and design details to occupancy or operating hours. The LPA must give reasons on its decision notice for every condition imposed.

At any time before a decision notice is issued by the LPA, the application may be withdrawn by the applicant. This may be done for a number of reasons but it is usually to avoid a refusal, often where the LPA requires more information to support the application which the applicant is unable to provide within the determination period. In these circumstances unless the application were withdrawn it would be refused.

The basis on which planning applications should be determined

As we have seen the primacy of the development plan means that unless other material considerations militate against it, planning determinations must be made in accordance with the development plan – in other words, in accordance with the planning policies of the local plan and any neighbourhood plan that is in place.

The caveat to that is found in Paragraph 11, NPPF which makes clear that decision-taking – the determination of planning applications – must be by reference to an *up-to-date* development plan.

The presumption in favour of sustainable development (Paragraph 11) applies to insist that *"where there are no relevant development plan policies, or the policies which are most important for determining the application are out-of-date"*, then planning permission should be granted *unless*:

   i. NPPF policies that protect areas or assets of particular importance provide a clear reason for refusing the development proposed; or ii. the adverse impacts of granting planning permission would significantly and demonstrably outweigh the benefits, when assessed against NPPF policies taken as a whole.

As will be emphasised throughout this book, because of the way the presumption in favour of sustainable development operates, the currency of the development plan – that is, having an up-to-date development plan – is critical for decision-takers but it is also essential for all neighbourhood plan-makers to keep in mind.

However, the NPPF does not tell us what constitutes an 'up-to-date development plan' or (except in relation to housing and then in a very convoluted way) when planning policies may be considered 'out-of-date'.

This dilemma at the heart of the NPPF, and the implications for neighbourhood planning, are considered further in *Chapter 6*.

Planning appeals and legal challenges

The refusal of a planning application may be appealed by the applicant. Any such appeal will focus on the reasons for refusal set out in the decision notice, though the inspector considering an appeal will also take into account other material considerations.

A planning appeal is therefore an appeal *de novo* – an appeal afresh or anew that takes into account all material considerations, not just the LPA's reasons for refusal. This is important because anyone taking part in an appeal, for example a parish council making representations as an interested party, should not necessarily limit its representations to the issues addressed in the reasons for refusal. It may be that factors other than those given in the LPA's reasons should weigh more heavily for or against the appeal proposal than the LPA recognised.

There is no third party right of appeal against the issue of a planning permission. Only the refusal or the non-determination of a planning application may be appealed, by the applicant. The only opportunity a third party, or objector, has to challenge a planning permission issued by an LPA is by way of a judicial review. An appeal against a planning appeal decision, whether made by the planning applicant or a third party must be via a statutory appeal to the High Court[11]. In either case, the legal challenge must be made within six weeks of the decision under challenge and can

---

[11] Section 288, TCPA.

only succeed if it can be shown that the decision was unlawful or otherwise unreasonable.

In many cases where a judicial review or statutory appeal against a planning permission is successful, the planning application will be remitted back to the LPA for the decision to be taken again.

Development management – summary and conclusions

The determination of planning applications – which should be made in accordance with an up-to-date development plan – is the most obvious element of the development management function.

However, development management also involves the imposition, monitoring and enforcement of planning conditions and planning obligations and the monitoring and enforcement of unauthorised development generally. This is dealt with in more detail below.

Chapter 3: Elements of Development Control

Planning conditions

Planning conditions are used to restrict or impose detailed requirements on a planning permission and, as we have seen, the reason(s) for imposing a condition must be set out by the LPA on the decision notice.

Reasonable and enforceable

Conditions must be *"relevant to planning and to the development to be permitted"*; they must also be *"enforceable precise and reasonable in all other respects"*.

These tests are set out at Paragraph 55, NPPF[1] and are generally self-explanatory. They mean that, generally, planning conditions must relate to the land to be developed or immediately adjacent land within the same ownership so that compliance is within the control of the owner or developer who implements the permission.

However, a condition may require that land adjacent to the application site is managed in a certain way by a third party, usually a public body such as a highways authority undertaking necessary highways works or improvements; this is known as a *Grampian*[2] condition.

Variation and appeals

It is possible to appeal against the imposition of a condition on a planning permission. The appeal must be lodged within 12 weeks of a permission for householder development, or six months for any other development. However, an appeal involves the reconsideration of the whole development so may result in the permission being rescinded.

Alternatively, an application can be made at any time to vary or discharge a planning condition under Section 73, TCPA. There are three possible

---

[1] See also Paragraph 003, PPG on '*Use of planning conditions*'.

[2] *Grampian Regional Council v City of Aberdeen District Council* (1984) 47 P. & C. R. 633.

outcomes to an application of this type; the LPA may either simply grant the application, it may refuse the application or it may impose one or more different conditions in place of, or in addition to, the condition the application seeks to vary or discharge.

Time-limiting condition

Every permission is, or should be, subject to the standard time-limiting condition restricting the currency of the permission to three years. This is significant principally because it means that the development permitted by the permission must be commenced within three years of the date on the decision notice, and if not then the permission expires and can no longer be invoked. The time-limiting condition cannot be appealed or varied. A permission is implemented by a 'material start' to the development in question.

In most cases this is straightforward but the question of lawful implementation of a planning permission can get complicated where the permission includes conditions precedent – that is, conditions that must be discharged before development starts – that have not been complied with.

It may also be difficult to determine if and when the permission has been implemented when it is a change of use permission, and the new use has not commenced clearly or consistently from a certain date.

Outline planning permissions contain conditions requiring that details of all the reserved matters be submitted within three years of the outline permission, and that development is commenced within two years of the approval of the last of the reserved matters details.

Pre-commencement conditions

A pre-commencement condition, otherwise known as a condition precedent, is one that must be discharged *before* development commences. A typical pre-commencement condition requires that "*no development shall commence until* ..." certain details have been submitted and approved by the LPA, for example a scheme for dealing with the remediation of contaminated land.

An important feature of a genuine condition precedent is that it relates to a matter of such fundamental importance that unless the details are resolved, the development in question should not be allowed to go ahead. Generally, the requirement for submission and approval of schemes covering secondary matters such as certain design details, do not require the use of, and therefore should not be imposed as, pre-commencement conditions. However, the imposition of such conditions where they are not strictly necessary has become widespread over recent years.

Pre-commencement conditions can be problematic where possible non-compliance calls into question whether the related permission has been lawfully implemented. This in turn can generate fundamental doubts and questions as to the lawfulness of the development overall. This is the subject of much legal discussion and case law largely beyond the scope of this book.

Suffice to say that a condition requiring the submission and approval of certain details before development commences should be signed off by the LPA before commencement of the development can occur. The development must then be in accordance with the approved scheme required by the condition.

As planning generally has become more complicated and needs to deal with an increasing number of issues, so the use of pre-commencement conditions has become more prevalent. Planning officers under pressure to determine applications within the statutory time period are able to defer the consideration of detailed elements of the proposal until after the permission is issued, by the expedient use of pre-commencement conditions. This generally has suited applicants, who are always keen to secure a permission.

However, the problem with this approach has been that once the permission is issued the process of negotiating and applying for the pre-commencement conditions to be discharged is time-consuming and inevitably causes delays to the development in question being commenced, even though it has the benefit of a planning permission.

This is particularly so when neither the applicant nor the LPA has quite the same motivation to resolve the details in question if the permission has already been issued. This in turn can lead to the aforementioned problem; the developer making a start on the development without first fulfilling the requirements of the pre-commencement condition. This leads to uncertainly over whether a development that does not comply with a pre-commencement condition has been lawfully implemented.

In an attempt to address these difficulties, new rules on pre-commencement conditions were introduced in 2018.[3]

Now, an LPA must notify the applicant of its intention to impose pre-commencement conditions, giving the applicant ten days from the date of the notice to respond, either by agreeing to or refusing to accept the proposed conditions. If the applicant fails to respond within ten days, then the LPA may impose the conditions. If the applicant responds by refusing to accept such conditions then the LPA cannot impose them, but this may cause the LPA to issue a refusal. In practice these rules are likely to prompt more detailed negotiations between LPA and applicant prior to, and which may delay, the issue of a permission.

Pre-commencement conditions have always been problematic and it must make sense to focus on the all-important details of fundamental issues before a permission is granted.

Details and restrictions

Many of the details of development are finalised via the imposition of planning conditions, such as specifications for certain design elements, access, landscaping and green transport. Conditions are also used to ensure compliance with, or mitigation relating to, other areas of regulation such as flood risk, contaminated land and wildlife protection.

Planning permissions for industrial or retail development often contain conditions restricting operating hours, vehicle movements or particular activities. Conditions may also expressly restrict the development to a particular planning use class.

However, conditions are not the most effective means of ensuring that continuing positive requirements are met, and they cannot be used to impose a financial payment in furtherance of a planning purpose. This is because conditions are essentially restrictive in nature and the means of enforcing conditions is limited. The alternative method of imposing certain planning requirements is the planning obligation, which is dealt with below.

Occupancy conditions

A defining feature of some development is who is allowed to occupy it.

---

[3] See the Town and Country Planning (Pre-commencement Conditions) Regulations 2018.

Agricultural dwellings, holiday homes, live/work units and manager's accommodation are all examples of this. Any restriction on occupation may be imposed by an occupancy condition.

Occupancy conditions can be very contentious. There are two main reasons for this. First, they are difficult to monitor and are therefore usually quite easily breached without detection by the LPA. Secondly, they have a significant negative effect on the value of the properties they affect so there is a real incentive to establish a breach as lawful by a continuous ten year period of non-compliance.

Occupancy conditions are the subject of much case law and must be carefully considered by all concerned; the LPAs that impose them and the owners and occupiers of properties affected by them. Due to the fundamental nature of occupancy restrictions they are often imposed by the dual control of a planning condition and a planning obligation.

Planning obligations

In parallel with the legal principle of property law that only restrictive covenants run with the land and affect subsequent purchasers, so it is that planning conditions – binding on the land once the related permission has been implemented – cannot impose positive obligations.

In planning terms positive obligations can only be imposed by means of a planning agreement or unilateral undertaking – known generally as 'planning obligations' – under Section 106, TCPA which provides that the owner and subsequent owners of the land are bound by the obligations.

Planning obligations are another area thoroughly tested by legal challenges that have resulted in a mass of case law. Essentially though, the purpose of a planning obligation is *"to make the development acceptable in planning terms"*.

Paragraph 56 NPPF makes clear that:

> *Planning obligations must only be sought where they meet all of the following tests:*[4]

---

[4] As set out in Regulation 122(2) of the Community Infrastructure Levy Regulations 2010.

a) necessary to make the development acceptable in planning terms;

b) directly related to the development; and

c) fairly and reasonably related in scale and kind to the development.

Individual planning obligations are typically provided by means of a planning agreement – or Section 106 agreement – entered into between the landowner and the LPA. If the applicant or developer is not the landowner, they may be joined into the agreement too as may any other parties involved in the planning obligations provided.

A developer can also offer planning obligations by way of a unilateral undertaking in circumstances where the LPA will not agree those obligations or for some reason is unwilling to enter into an agreement with the developer. A unilateral undertaking is used, for example, where the LPA has refused the related planning application and the developer submits proposed planning obligations unilaterally as part of the appeal case. A permission granted on appeal may then be based on the planning obligations provided by the undertaking.

Whether by way of an agreement or an undertaking, a planning obligation under Section 106 is a legal deed which is registered as a Local Land Charge and should therefore come to the attention of any purchaser of a legal interest in the land.

Section 106 agreements have been typically used to provide financial contributions towards various infrastructure requirements such as education provision, highways improvements and public open space, as well as for affordable housing. However, for the payment of off-site contributions Section 106 agreements and undertakings are being replaced by the Community Infrastructure Levy ("CIL").[5]

However, a planning obligation may take many forms and may be the means via which unusual solutions are found to difficult planning problems.

Although the occupancy conditions relating to affordable housing could be imposed by condition, the provision of an agreed number of houses to be built as affordable homes is seen very much as a positive obligation on the developer; a form of 'planning gain' which along with the detailed pricing restrictions is best tied up in a legal deed. On-site obligations and

---

[5] See PPG on *'Community infrastructure levy'*.

occupancy restrictions cannot be provided by the CIL.

For other types of occupancy, such as an agricultural occupancy restriction, a planning condition alone may be imposed and may adequately maintain the restriction. However, there are circumstances in which a condition may be lifted (via a Section 73 Application[6]), or where occupation in breach of the condition may become lawful. That is why some LPAs impose the 'dual control' of a planning obligation as well as a planning condition to reinforce an occupancy restriction – in case the effect of the condition is lost.

A Section 106 agreement or undertaking may be discharged or varied upon an application to the LPA. The refusal of such an application can be appealed. In determining an application to vary or discharge, the LPA should consider whether the obligation *"still serves a useful purpose"*.[7]

Whereas most breaches of planning can only be dealt with by the planning enforcement regime, a breach of the obligations in a Section 106 agreement can be enforced through the statutory remedies under Section 106 itself or, where appropriate, as a breach of contract. In practice, this may mean that sums due under a planning obligation may be recovered by the LPA, or an injunction may be issued to prevent further development or to require compliance with the planning obligation, or the LPA may enter the land in question, undertake the necessary works and then recover the reasonable costs of doing so.

Planning enforcement

A fundamental element of any regulatory system is the regime in place to enforce the rules and ensure there are remedies to deal with those who do not comply. Planning enforcement is a fascinating but complicated subject in its own right; one that is forever evolving as a result of new legislation and, by the nuances that arise from difficult cases, through case law. Here we consider the main principles.

Enforcement investigations

Every LPA has a range of statutory powers to enable it to investigate and

---

[6]   Under Section 73, TCPA.

[7]   Section 106A(6)(b), TCPA.

take action against unauthorised development. Each LPA vests those powers and the responsibilities that go with them in a dedicated team of planning enforcement officers.

Unauthorised development, or a breach of planning, will be either operational development which is wholly unauthorised or fails to accord with the details of a planning permission, an unauthorised material change of use or the breach of a planning condition. Planning enforcement officers also deal with offences relating to listed buildings and conservation areas whilst specialist tree officers usually deal with breaches of Tree Preservation Orders.

The LPA should respond to every report or complaint about unauthorised development by instigating an enforcement investigation into the matter. The investigation will be given a reference number and the complainant should be told by the LPA how the investigation is progressing or at least how it is concluded. An enforcement investigation, with the basic details of the complaint, used to appear on an LPA's online planning register but the GDPR[8] is now interpreted as a reason to withhold such information from the planning register accessible to the public – and as a result, a vital element of an LPA's planning function is no longer subject to the transparency or public scrutiny that it ought to be.

Planning enforcement officers have a variety of statutory powers, some equivalent to those of the police and the Crown Prosecution Service, for investigating and prosecuting unauthorised development. They may enter onto private land for the purposes of an investigation and may interview under caution persons suspected of a breach.[9]

Enforcement officers may issue formal written requests for information, responses to which must be made within specified time periods, and which make clear that knowingly giving false information is itself a criminal offence. If the LPA requires more information about a suspected planning breach, or the ownership of land affected by it, it may serve a *Planning Contravention Notice* ("PCN") on an owner or occupier. A failure to duly provide the information requested in the PCN may be a criminal offence.[10]

---

[8] General Data Protection Regulation 2016/679 – an EU Regulation brought into effect in UK law by the Data Protection Act 2018.

[9] Sections 196A to 196C, TCPA.

[10] Sections 171C and 171D, TCPA.

There is no doubt that breaches of planning and the investigations into them are of real interest to many parish councils which, quite rightly, regard themselves as the eyes and ears of their local community.

Given that in all of their planning functions LPAs are increasingly under-resourced and none more so than their enforcement teams, it could be argued that there is an increased need for local vigilance. It is certainly not the case that planning enforcement officers patrol their areas looking for breaches of planning. Most enforcement investigations are in response to complaints from members of the public, usually aggrieved neighbours.

The often less than enthusiastic attitude of LPAs to their enforcement responsibilities is perhaps understandable given the changing culture of the planning system, from an essentially regulatory regime to one that is increasingly permissive. Planning enforcement is seen by many LPAs as a costly, no-win function which carries considerable risks for the authority particularly when up against well organised developers with clear commercial incentives to fight what they often consider to be the minor obstacles of the planning system.

Ultimately though, the reason planning authorities can afford to be lacklustre when it comes to enforcement is that whether or not they take enforcement action in response to a breach is entirely discretionary. That means that if an LPA decides not to take enforcement action in a particular case, it cannot be compelled to do so. Unlike the determination of a planning application, a decision not to take enforcement action is not a formal decision of the LPA, but merely an exercise of its discretion for which it need give no reasons at all. The corollary is that if an LPA refuses to take enforcement action, however unreasonable that may seem, it cannot be subject to legal challenge.

The significance of enforcement in today's planning system is reflected in a single paragraph – Paragraph 58 – of the NPPF:

> *Effective enforcement is important to maintain public confidence in the planning system. Enforcement action is discretionary, and local planning authorities should act proportionately in responding to suspected breaches of planning control. They should consider publishing a local enforcement plan to manage enforcement proactively, in a way that is appropriate to their area. This should set out how they will monitor the implementation of planning permissions, investigate alleged cases of unauthorised development and take action where appropriate.*

The local focus encouraged by the NPPF indeed means that enforcement teams adopt their own approach, which will inevitably vary from one LPA area to another. Most LPAs maintain that before taking any enforcement action, there must be – as well as strong evidence of a breach – real 'planning harm' resulting from it. What constitutes planning harm is obviously subjective.

When an LPA does decide to take enforcement action, it has a variety of tools at its disposal.

Enforcement remedies

Where an LPA concludes that unauthorised development has taken place and should be remedied, the first recourse in many cases will be to encourage the developer to submit a retrospective planning application, that is, unless the development is so offensive as to not stand any chance of gaining a planning consent. In all other cases, a retrospective application gives the developer the opportunity of testing the merits of the development and perhaps obtaining permission for it.

If a retrospective application is refused, it can be appealed – a further opportunity for the offending development to be regularised. If an appeal also fails then at least the planning merits and all associated issues will have been thoroughly scrutinised and reasons given for the conclusions reached. By that stage the LPA is likely to be on solid ground in pursuing formal enforcement action by any appropriate means.

An *Enforcement Notice*[11], which should be served on all and any owners of the land in question, must specify the breach, what must be done to remedy the breach and the time period within which that compliance must take place.

An enforcement notice must be served at least 28 days before it comes into effect, and *at any time before the effective date* the landowner can appeal against the notice. That is the only opportunity for the notice to be appealed. If it is not appealed (or is unsuccessfully appealed) then unless it is unilaterally withdrawn by the LPA, which is unlikely, the notice takes effect in perpetuity.

There are several grounds of appeal against an enforcement notice. The main grounds are: the notice is factually incorrect; the alleged breach is

---

[11] Sections 172 to 179, TCPA.

not unlawful (in other words, the notice is legally incorrect); the alleged breach has become immune from enforcement; and the development should be granted planning permission. If the latter ground is invoked, then that part of the appeal will be considered in much the same way as a planning application – on the merits of the development in question.

Once an enforcement notice takes effect, it is registered as a Local Land Charge and as such should come to the attention of anyone checking the Register of Local Land Charges such as a prospective purchaser of the land in question. This is significant because it means that even after the notice has been complied with, it not only remains in full effect to deter any repeat breaches of the same type but it stands as a 'black mark' against the property.

Failure to comply with an effective enforcement notice is a criminal offence which will be liable to a prosecution by the LPA. Most LPAs in most cases allow more time than is specified on the notice for it to be complied with, but if the failure to comply still persists then a prosecution may follow.

A *Stop Notice*[12] may be served by the LPA, only in conjunction with an enforcement notice, to prevent the unauthorised development specified being undertaken before the enforcement notice takes effect. A stop notice is therefore used to stop particularly objectionable, damaging or irreversible development immediately, and it will therefore usually come into effect within a few days. The LPA may specify an effective date less than three days ahead in certain circumstances provided it gives clear reasons for doing so.

A *Temporary Stop Notice*[13] may be served to prevent with immediate effect development considered by the LPA to be unlawful, where such urgency is needed. The breach of a stop notice or temporary stop notice is an offence.

If a stop notice is served in support of an enforcement notice that is subsequently quashed, varied or withdrawn, or if the stop notice is withdrawn, then the developer may claim compensation from the LPA for "*any loss or damage directly attributable to the prohibition contained in the notice*".[14]

---

[12] Sections 183 to 187, TCPA.

[13] Sections 171E to 171H, TCPA.

[14] Section 186, TCPA.

There are similar compensation provisions for a temporary stop notice.[15]

A *Breach of Condition Notice*[16] is in a similar form to an enforcement notice but comes into effect via a more expedited procedure. A breach of condition notice cannot be appealed. It simply specifies breaches of condition, often occupancy conditions, that must cease in order to restore compliance with the condition(s) specified. Non-compliance with a breach of condition notice is a criminal offence, so provided it is legally valid it enables the LPA to prosecute for any continuing or further breaches of the type specified.

An *injunction*[17] may be sought by an LPA where it is considered necessary, expedient and proportionate to restrain any actual or apprehended breach of planning. The LPA must apply to the High Court or County Court for an injunction and is only likely to do so where other enforcement remedies are unlikely to be effective.

A *Listed Buildings Enforcement Notice*[18] works in the same way as a planning enforcement notice to require unauthorised works to a listed building to be removed or remedial works undertaken. It is an offence to undertake any works to a listed building, inside or externally, without a listed buildings consent so the LPA may prosecute in respect of any unauthorised works as well as serving a listed buildings enforcement notice.

A *Section 215 Notice*[19] may be served by an LPA to require the tidying of any land or building which is adversely affecting the amenity of the area. These notices are usually used to compel the tidying of land in residential areas but are not limited to that and may be served on the owners of agricultural land to require the removal of unsightly dumping and even untidy external storage that adversely affects rural amenity.

The procedure for a Section 215 notice is relatively straightforward and there is a right of appeal to the Magistrates Court. Upon the notice taking effect, non-compliance constitutes a criminal offence. However, research has shown that Section 215 notices are often complied with and that

---

[15] Section 171H, TCPA.

[16] Section 187A, TCPA.

[17] Under Section 187B, TCPA.

[18] Section 38, Planning (Listed Buildings and Conservation Areas) Act 1990.

[19] Sections 215 to 219, TCPA.

even the threat of one usually has the desired effect. If not complied with, accompanying powers enable the LPA to undertake the tidying up and charge the owner for the costs incurred, enforced if necessary by a charge on the property.

Immunity from enforcement

One of the most interesting, contentious and complex features of the planning system is the concept of immunity from enforcement – if an unauthorised development or breach of planning has continued uninterrupted for a certain period of time it cannot be enforced against and becomes lawful. The time periods needed to gain immunity are laid down in statute though many of the very significant nuances in this area have evolved through case law.

There are three 'categories' of immunity from enforcement:[20]

- for *operational development* immunity is gained four years after completion of the unauthorised development;

- for a *material change of use or breach of condition* immunity is gained ten years after a continuous and uninterrupted change of use or breach of condition

- *change of use of a building to use as a single dwelling:* this very specific unauthorised change of use must continue uninterrupted for at least four years to become immune from enforcement.

On the face of it the operation of these time periods and the concept of immunity in each case appears uncomplicated, yet apparently simple questions often arise that can be far from straightforward to answer.

When was a particular building completed, to trigger the start of the four year period? On what date did the unauthorised change of use become material? Did it apply across the whole planning unit? Was the change of use in fact permitted development for some or all of the period claimed?

For immunity to be gained the breach of planning must have been capable of being enforced against for the whole of the requisite period – the enforcement period. The simple test is, would there have been a breach obvious to a visiting planning enforcement officer at any time during the

---

[20] Section 171B, TCPA.

claimed period? If, for example, a breach of condition is claimed over a ten year period but for a couple of weeks in the middle of the claimed period there was compliance with the condition and no breach persisted, then the time period needed only starts to run from when the breach is resumed.

Immunity from enforcement can be invoked in one of two ways; either as a defence to enforcement action (if an enforcement notice has been served the immunity must be claimed in an appeal against the notice), or in an application for a Certificate of Lawfulness of Existing Use or Development.

Certificates of lawfulness

There are two types of certificate of lawfulness; a *Certificate of Lawfulness of Existing Use or Development* ("CLEUD") and a *Certificate of Lawfulness of Proposed Use or Development* ("CLOPUD").[21]

A certificate of lawfulness may establish the lawfulness of any existing or proposed development, or use or activity in relation to a development. A certificate may therefore be useful in a number of different situations, for example, to support a defence to enforcement action, to confirm that a particular development is permitted development, to certify that a planning permission has been implemented or to establish the lawful planning use or status of land, perhaps for marketing purposes.

An application for a certificate of lawfulness is a different type of planning application in that it should not be determined on its planning merits, or by reference to planning policy, but simply on the lawfulness of what is set out in the application. The lawfulness of the proposed or existing development in question must be established on the balance of probability by evidence submitted with the application. If such evidence exists but is not submitted, the application should be refused.

Only lawyers are trained to consider and weigh evidence in this way, which is why only the specialist planning solicitors or legal officers at an LPA should determine such applications. This always used to be the case but as LPAs have become increasingly under-resourced, now planning officers often determine CLEUD or CLOPUD applications and some even go before the planning committee! This often results in very poor decisions being made and planning abuses being certified as lawful because the evidence submitted with the application is accepted without its credibility or the weight to be attributed to it being properly considered.

---

[21] Sections 191 to 196, TCPA.

A common misapprehension is that any unopposed evidence presented by the applicant establishes lawfulness. It does not. Only evidence that establishes lawfulness on the balance of probability is sufficient. If the evidence submitted with the application lacks fundamental credibility or veracity, perhaps because it is contradicted by other evidence known to the LPA as a matter of public record, then it does not establish lawfulness.

Evidence submitted by the applicant in support of the application may also be countered or discredited by representations or evidence submitted by members of the public, or by parish councils for that matter. CLEUD and CLOPUD applications are publicised by the LPA in much the same way as any other planning application, to enable public scrutiny and comment.

If the evidence is insufficient to establish lawfulness on the balance of probability, the application should be refused.

The refusal of a certificate of lawfulness application may be appealed by the applicant but there is no third party right of appeal against a certificate granted by an LPA. However, a certificate that is legally flawed may be challenged by judicial review, an application for which must be made within six weeks of the certificate of lawfulness being issued by the LPA.

The LPA has statutory powers to revoke a certificate[22] if it can be shown to have been based on false evidence though most LPAs rarely, if ever, use this power of revocation.

CLEUD and CLOPUD applications are widely misunderstood, partly because of their hybrid nature; part planning application, part legal certification. They are also often contentious and are regarded by some, including many planning officers, as tools of planning abuse. Most types of lawfulness are only established after being hidden from the LPA for a number of years under circumstances in which the applicant would never have obtained a planning permission on the merits of the development in question.

There are certainly cases where the circumstances underpinning the lawfulness applied for occur as a matter of course or even by chance but there are many more where the unauthorised development is planned and carefully contrived with the intention of obtaining a CLEUD once the statutory enforcement period of either four or ten years has expired.

---

[22] Section 193(7), TCPA.

Two cases that fall firmly into the latter category are a couple of the most significant planning cases of recent times, partly because they prompted a change in the law. Between them they also demonstrate many aspects of the law on planning enforcement and immunity from enforcement and are therefore worth considering in a little more detail.

Mr Fidler and his castle[23]

In 2001 on his property in the village of Salfords, near Reigate, Mr Fidler built without planning permission a large home with castellated turrets completely hidden behind walls of straw bales and a tarpaulin 'roof'. This gave the outward appearance of a massive stack of bales with a cover over it. He and his wife lived in their concealed castle-like dwelling for just over four years before the LPA – Reigate and Banstead District Council – discovered it and issued an enforcement notice requiring him to demolish it.

Mr Fidler was no stranger to planning enforcement. The district council had previously served enforcement notices against various business uses at his premises, Honeycrock Farm, in the Surrey countryside.

His appeal against the enforcement notice requiring demolition of his 'castle' was upheld on the basis that the dwelling had been substantially complete – albeit behind the bales – for more than four years, and so had become immune from enforcement under the four year rule that applies to operational development.

The council then appealed the appeal inspector's decision to the High Court where it was decided, in 2010, that the building was *not* substantially complete, for the purposes of triggering the four year enforcement period, until the screen of bales was taken down. Only then had the four year period started to run and as four years had not elapsed between then and the enforcement notice being served, the notice took effect and the building had to be demolished.

The determined Mr Fidler still refused to demolish his home and a protracted legal saga followed in which the council had to wield most of the enforcement tools at its disposal. It sought and was granted a court injunction ordering the building to be demolished and when Mr Fidler failed to comply with that, he was served with contempt of court proceedings. He was also prosecuted for failure to comply with the enforcement notice and given a suspended sentence pending a final deadline for

---

[23] *Fidler v SoS for Communities and Local Government & Anor* [2010] EWHC 143 (Admin).

demolition.

After unsuccessfully claiming that the presence of protected species (bats and newts) on the site prevented him complying with the enforcement notice, in 2016 he finally demolished the building he had lived in for 15 years.

Mr Beesley and his barn[24] (the "Welwyn" case)

At around the same time that the Fidler enforcement notice was upheld by the High Court, Mr Beesley's case was in the Court of Appeal. His dwelling was an altogether more sophisticated contrivance and although a less dramatic construction, the case is arguably more interesting from a legal perspective and has certainly had a greater impact on the law in this area. In fact, were it not for Beesley and his barn, Fidler's castle may still be standing.

In December 2001, pursuant to a planning application, Welwyn Hatfield Borough Council granted Mr Beesley planning permission to construct a hay barn on his land near Potter's Bar in Hertfordshire. The permission was subject to the condition that: *"The building hereby permitted shall be used only for the storage of hay, straw or other agricultural products and shall not be used for any commercial or non agricultural storage purposes"*.

The permission was clearly for an agricultural building, to be *used* as an agricultural building. In making sure the permission was subject to the condition restricting its planning use, it appears the council anticipated that Mr Beesley had ulterior motives for a storage or general industrial use.

However, given that the building permitted was designed and built, externally at least, as a large modern agricultural shed, it could not have been anticipated that it would be lived in as a dwelling. Yet, having fitted it out internally as a dwelling, that is exactly what Mr Beesley did.

After living there for four years he then applied for a CLEUD for the change of use of a building to use as a dwelling under Section 171B(2), TCPA, which provides that: *"Where there has been a breach of planning control consisting in the change of use of any building to use as a single dwellinghouse, no enforcement action may be taken after the end of the period of four years beginning with the date of the breach"*.

---

[24] *SoS for Communities and Local Government & Anor v Welwyn Hatfield BC* [2011] UKSC 15.

The council refused the CLEUD application on the basis that Section 171B(2) did not apply and that Mr Beesley needed to have lived in the dwelling for at least ten years to gain immunity from breach of the condition restricting the use of the barn to an agricultural use.

Mr Beesley successfully appealed the CLEUD refusal. The inspector held that Section 171B(2) did apply and that Mr Beesley had shown he had lived in the dwelling for four years unopposed. The council then appealed successfully to the High Court, that court finding that there had been no change of use and therefore Section 171B(2) was not relevant. Mr Beesley and his co-appellant, the Secretary of State supporting his inspector's upholding of the CLEUD appeal, were given leave to appeal to the Court of Appeal.

Not for the first time the Court of Appeal got itself in a bit of a muddle on some fundamental principles of planning law. The court held that there had been a change of use to use as a dwelling because there had been a change of use from the permitted agricultural use or, alternatively it said, from a period of "no use" that occurred between completion of the building and its residential occupation. The problems with this reasoning are two-fold.

First of all, where there is a difference between the permitted use and the actual use (as there was here – that was the essence of the breach and not in dispute) then in deciding whether there was a *change* of use, one must consider the *actual use* rather than the permitted use. Although Mr Beesley's dwelling had planning permission as an agricultural barn and although it looked from the outside to be a barn, it was never used as a barn or for any other agricultural purpose, so it only ever had one planning use; as a dwelling. There was therefore no change of use to use as a dwellinghouse, as that was what it had always been.

Secondly, the concept of "no use" seems to be one recognised only by the Court of Appeal in this case. Whether or not a building is occupied or until it is occupied after completion of construction, it can still be attributed with an actual, and a planning, use. An unoccupied dwelling is still a dwelling and its planning use class is C3, residential.

Fortunately, the council appealed to the Supreme Court and common sense was restored in a very significant judgment. There were two grounds to the Supreme Court decision. Most commentators understandably concentrate on the second as that led to the significant legislative changes considered below. However, the first ground and the reasoning behind it – relating to the application of Section 171B(2) – was also very important and, as the Supreme Court judgment made clear, was on its own sufficient to determine the outcome of the case in the council's favour.

The Supreme Court followed the reasoning of the High Court judge and the council. Despite its outward appearance, and its permitted use, which was irrelevant to whether a change of use had occurred, Mr Beesley's 'barn' was constructed and used as a dwelling – exactly as he had always intended. It was never anything other than a dwelling and therefore there had not been any change of use of a building to use as a single dwelling, because quite simply there had been no change of use. The council had been right to refuse the CLEUD because Mr Beesley had not gained immunity from enforcement against the residential use.

It seems that the second ground of appeal before the Supreme Court was only pleaded by the council because the Court of Appeal had expressed some surprise that it had not been raised before. That was whether Mr Beesley's deception was deliberate and intended and if so, it raised the question of whether, as a matter of principle, he should be allowed to profit from it by gaining immunity from enforcement.

So why had such an obvious and fundamental matter – deliberate deception – not been an issue before the court at an earlier stage of this legal battle?

The answer is that it is generally acknowledged by planning professionals that in many, if not most, cases involving certificates of lawfulness and immunity from enforcement there is some form of deception, and often the deception is deliberate and carefully contrived. Until *Welwyn*, planning law just accepted this and it was simply the case that if an unauthorised development survived the statutory enforcement period, then however deliberately it had been concealed in order to gain that immunity was completely irrelevant. This was expressly recognised by the Supreme Court in its judgment.

However, concealment and deception tend to undermine the principal rationale behind immunity which is that if the breach of planning has gone unnoticed by a planning authority for a number of years, then it cannot be that bad and should be allowed to remain.

There is no doubt that both the *Fidler* and *Welwyn* cases and the media attention they attracted brought this dichotomy – whether the breach goes unnoticed because it is harmless or because it has been concealed

– to the fore. In the public consciousness it could not be right that two apparently well-to-do landowners could deliberately set out to deceive their local planning authority, and to their considerable financial advantage succeed, with no legal redress or sanction against them whatsoever.

So, it was against this background that when asked to do so, the Supreme Court tackled the issue head on in a classic example of what lawyers refer to as judge-made law.

The court invoked the *Connor* principle, derived from a 1981 decision of the High Court which ensured that a widow's claim for a widow's allowance failed, despite her apparently absolute statutory entitlement, because her widowhood derived from the manslaughter of her husband of which she had been convicted.

The *Connor*[25] case was nothing to do with planning or even deception as such. Its application to planning was on an even broader basis, that an illegal or fraudulent act should not be allowed to facilitate a benefit accruing to the perpetrator from a regime of public law. The dishonest manipulation of the planning system to facilitate otherwise unattainable private profit was no more acceptable in public policy terms than an individual securing a state welfare benefit as a direct consequence of her criminal act.

The Supreme Court therefore held that even if on the face of it Section 171B(2) had applied to confer immunity from enforcement, that statutory provision could not have been intended to facilitate such a deliberate and contrived fraud as Mr Beesley had engaged in. He did not get his CLEUD which meant that his unauthorised residential use could be enforced against.

As a result of the Supreme Court judgment, in its application to the law on immunity from planning enforcement the *Connor* principle is now known as the *Welwyn* principle. More significantly still, the government followed the lead taken by the lawlords by deciding that deliberate deception of the type perpetrated by Messrs Fidler and Beesley warranted new legislative provision.

Planning Enforcement Orders

The Localism Act 2011 inserted a new Section 171BA into the Town and

---

[25] *R v Chief National Insurance Commissioner, Ex p Connor* [1981] QB 758.

Country Planning Act 1990 dealing with time limits for enforcing concealed breaches of planning control, by way of a *Planning Enforcement Order* ("PEO").

Whether or not the statutory four or ten year enforcement period has elapsed the LPA may apply to the magistrates' court for a planning enforcement order. If a PEO is made it gives the LPA a further year and 22 days from the date of the order in which to take enforcement action; a further enforcement period referred to in the legislation as "the enforcement year".

However, the key to this new enforcement power is that the breach of planning control to which the PEO application relates must be one that has been "deliberately concealed".

Section 171BC provides that:

(1) A magistrates' court may make a planning enforcement order in relation to an apparent breach of planning control only if –

(a) the court is satisfied, on the balance of probabilities, that the apparent breach, or any of the matters constituting the apparent breach, has (to any extent) been deliberately concealed by any person or persons, and

(b) the court considers it just to make the order having regard to all the circumstances.

A breach of planning that has not been deliberately concealed cannot be subject to a PEO, and only the normal four or ten year enforcement period will apply within which time any enforcement action must be taken.

Furthermore, because deliberate concealment is the essential ingredient, the LPA can only apply for a PEO if it does so within six months of becoming aware of the breach. For the purposes of proving when the LPA first had knowledge of the apparent breach, a certificate signed on behalf of the LPA giving the date on which evidence sufficient in the authority's opinion to justify the application came to its knowledge is conclusive evidence of that fact.[26]

When an LPA applies for a PEO, copies of the application must be served

---

[26] Section 171BB(2), TCPA.

on the owners and occupiers of the land, and on anyone else with an interest in the land who may be affected by the taking of enforcement action in respect of the breach, all of whom have a right to appear before, and be heard by, the court hearing the application.

The effect of the PEO provisions on a CLEUD application is as follows. If the LPA could still apply for a PEO in respect of any of the evidence or matters claimed in support of the application, because the LPA's knowledge of those matters is not more than six months old, or if an application for a PEO has been made but not yet determined or withdrawn, or if a PEO has been made but the enforcement year not expired, then the CLEUD cannot be granted.

Case law since *Welwyn* has established that in a case of deliberate conceal-ment, even where the LPA has not applied for a PEO, the *Welwyn* principle can still apply to prevent the unauthorised development concealed by deception from becoming lawful.

That reflects the practical reality, which is that in most cases the first time the LPA will be aware of a concealed planning breach is when it is asked to consider a CLEUD application. Before *Welwyn* and the introduction of PEOs, a CLEUD applicant confident of establishing the necessary period of immunity for a breach – of four or ten years – could be fairly confident of obtaining the certificate. Now they need to consider whether the LPA and a court might find there has been *deliberate concealment* that would render the breach thought to be immune, subject to enforcement after all; quite a turnaround from the pre-*Welwyn* position.

Exactly how the *Welwyn* principle works alongside the new statutory provisions on PEOs is not entirely clear in all cases, and there are some obvious legal points and questions that may well arise in future.

What is clear is that where a breach, concealed or not, comes to the attention of the LPA within the four or ten year enforcement period, then the LPA can take enforcement action anyway and there would seem little point in applying for a PEO.

If a CLEUD application (which by its very nature is usually made outside of the intended four or ten year period) is refused because the LPA con-siders there has been deliberate concealment, it must make sense that an appeal against that refusal can be dismissed on the basis of the deliberate concealment even if the LPA has not applied for a PEO. It may be that the LPA has not had time to apply for a PEO when the appeal is made.

However, on becoming aware of a concealed breach via a CLEUD application, the LPA should then act by applying for a PEO and taking enforcement action within the enforcement year. The refusal of a CLEUD application simply means the LPA does not recognise the development in question as lawful. Enforcement action against the breach still needs to be taken if the LPA wants it stopped or got rid of, and a PEO simply gives the LPA more time in which to do that.

The plain statutory effect of the PEO is that it creates a further period, the "enforcement year", after which even concealed breaches become immune from enforcement. If after becoming aware of a concealed breach the LPA does not apply for a PEO or does not take enforcement action within the enforcement year pursuant to a PEO, then it would appear that even a concealed breach does finally become immune from enforcement.

The obvious question which follows from that is if a further CLEUD application is made after the end of the enforcement year (in which the LPA took no enforcement action) on exactly the same basis as an earlier CLEUD that triggered the LPA's PEO application, should the CLEUD be granted second time around?

If the LPA refuses the second CLEUD, could an inspector or a court still uphold that refusal on the *Welwyn* principle alone, even though the enforcement year has expired and the statutory remedy against the breach has been exhausted?

Also, what about a second CLEUD in very similar circumstances but where the magistrates refused to make a PEO because they took the view it was not 'just' to do so – could a higher court take a different view and nevertheless invoke the *Welwyn* principle to override the PEO provisions?

Another question that arises is whether a certain level or severity of deception, the deception that constitutes concealment, is required to invoke the *Welwyn* principle? Some commentators suggest there is but others argue that any contrived deception that leads to concealment will do.

This point was addressed in the Supreme Court decision in *Welwyn*. It was suggested that some of Mr Beesley's acts of deception, of a sort typically engaged in to conceal unauthorised residential use (such as not applying for building regulations consent for a dwelling and failing to pay council tax) were merely "*ancillary to the plan of deception* [that] *would not, at least without more, disentitle reliance*" on immunity after four years. In the eyes of the court, it was the "*positive deception in the making and obtaining of fraudulent planning applications"* that 'did it' for Mr Beesley.

Under the *'Enforcement and post-permission matters'* section, PPG[27] suggests that a planning enforcement order should only be made where there is:

> ... *evidence that the developer has taken positive steps to conceal the unauthorised development, rather than merely refraining from informing the local planning authority about it* [and] *it is expected that planning enforcement orders will be focused on the worst cases of concealment.*

The irony is that a failure to apply for and obtain building consent (which may have serious health and safety implications) or a failure to pay council tax appear to be considered in a less serious category of deception that would probably not cause the *Welwyn* principle to be invoked. Yet in each case, such deception by omission or failure to act may constitute a criminal offence. On the other hand, a fraudulent planning application with no wider consequences than an abuse of the planning system is considered much more serious simply because it is a positive act.

Nonetheless, the law is as stated by statute and the wording of that is quite different from the PPG. The requirement for a PEO under Section 171BC is clear. It is simply that the apparent breach, or any of the matters constituting it: *"has (to any extent) been deliberately concealed".* The words 'to any extent' are significant and self-explanatory.

Unlike the PPG, the statutory provision does not require the developer to have *"taken positive steps to conceal".* On the contrary, if the breach *"has (to any extent) been deliberately concealed"* a PEO can be made provided the magistrates consider it just in all the circumstances to do so.

In conclusion, if *deliberate concealment* has occurred, whether by omission or positive steps taken, a PEO can be made. Only where there has been no attempt at deliberate concealment can the developer or landowner have any confidence that the LPA will not obtain a PEO. In all other cases, until the LPA has been made aware of the breach or the matters constituting its concealment, the time period within which the LPA may take enforcement action is, in effect, unlimited. This amounts to a significant change in the law.

---

[27] Paragraph 026, Reference ID: 17b-026-20140306.

Orders requiring completion, revocation etc

Under various statutory provisions[28] LPAs have discretionary powers to enable them, if necessary, to retrospectively control development for which planning permission has been granted. The LPA, and in some cases the Secretary of State, may restrict or withdraw an element of a permission previously granted subject to the potential need to pay compensation. The threat of compensation, opposed orders and as a consequence, lengthy procedures, means that LPAs only very rarely and reluctantly use these powers.

Completion Notices

Section 94 provides that if an LPA is of the opinion that a development that has been started in accordance with a planning permission will not be completed within a reasonable period, it may at any time until the development is completed serve a *Completion Notice*.

A completion notice requires that the development must be completed within the period specified in the notice; the specified period must be at least 12 months after the notice takes effect. A completion notice must be confirmed by the Secretary of State who may extend the period specified in it.

The notice can only take effect – that is, be confirmed – not less than 28 days from the date it is served. That is to give any owner, occupier or interested party the opportunity to oppose the notice at a hearing conducted by an inspector appointed by the Secretary of State.

Upon expiry of the specified period in a notice that has been duly confirmed, the planning permission to which it relates is rendered invalid and further development pursuant to it will be unauthorised. The notice therefore encourages completion of the development within the specified period – which is in effect the deadline for completion – but it does not and cannot compel completion of the development.

The Secretary of State has the power to serve a completion notice under Section 96.

---

[28] Sections 94 to 107, TCPA.

Revocation and Modification Orders

If it appears expedient to an LPA to revoke or modify any planning permission, it may serve an order to that effect – this is also known as a *Section 97 Order*. However, such orders are rarely used because they render the LPA liable to pay compensation.

The owner, occupier and anyone else affected by a Section 97 Order may oppose, effectively appeal, it by reference to the Secretary of State.

In any case, the Secretary of State may make a revocation or modification order in exactly the same way as the LPA, under Section 100.

Discontinuance Orders

Under Section 102, if an LPA considers that it is expedient in the interests of the proper planning of their area, including the interests of amenity, it may serve an order requiring discontinuance of use or alteration or removal of buildings or works; a *Discontinuance Order*.

An order under this section need not necessarily relate to any planning permission previously granted by the LPA but the order *"may grant planning permission for any development of the land to which the order relates, subject to such conditions as may be specified in the order"*.

Conservation Areas and Listed Buildings

Conservation Areas and *Listed Buildings* are covered by their own Act of Parliament. The relevant statutory provisions, requirements and procedures are set out in the Planning (Listed Buildings and Conservation Areas) Act 1990.

A conservation area is designated for an area of historic or architectural importance in order to protect and enhance its layout and architectural features by imposing additional planning restrictions and requirements.

The LPA will usually prepare a conservation area management plan and, or, a design guide identifying important buildings and features and how they should be preserved.

An *Article 4 Direction*[29] may be made by the LPA to remove certain permitted development rights within a conservation area, thereby making it necessary to obtain planning permission for development that would not otherwise need it.

Planning permission may be required for prescribed works, such as demolition and the removal of certain types of enclosure (gates, fences and walls). Demolition of a building in a conservation area without planning permission is a criminal offence. Other unauthorised works in a conservation area may be subject to planning enforcement action.

In a conservation area the LPA must be informed of any intended works to trees[30] (even if no TPO applies) under a prior notification procedure which gives the LPA time to make a TPO if they consider it necessary.

Listed buildings are designated by the Secretary of State on the advice of Historic England. Spot listing often occurs if a threat to a historic building is perceived. Virtually any work, internal or external, to a listed building requires listed building consent.

Undertaking works to a listed building without consent is an offence[31] and prosecution is often seen by the LPA as the most effective deterrent against repeat offences. In addition, or alternatively, unauthorised works may be tackled with a listed building enforcement notice[32] setting out remedial measures. In contrast to planning enforcement, there is no possibility of immunity from listed building enforcement through lapse of time.

Historic England and LPAs have an array of statutory powers, including compulsory purchase, to enable them to act to preserve and maintain listed buildings. Although some LPAs are reluctant to invoke them for fear of lengthy and costly legal battles, there is generally a much stricter approach to listed buildings enforcement, perhaps because LPAs are usually supported in their efforts by Historic England.

---

[29] Under Article 4, The Town and Country (General Permitted Development) (England) Order 2015.

[30] Section 211, TCPA.

[31] Under Section 9, Planning (Listed Buildings and Conservation Areas) Act 1990.

[32] Under Section 38, Planning (Listed Buildings and Conservation Areas) Act 1990.

Tree Preservation Orders

Tree Preservation Orders, or TPOs, are made under planning legislation with the specific objective of protecting amenity trees from any form of damage or unauthorised work. A TPO should only be made to protect a tree or trees *"if it is expedient in the interests of public amenity"*.[33] Therefore, a tree completely hidden from public view – however impressive a specimen it may be – is unlikely to be protected by a TPO unless within a woodland covered by a Woodland TPO.

The many detailed provisions of the TPO regime are beyond the scope of this book but essentially a TPO is made by an LPA to protect an individual tree, a group of trees or a woodland. An individual or group TPO must specify by reference to species, and location on a plan, each tree covered.

A woodland TPO, used where the whole woodland is considered to be of amenity value as a woodland, covers every tree growing at the time the TPO is made (although this can be difficult to determine and administer).

An 'area' TPO should really only be used as an expedient, emergency measure to give the LPA time to identify individual specimens and groups worthy of protection and to make 'individual' or 'group' TPOs accordingly.

Subject to only a few very specific exemptions, it is a criminal offence to wilfully or recklessly damage, or undertake any works to, a TPO-protected tree or trees, an offence which in severe cases is punishable by imprisonment.

To undertake any work to a tree covered by a TPO, an application for consent must be made to the LPA specifying the work intended in some detail. Such an application may be granted, with conditions imposed, or refused. A refusal, or the imposition of conditions, may be appealed.

---

[33] Sections 198 to 210, TCPA.

Chapter 4: Neighbourhood Planning

Origins and evolution

Just before the May 2010 general election, the Conservatives published their Planning Green Paper, 'Open Source Planning' which proposed radical reforms to *"restore democratic and local control over the planning system, rebalance the system in favour of sustainable development and produce a simpler, quicker, cheaper and less bureaucratic planning system"*.

Some of the proposed reforms, such as residents' appeals against unacceptable major development, were abandoned but nonetheless the Green Paper was widely publicised as representing the possibility for genuine reform by 'bottom-up' plans or 'modules' of the local plan being prepared by communities at neighbourhood level.

Under the subsequent coalition government the bottom-up philosophy for planning was if anything broadened slightly and the resultant Localism Act 2011 was a comprehensive piece of legislation that was clearly aimed at, and has been largely successful in, enfranchising communities and empowering local authorities in a number of ways.

Localism Act 2011

Section 1 gives an indication of how radical the Localism Act ("the Act") was conceived to be. More philosophical proposition than statutory requirement, the local authority's general power of competence provides that *"a local authority has power to do anything that individuals generally may do"*, including engaging in any form of commercial activity provided it is lawful.

Arguably, all this really does is confirm the pre-existing legal position, that local authorities are not limited in law by the constraints they may, as a matter of convention, have considered themselves bound by. The real purpose behind Section 1 and its general power of competence is political encouragement to local authorities to engage in more commercial activities for the benefit of their respective communities and, from a more cynical perspective, to offset public spending cuts through commercial acumen.

Part 6 of the Localism Act is dedicated to 'Planning' and it is under this Part (at Chapter 3 of the Act) that the neighbourhood planning regime is introduced and the enforcement provisions introducing planning enforcement orders are brought into effect (Chapter 5).

Also at Part 6 are the provisions to abolish Regional Spatial Strategies (previously part of the statutory development plan) and to introduce a duty on planning authorities to cooperate on the planning of cross-boundary strategic development (Chapter 1). There is also provision for a duty on developers of major development to engage in pre-application public consultation (Chapter 4) and for a regime for the consideration of nationally significant infrastructure projects (Chapter 6).

There are other main parts of the Act that also have a significant bearing on planning, most notably under the various 'community empowerment' provisions of Part 5 the introduction of a regime for the listing of community assets. From a planning perspective the listing of community assets is significant because it is closely related to neighbourhood planning and the interests of local people.

However, the most radical feature of the Localism Act is undoubtedly the introduction of neighbourhood planning.

The Neighbourhood Development Plan

There is plenty of scope for discussion about just how important neighbourhood planning is, but there is no doubt that the neighbourhood plan or *Neighbourhood Development Plan* is, for two principal reasons, a significant and potentially highly influential concept.

First of all, once made – the technical term for adoption of an NDP – a neighbourhood development plan becomes part of the statutory development plan, alongside the local plan, to which every planning decision-maker must have regard in the making of their planning determinations.

Regional spatial strategies (abolished by the Localism Act) and before them, structure plans at county level were part of the statutory development plan, but both were above the local plan in the development plan hierarchy. These plans were therefore intended to provide guidance on strategic and regional matters across district boundaries.

The second very significant, and particularly distinctive, feature of an NDP is that it is a local level plan, produced by the local community. For the very first time in the UK planning system a development plan with full statutory effect can be produced by local people for the benefit of their local area and its community. Unlike parish plans, village plans or local design guides, a neighbourhood plan has a statutory basis and therefore the potential to have real planning influence at a local level.

These fundamentally important features of a neighbourhood development plan are embraced by statute, specifically Section 38A, Planning and Compulsory Purchase Act 2004 (as amended), which is as follows;

Meaning of "neighbourhood development plan"

(1) Any qualifying body is entitled to initiate a process for the purpose of requiring a local planning authority in England to make a neighbourhood development plan.

(2) A "neighbourhood development plan" is a plan which sets out policies (however expressed) in relation to the development and use of land in the whole or any part of a particular neighbourhood area specified in the plan.

Due to the legal significance of an NDP, there is now an attendant maze of regulations, procedural rules and practice notes. The law on neighbourhood planning comprises parts of several acts of parliament and a myriad of secondary legislation. Some of the detailed requirements and rules of procedure are already too complex – or at least too dispersed throughout the various legislative sources – to be readily understood, even by lawyers.

In one sense this increasing complexity is worrying because it threatens to undermine what was intended to be, and in essence still is, the simplicity of the concept. On the other hand, it serves to underpin a regime of local empowerment as one that is here to stay. If neighbourhood plans are to have real and lasting influence then they must, however unfortunately, be subject to similar rules and requirements as higher level plans.

A qualifying body

Any development plan needs a plan-making body that also has statutory recognition. The plan-making body for a local plan is the LPA, and for a neighbourhood plan the plan-making body is known as the *Qualifying*

Body. In parished areas, the qualifying body is the town or parish council (known as 'local councils', and for the purposes of the legislation the area of a town council is a parish and the term 'parish council' includes town councils).

A parish council is the obvious plan-making body because it is funded from the council tax, is already part of the government family and is a statutory consultee on all planning applications within its area. In a parish, only the parish council can be the qualifying body for an NDP.

In an unparished area, where there is no existing body with a recognised planning function, a *Neighbourhood Forum* may be formed for the purposes of making a neighbourhood plan. The requirements for the constitution of a neighbourhood forum are set out in the legislation,[1] to ensure that such a body has sufficient members with a local connection, and is an appropriate body to represent the interests of the area it claims jurisdiction over.

It is highly significant that there is a statutory duty imposed on every LPA to *"give such advice or assistance to qualifying bodies as, in all the circumstances, they consider appropriate for the purpose of, or in connection with, facilitating the making of proposals for neighbourhood development plans in relation to neighbourhood areas within their area".*[2]

The Neighbourhood Area

The first formal step towards a neighbourhood plan is an application to the LPA for designation of a *Neighbourhood Area*, the area to be covered by the plan.

It is worth considering the law on neighbourhood areas in some detail. As the area to be covered by the plan, the neighbourhood area is the basis and starting point for the whole project. If you, as a parish council or neighbourhood forum, want to make a neighbourhood plan for your area and are then told that your NDP can only apply to a smaller area, that may undermine the whole purpose behind it.

Where the application is made by a parish council for the whole or part of the parish to be the neighbourhood area, designation should be an

---

[1] Section 61F(5), TCPA.

[2] Paragraph 3, Schedule 4B, TCPA.

administrative formality and in most cases a parish council does apply for designation of the whole parish. However, it is not uncommon for two or more parish councils to jointly produce an NDP, and provided the area applied for is within their parishes, designation should also be straightforward.

In an unparished area, neighbourhood area designation is a little more complicated because the group making the application for the area must at the same time establish its standing as a neighbourhood forum. Designation of the neighbourhood forum and its neighbourhood area are inextricably linked; whether the forum is properly constituted can only be assessed, under the relevant statutory provisions, by reference to the area applied for.[3]

Even for a neighbourhood forum application the issues involved in area designation should not be particularly difficult. However, ambiguity in the legislative provisions and an unfortunate judicial decision in *Daws Hill*[4] caused unintended complications that secondary legislation has had to resolve.

Daw's Hill – neighbourhood planning, but not for all

The one thing that can be said for the *Daw's Hill* case is that it flushed out consideration of some fundamental neighbourhood planning principles.

The facts in *Daw's Hill* were unusual in that a group of residents in an unparished suburb of High Wycombe sought to oppose the major residential redevelopment of two redundant MOD sites by applying to be a neighbourhood forum (the Daw's Hill Residents' Association – "DHRA") for a neighbourhood area that included both sites. The LPA approved DHRA as a neighbourhood forum but designated a smaller neighbourhood area excluding the two MOD sites because it considered them strategic sites as they were already allocated for housing in the local plan.

DHRA unsuccessfully challenged the decision to designate only the smaller neighbourhood area, first in the High Court, then in the Court of Appeal. On the face of it, the LPA's refusal to include in a neighbourhood area applied for by a neighbourhood forum two large sites (strategic or

---

[3]   Under Section 61F, TCPA applied to neighbourhood plans by Section 38C, PCPA.

[4]   *Daw's Hill Neighbourhood Forum & Others v Wycombe DC & Others* [2014] EWCA Civ 228.

not) to which the neighbourhood forum had no direct connection could be justified by the rules that require a neighbourhood forum to establish a sufficient connection with an appropriate neighbourhood area.

However, instead of applying such a straightforward analysis, the Court of Appeal indulged in a mischievous attempt at judicial law-making by suggesting it was not Parliament's intention to create universal coverage of neighbourhood areas and that when considering a neighbourhood area application, the LPA has a wide discretion to designate a smaller area.

Most planning professionals would agree that for the planning system to work at all there must be universal coverage of the development plan. There are obvious and fundamental difficulties in making neighbourhood planning of universal coverage, and a number of pragmatic reasons why the legislation does not make neighbourhood plans compulsory.

Foremost amongst them is that there are many unparished areas where there may be no group willing to form a neighbourhood forum, and for which there is therefore no qualifying body. Furthermore, where there is a potential qualifying body – parish council or neighbourhood forum – it will be comprised entirely of volunteers so it is unrealistic to impose a absolute plan-making duty upon it in the same way that an LPA is under a duty to produce a local plan.

These fairly plain and obvious realities create all sorts of difficulties for parliamentary draftsmen trying to introduce an entirely new tier of the development plan to be administered by two completely different types of organisation with very different characteristics, parish councils and neigh-bourhood forums. Those difficulties are compounded when attempting to confer on LPAs the necessary statutory duties to administer that process with sufficient authority.

As a result, the statutory rules on the designation of neighbourhood areas are far from clear and are certainly open to different interpretations. However, one pronounced and distinctive feature of the relevant statu-tory provisions is the positive power of designation it confers on an LPA considering the extent of the neighbourhood area it should designate.[5]

Many would argue that the LPA's power of designation was as far as the legislation could possibly go in empowering LPAs to achieve maximum coverage of neighbourhood plans even if universal coverage may not

---

[5] Section 61G, TCPA.

ultimately be achievable. Parliament's intention seems to be that it is only really in cases where part of the area applied for by a neighbourhood forum is not appropriate to that neighbourhood forum that LPAs should not use the power of designation to designate the whole area applied for.

Notwithstanding all of this, the Court of Appeal in *Daw's Hill* adopted a very narrow interpretation of the legislation which had little regard for the purpose behind it. The court held that the LPA has a wide and general discretion to refuse to designate any part of the area applied for. However, this had somewhat predictable consequences for parish councils seeking to have whole parish areas designated in the face of commercial opposition.

After all, most landowners and developers would prefer not to have to deal with a neighbourhood plan as they tend to see it as another layer of planning policies that they would rather not have to negotiate. Some will therefore take any opportunity to stop an NDP at the first hurdle unless they are confident that their development proposals will gain local support. Some landowners latched onto the *Daw's Hill* judgment to argue their land was 'strategic' and should be excluded from the neighbourhood area, and therefore from the effect of the related neighbourhood plan. In the immediate light of *Daw's Hill*, LPAs were powerless to resist such claims.

This was exactly the opposite of what was intended by the Localism Act and within weeks of the *Daw's Hill* decision the government took steps to consolidate the law in accordance with the original parliamentary intention.

The 2016 amendment Regulations – designation of the whole parish area

The amending Regulations,[6] The Neighbourhood Planning (General) and Development Management Procedure (Amendment) Regulations 2016, (the "2016 amendment Regulations") now provide that where a parish council applies for the whole or any part of its parish area that is not

---

[6] The statutory procedure for NDPs and NDOs is governed by The Neighbourhood Planning (General) Regulations 2012 ("the 2012 Regulations as amended") which have subsequently been amended by various primary and secondary legislation including The Neighbourhood Planning (General) (Amendment) Regulations 2015 ("the 2015 amendment Regulations") and The Neighbourhood Planning (General) and Development Management Procedure (Amendment) Regulations 2016 ("the 2016 amendment Regulations").

already designated, the LPA *"must designate the whole area as a neigh-bourhood area".*[7]

The LPA has no discretion in the matter; it cannot refuse such an application or exclude any part of the area applied for. Unfortunately, there is no prescribed time period within which the LPA must make such a designation; an obvious omission which may cause some difficulties, but perhaps that too will be remedied in due course.

The relevant PPG on *'Neighbourhood Planning'* under the heading *'Designating a Neighbourhood Area'* has been revised to take account of the amended Regulations[8] but anomalies remain.

Although Paragraph 036, PPG has been revised (in May 2019) since the statutory amendment for whole area designation, it remains somewhat ambiguous. It reads as follows:

Can a neighbourhood area include land allocated in strategic policies as a strategic site?

A neighbourhood area can include land allocated in strategic policies as a strategic site. Where a proposed neighbourhood area includes such a site, those wishing to produce a neighbourhood plan or Order should discuss with the local planning authority the particular planning context and circumstances that may inform the local planning authority's decision on the area it will designate.

A neighbourhood plan must be in general conformity with, and plan positively to support, the strategic policies of the development plan

However, the 2016 amendment Regulations make absolutely clear that where a parish council applies for designation of the whole parish as a neighbourhood area, that area must now be designated by the LPA – whether or not it contains land allocated as a strategic site.

Notwithstanding the now clear statutory provision for whole area designation of parish areas, PPG Paragraph 036 still suggests that the LPA may even in these circumstances decide to designate a neighbourhood

---

[7] Regulation 2 of the 2016 amendment Regulations introduces a new Regulation 5A into the 2012 Regulations as amended for the 'Designation of the whole of the area of a parish council'.

[8] See for example Paragraph 035, PPG.

area that excludes strategic sites. This is unnecessarily confusing and anomalous.

Even in relation to a neighbourhood area applied for by a neighbourhood forum, given that an NDP must conform to the strategic objectives of the local plan, what does it matter if a neighbourhood area happens to include – as is almost inevitable – strategic sites? The NDP policies cannot override strategic policies in any event.

Furthermore, if a neighbourhood forum can establish a sufficient connection with an area so as to make its standing to produce a neighbourhood plan equivalent to that of a parish council, why should land allocated as a strategic site interfere with the designation of a neighbourhood forum area when it cannot have any effect on the designation of a parish area? It remains to be seen whether these anomalies will be dealt with in further amending legislation and, or, revisions to the PPG.

There is another remaining legacy of *Daw's Hill* which has arguably always been as Parliament intended and is certainly untouched by the 2016 amendment Regulations. That is that where the LPA refuses to designate part of the neighbourhood area applied for by a neighbourhood forum, there will be some left with no opportunity to be involved in the making of a neighbourhood plan covering the area in which they live.

Whether intended or not, this is an anomaly and is not consistent with the underlying ethos of neighbourhood planning which is one of community involvement and enfranchisement.

Compliance with the basic conditions

Once a fledgling NDP has had its neighbourhood area designated, the next formal stage under the statutory procedure is the publication of a draft NDP by the LPA. However, most of the work in producing the draft plan is likely to take place between those two events – area designation and LPA publication – so that is when the essence of an NDP, what the plan is going to be all about, needs to be considered and formulated. It is the 'blank canvas' stage!

Neither the law, planning policy or even good practice guidance is actually very prescriptive about what your neighbourhood development plan should contain or what it should try to achieve. In fact, the only prescribed constraints are the basic conditions.[9]

There are five basic conditions with which an NDP must comply. Paragraph 065 of the PPG on 'Neighbourhood Planning' sets out the basic conditions as:

1. ***having regard to national policies and advice contained in guidance issued by the Secretary of State it is appropriate to make the neighbourhood plan***. This means, quite simply, compliance with the NPPF.

2. ***the making of the neighbourhood plan contributes to the achievement of sustainable development***. Unfortunately, 'sustainable development' has become a very woolly concept so this basic condition is really rather hollow and certainly adds nothing to the above, compliance with the NPPF.

3. ***the making of the neighbourhood plan is in general conformity with the strategic policies contained in the development plan for the area of the authority (or any part of that area)***. This is really the one to watch and the precise wording should be carefully considered – 'the development plan for the area' means the local plan.

4. ***the making of the neighbourhood plan does not breach, and is otherwise compatible with, EU obligations***. This relates essentially to European environmental legislation (considered in more detail in *Chapter 5*).

5. ***the prescribed conditions are met in relation to the plan and prescribed matters have been complied with in connection with the proposal for the neighbourhood plan***. This is entirely concerned with the administrative and procedural requirements as laid down by statute, most of which are essentially the responsibility of the LPA.

We deal with some of these and the controversial issues that arise from them in other parts of this book but even this relatively short list of five basic conditions is intimidating for many local councils and neighbourhood forums in the early stages of an NDP, and may deter some from even starting that process.

---

[9] Stipulated by Paragraph 8(2), Schedule 4B, TCPA.

The best advice to those making an NDP is to keep in mind the essential basic condition that a neighbourhood plan must be in general conformity with the strategic policies of the local plan.

It is not that the other basic conditions can be disregarded but rather that they will tend to follow from or be closely linked to this one. The only other part of the statutory development plan is the local plan. Every local plan must pass an examination of its soundness; a rigorous and often lengthy legal test of its compliance with the NPPF (and the presumption in favour of sustainable development) and with EU law. Therefore if an NDP is in general conformity with the strategic objectives of the local plan, and provided it has met the prescribed conditions of procedure, it is more likely – though it will not necessarily follow – that it also complies with the NPPF, with EU law and with the presumption in favour of sustainable development.

General conformity with the strategic policies of the local plan

Whilst general conformity is arguably the most fundamental of the basic conditions as compliance with it implies the other basic conditions have also been met, as with other flagship principles of neighbourhood planning general conformity is nuanced and requires further consideration.

The difficulties arise when the adopted local plan is out-of-date (even though it is still the development plan for the area) and due to be replaced. There is no point at all in the NDP being in general conformity with an out-of-date local plan which will obviously only contain similarly outdated strategic policies, because that would not be consistent with the NPPF.[10]

On the other hand the legal test of general conformity is not satisfied by conformity with an emerging local plan because its strategic policies will, by definition, only be in draft form until that emerging local plan passes its examination and is adopted as part of the development plan.

---

[10] The presumption in favour of sustainable development at Paragraph 11 NPPF requires planning approvals to follow only an up-to-date development plan; where planning policies are not up-to-date, planning permission should be granted unless the adverse impacts of doing so would significantly and demonstrably outweigh the benefits, considered by reference to other NPPF policies. If planning decision-takers (meaning planning officers, planning committees and appeal inspectors appointed by the Secretary of State) should not have regard to a local plan that is not up-to-date, there is little point in a neighbourhood plan or for that matter an emerging NDP, being in conformity with such a plan.

The qualifying body will first need to establish whether the adopted local plan is up-to-date for NPPF purposes and if not, whether the emerging NDP is likely to be made before or after adoption of a new local plan. If the NDP is intended to be made before a new local plan is adopted, then the emerging NDP should be aiming for general conformity, or at least not undermining that conformity, with the strategic scheme of the emerging local plan.

It can be difficult for the qualifying body of an emerging NDP to know what is an up-to-date local plan or when the policies of an existing local plan are *not* up-to-date for NPPF purposes. The NPPF provides no absolute rules on what constitutes an up-to-date local plan, though by reference to a five year supply of housing it does prescribe what should be considered to be up-to-date strategic policies for housing delivery[11] and, in the same context, when a neighbourhood plan will be considered up-to-date.[12]

The NDP qualifying body should liaise closely with their LPA to at least understand what it considers the up-to-date strategic policies to be, even if only the emerging local plan policies can be considered to have sufficient currency.

At least in all respects other than housing policies, it is reasonable to assume that a local plan recently adopted in accordance with the NPPF, is up-to-date. However, a local plan adopted prior to the 2012 NPPF is to all intents and purposes obsolete and due to be replaced, and in those circumstances it will generally be the emerging local plan that an NDP should be looking to synchronise with.

It is well established that a neighbourhood plan may be made whilst a new local plan is still emerging and before it is adopted, that is, when there is no other part of the development plan and no strategic policies in place. That is confirmed by the decisions of the High Court in *BDW Trading*[13] and *Gladman Developments*,[14] which arose from very similar circumstances.

---

[11] Section 5 and Paragraphs 67, 73 and 74, NPPF.

[12] Paragraph 14, NPPF.

[13] *BDW Trading Ltd v Cheshire West and Chester Borough Council* [2014] EWHC 1470 (Admin).

[14] *R (on the application of Gladman Developments Ltd) v Aylesbury Vale District Council* [2014] EWHC 4323 (Admin).

In both cases, one of the main grounds of challenge to the neighbourhood plan was that because the emerging local plan was not yet adopted and there were therefore no strategic policies in place for the NDP to be in general conformity with, the neighbourhood plan failed to comply with that basic condition and should not be made.

In *Gladman* it was held that the examiner *"was entitled ... to conclude that the Neighbourhood Plan satisfied basic condition 8(2)(e) of Schedule 4B to the 1990 Act as it was in conformity with such strategic policies as were contained in development plan documents notwithstanding the fact that the local planning authority had not yet adopted a development plan document containing strategic polices ..."*.

What follows from this is a different but equally significant feature of general conformity expressed in the judgment in *BDW Trading*[15] which is *"that the Neighbourhood Plan as a whole should be in general conformity with the adopted Development Plan as a whole* [and that] *whether or not there was any tension between one policy in the Neighbourhood Plan and one element of the eventual emerging local plan was not a matter for the Examiner to determine"*. That is because tension between a neighbourhood plan policy and a local plan policy does not necessarily mean the former is not in general conformity with the latter.

The judgments in *Gladman* and *BDW* on general conformity were endorsed by the Court of Appeal in the *DLA v Lewes District Council* case,[16] where it was held that the requirement for general conformity with the strategic policies of the development plan simply means general conformity with any such strategic policies that exist, and that (at paragraph 25 of the judgment):

> ... [the legislation] *does not require the making of a neighbourhood development plan to await the adoption of any other development plan document. It does not prevent a neighbourhood development plan from addressing housing needs unless or until there is an adopted development plan document in place setting a housing requirement for a period coinciding, wholly or partly, with the period of the neighbourhood development plan. A neighbourhood development plan may include, for example, policies allocating land*

---

[15] Paragraph 82, *BDW Trading Ltd v Cheshire West and Chester Borough Council* [2014] EWHC 1470 (Admin).

[16] *R (on the application of DLA Delivery Ltd) v Lewes District Council and Newick Parish Council* [2017] EWCA Civ 58.

> for particular purposes, including housing development, even when
> there are no "strategic policies" in the statutorily adopted develop-
> ment plan to which such policies in the neighbourhood development
> plan can sensibly relate. This may be either because there are no
> relevant "strategic policies" at all or because the relevant strategy
> itself is now effectively redundant, its period having expired. The
> neighbourhood development plan may also conform with the strat-
> egy of an emerging Local Plan. It may, for example, anticipate the
> strategy for housing development in that emerging plan and still not
> lack "general conformity" with the "strategic policies" of the existing
> development plan.

Furthermore, the requirement for general conformity is not for slavish
adherence to all local plan policies or even to all strategic policies in the
local plan,[17] but conformity with the strategic objectives of a local plan
as illustrated by its strategic policies.

By no means is every local plan policy a strategic policy, and neither is a
planning policy strategic simply by being labelled as such. The NPPF now
clearly sets out[18] the proper context for strategic policies, non-strategic
policies and how both should be accommodated in the development plan.

The main function of local plans is strategic planning via strategic policies,
whilst neighbourhood plans should look to add the detail to that framework via non-strategic policies. However, as neighbourhood plan-making
is not compulsory and many areas do not have an NDP, local plans may
also contain non-strategic policies.

Strategic policies are those that facilitate the delivery of development
identified as necessary to fulfil strategic objectives.[19] Planning policies
that relate to other aspects of such development – such as scale, form,
access and design details – are generally not matters for strategic policies.

---

[17] See judgment of Howell J in *Hoare v The Vale of White Horse District Council* [2017]
EWHC 1711 (Admin) at paragraph 127: "*The mere fact that there is a conflict between
one policy in a neighbourhood plan and one strategic policy in the development plan
does not necessarily mean that the policies in the neighbourhood plan collectively are
not in general conformity with the strategic policies in the development plan as a whole.
It is necessary to consider what the conflict relates to and how important it may be
in the context of the policies in the neighbourhood plan collectively and the strategic
policies in the development plan as a whole*".

[18] At Paragraphs 17 to 23 and 28 to 30.

[19] Paragraph 20, NPPF.

A site identified in a local plan for strategic development will be a strategic site, and the local plan policy that allocates the site in fulfilment of strategic objectives will be a strategic policy. On the other hand, a local plan policy that simply sets out general prerequisites for acceptable development is not a strategic policy. The NPPF says that [local] *"Plans should make explicit which policies are strategic policies"*[20] and that *"the non-strategic policies should be clearly distinguished from the strategic policies".*

The heavily revised NPPF guidance on strategic policies and the implications for plan-makers is very clear and very welcome for that. That guidance should also be kept in mind when considering the planning policies of local plans adopted pursuant to the 2012 NPPF which said little about the significance of strategic policies.

Some LPAs tried to confer strategic significance by labelling almost every local policy as 'strategic' whether or not it actually is. There is no doubt that many LPAs have been less enthusiastic about neighbourhood planning than they should be.[21] Dealing with non-strategic issues as strategic is often an attempt to retain control over planning issues that are now within the remit of neighbourhood planners.

This approach is, unwittingly or not, supported by some NDP examiners who take LPA-labelled strategic policies in local plans at face value. When testing the conformity of a draft NDP policy, examiners are often unwilling to discern a local plan policy that genuinely seeks to pursue strategic objectives from one that does no such thing but happens to be called a strategic policy.

Given that a typical plan period is at least 15 years, it is essential that NDP examiners have regard to the current NPPF and are more discerning in differentiating strategic from non-strategic local plan policies when testing the general conformity of a neighbourhood plan.

So, the proper context in which to consider general conformity is that of conformity with the strategic objectives of the emerging or adopted

---

[20] Paragraph 21, NPPF.

[21] Under Section 38A(3), TCPA (applying Section 61E(3), TCPA on Neighbourhood Development Orders to Neighbourhood Development Plans), a local planning authority must give such advice or assistance to qualifying bodies as, in all the circumstances, they consider appropriate for the purpose of, or in connection with, facilitating the making of proposals for neighbourhood development [plans] etc.

development plan as a whole, rather than close adherence to individual policies. General conformity is a principle that allows there to be some tension or even inconsistency between an NDP policy and strategic policies.

Given that, as we have seen, general conformity may be relevant to the timing of a neighbourhood plan in relation to an emerging local plan, the qualifying body should not forget the importance of Section 38(5) Planning and Compulsory Purchase Act 2004:

> *If to any extent a policy contained in a development plan for an area conflicts with another policy in the development plan the conflict must be resolved in favour of the policy contained in the last document to be adopted.*

Here the issue is not conformity but conflict. Where an NDP policy conflicts with a non-strategic policy of a subsequently adopted local plan, even though no question may arise as to the NDP's compliance with the basic conditions, the conflicting NDP policy could, and arguably should, be ignored by decision-makers.

If it is anticipated that this situation may arise, it may be better for the NDP to be made after the local plan is adopted.

The content of an NDP

What the basic conditions and the principle of general conformity do not tell us is what the plan should contain. Once the neighbourhood area has been designated, if not before, that should be the main focus.

A neighbourhood plan can only directly influence local planning matters. It cannot have a direct effect on planning issues beyond the neighbourhood area or on what are sometimes considered to be matters closely related to planning such as highways and transport issues including bus times, speeding or even public rights of way.

The way an NDP seeks to address local planning concerns may have an indirect effect on matters strictly beyond its remit and it may even contain aspirational objectives on such issues, but the real purpose of a neighbourhood plan is to set down – as part of the development plan for the area – effective local planning policies.

This is so important that we will return to it in more detail, but if your parish council or neighbourhood forum is just embarking on the NDP project and wondering where to start, the principal and overriding focus should be; *what do we need local planning policies to cover?* Those who join an NDP steering group primarily to reduce littering, dog fouling or speeding, important as those things may be, need to change focus.

The ever increasing volume of legislation on neighbourhood plans will not help you here. Neither, to any great extent, will the various sources of guidance be of much use in formulating the specific content, and in particular the local planning policies, of your NDP. Those sources will tell you that after area designation, the next statutory stage of the process is pre-submission consultation and publicity of the draft plan.

However, it is between the area designation and pre-submission consultation stages that the main input into the plan occurs and when the NDP really takes shape. This happens via a combination of public consultation, assessment of evidence and executive decision-making by the qualifying body, the requirements of which will be explained in the next chapter. For now, suffice to say that this part of the process – what may be called the input stage – is usually the most time-consuming and, particularly in the absence of professional support, difficult to manage. It is at this stage where many neighbourhood plans, however enthusiastically commenced, are weighed down by inertia and a lack of direction and as a result of that it is not uncommon for an NDP to be put on hold or abandoned completely.

Once a coherent draft of the neighbourhood plan in final form has been produced it must be publicised by the qualifying body under Regulation 14 of the Neighbourhood Planning (General) Regulations 2012 ("the 2012 Regulations").

The unwieldy maze of the statutory process

Regulation 14 is the start of the statutory process for formal scrutiny of a neighbourhood plan, yet in some ways the 2012 Regulations are rather misleading and should be fully understood before going public with your draft NDP.

In fact, at this stage of an NDP – just when an often inexperienced qualifying body has to grapple with the legislative process for the first time – the various procedural rules become particularly complicated and confused. One of the reasons for this is that there are simply too many legislative sources and it is difficult to get an overall picture of how the process works in practice.

The principal legislation for the procedural rules on neighbourhood plans is Schedule 4B of the Town and Country Planning Act 1990, as amended ("TCPA"), imported into the Act by Schedule 9 of the Localism Act 2011. Though the lengthy and detailed rules under Schedule 9 only actually relate to Neighbourhood Development Orders, they apply to NDPs, with various modifications, by virtue of provisions in Schedule 10 of the Localism Act. Then there are the 2012 Regulations and the various amending Regulations, and subsequently the Neighbourhood Planning Act 2017.

Finally, the PPG on *'Neighbourhood Planning'* attempts, and generally fails, to distil the foregoing statutory rules into a number of easily digestible paragraphs. The problem is that the PPG is modular; within each section of the PPG there are a number of paragraphs that are introduced, or revised, separately and at different times so it is not guidance prepared as a whole and presented in a logical sequence. In any case the PPG is merely guidance, not a definitive statement of the law. For that … you need to go back to square one, the TCPA!

Before considering them in detail, it is worth providing a brief summary of the key Regulations, interpreted so as to make some sense of them.

Making sense of Regulations 14, 15, 16 and 17 and how they operate

The key to understanding Regulation 14 is in its heading: *'Pre-submission consultation and publicity'*.

Regulation 14 sets out the requirements for the qualifying body to publicise and consult on the draft plan *"before it is formally submitted to the LPA"*, even though Regulation 14(c) requires *"a copy of the proposals for a neighbourhood development plan"* – meaning a copy of the draft plan – to be sent to the LPA. However, this is not the submission of the draft plan to the LPA.

Before we consider what *'Plan proposals'* under Regulation 15 actually relates to, we should look at Regulation 16.

Somewhat disguised under the rather misleading heading of *'Publicising a plan proposal'*, and although it doesn't actually say so, Regulation 16 deals with the formal submission of the draft plan to the LPA for the first time. This is very significant for a number of reasons not least because it is at this point that the qualifying body loses control of its draft NDP almost completely.

Given the significance of this, for the qualifying body at least, it is somewhat surprising that Regulation 16 itself does not refer to the submission of the draft plan to the LPA, as that is exactly what Regulation 16 deals with.

So, whilst at first glance the Regulation 15 details required of '*Plan proposals*' may appear to relate to the proposals under Regulation 14, they do not. The detailed requirements of Regulation 15 relate to the submission of the draft NDP under Regulation 16.

Where there is some sense in this statutory sequence is that the requirements of Regulations 14 and 15 are strictly the responsibility of the qualifying body, whilst those under Regulations 16 and 17 ('*Submission of plan proposal to examination*') are entirely the responsibility of the LPA.

However, given that most qualifying bodies are at least in need of LPA advice, if not more involved assistance, by the time they get to Regulation 14, and that LPAs are under a statutory duty to assist throughout anyway, in practice any division of responsibility between the qualifying body and the LPA is already somewhat blurred by the time the Regulation 14 stage is reached.

The Regulation 15 details required of '*Plan proposals*' could be read as applying to Regulation 14 pre-submission consultation and publicity as well as Regulation 16 post-submission publicity.

However, qualifying bodies should note that pre-submission (Regulation 14) and post-submission (Regulation 16) publicity are two very different exercises, with the qualifying body only responsible for the former. There are also sound practical reasons (dealt with below) for the qualifying body not applying the strict Regulation 15 requirements to the Regulation 14 proposals.

Pre-submission publicity and consultation under Regulation 14

Before submitting the proposed NDP to the LPA, the qualifying body must publicise it in a way that is likely to bring it to the attention of people who live, work or carry on business in the area (this will usually be on a website although that is not expressly required). The publicity must include details of where the draft plan can be inspected and how representations on it may be made for a period of at least six weeks from the date of publication.[22]

The qualifying body must also consult with any consultation bodies (listed under Schedule 1 of the 2012 Regulations) whose interests are potentially affected by the draft plan, by notifying them of the proposals and considering their responses.

A copy of the proposed NDP must also be sent to the LPA at this stage. In practice the LPA will usually publicise the draft NDP on its website once it receives it but the responsibility for ensuring the draft NDP is properly publicised, and for dealing appropriately with any consultation representations, remains firmly with the qualifying body at this stage.

If the qualifying body makes material amendments to the plan as a result of the consultation representations, so that the draft plan proposed to go forward to the next stage is different from the one publicised for the Regulation 14 consultation, then the Regulation 14 consultation should be re-run giving the public and the consultation bodies the chance to make representations on the 'new' amended plan. It is easy to see how this could turn into a never-ending, circular process – all the more reason to refine the draft plan as keenly as possible prior to Regulation 14 publicity.

Publicising a plan proposal under Regulation 16

Having consulted on the draft NDP under Regulation 14 and taken account of the consultation responses by appropriate amendments where necessary, the proposed NDP is then submitted to the LPA for publication on its website, under Regulation 16.[23]

Representations may then be made on the publicised draft during a consultation period of at least six weeks. Any consultation body must be notified that the LPA has received the proposed NDP under Regulation 16.

When submitting the proposed NDP to the LPA under Regulation 16, the qualifying body must include a consultation statement[24] containing details of persons and bodies consulted on the NDP and how they were consulted. The consultation statement must also summarise the main issues and concerns, how they have been considered and, where relevant,

---

[22] Regulation 14, 2012 Regulations.

[23] Regulation 16, 2012 Regulations.

[24] Regulation 15(1)(b) and (2), 2012 Regulations.

addressed.

The consultation statement is an important document that should deal with all the consultations conducted throughout the process of the draft NDP and not just the Regulation 14 consultation. It should be considered at the examination and where elements of the NDP are contentious should provide vital evidence for the examiner of how those issues were consulted upon and how any representations made were taken account of.

Although in practice the requirements and process for Regulation 14 and Regulation 16 are very similar, it is under Regulation 16 that the qualifying body is formally submitting the draft NDP to the LPA, for the LPA in turn to submit the draft plan for examination under Regulation 17.

The implications of this and how the qualifying body should anticipate the potential problems it creates are dealt with in the next chapter under *'Potential pitfalls with Regulation 16 and the examination process'.*

The examination stage – submission by LPA under Regulation 17

It is the LPA that submits the proposed NDP for examination, under Regulation 17,[25] once the Regulation 16 consultation is complete. The detailed rules governing the examination and the criteria by which the draft plan is to be examined are to be found in Schedule 4B, TCPA.

Along with the draft plan the examiner will be sent the various other documents arising from the NDP process and produced by the qualifying body including a consultation statement and a basic conditions statement.

The LPA appoints the examiner – who should be independent of the LPA – and will consult with the qualifying body on that appointment. If it cannot be agreed, the Secretary of State will appoint an examiner. Generally, though, the qualifying body will have no reason to question the examiner(s) proposed by the LPA and it is unlikely to cause disagreement.

Where the examiner considers that the consideration of oral representations is necessary to ensure adequate examination of an issue or to ensure that a person has a fair chance to put a case, the examiner must hold a public hearing to allow adequate examination. The examiner will determine how such a hearing is to be held and how any questioning of those

---

[25] Regulation 17, 2012 Regulations.

involved is to be conducted. If a hearing is held then both the qualifying body and the LPA are entitled to attend and make oral representations.

However, hearings are unusual and in most cases the examination is dealt with by way of written representations. The written representations to be considered by the examiner are those made and received in response to the Regulation 16 publicity of the proposed plan by the LPA. The examiner should also consider the Regulation 15 consultation statement produced by the qualifying body describing how any issues raised by the statutory consultees are addressed by the plan proposal.

Once the examination deliberations, whether by a hearing or written representations, are complete the examiner produces a report on the examination to the LPA (see below – *The examiner's report on the examination*).

Having completed his or her deliberations, the examiner will usually produce a draft report for the LPA giving it the opportunity to correct any obvious factual errors but that currently seems to be the only purpose of a draft report. There is currently no statutory obligation on the examiner to produce a draft report and no need at all for a draft report to be shown to or discussed with the qualifying body.

Section 7 of the Neighbourhood Planning Act 2017 provides for regulations to be made that will impose a responsibility on an examiner to produce a draft report for discussion at a meeting or meetings to which the qualifying body must be invited. This is a noteworthy provision in that it seems to acknowledge that the qualifying body is currently cut out of the process but as yet there is still no secondary legislation to give effect to Section 7.

The aspects of the examination procedure that the qualifying body should try to anticipate are dealt with in the next chapter under *Problems for the qualifying body in the examination process*.

The examiner's report on the examination

Upon completion of the examination, the examiner makes a report on the draft plan containing a recommendation either for it to be submitted to a referendum as proposed, or that modifications as specified in the report are made to it and then the draft plan as modified is submitted to a referendum. The third possibility is that the proposal for the NDP is refused altogether.

The report cannot recommend that the draft plan is submitted to a referendum unless it meets the basic conditions and conversely the only modifications the report can make – other than to correct errors and ensure compliance with the European Convention on Human Rights ("the Convention") – are those required to comply with the basic conditions.[26]

In essence and as we have seen above a neighbourhood plan must be in general conformity with the strategic policies of the local plan and any modifications by the examiner, if necessary at all, must be necessary for the purposes of achieving conformity. There is no justification or any sound basis for examiner modifications that are not made to secure general conformity or compliance with the Convention, unless merely for the correction of errors.

However, there is no escaping the fact that examiners do make modifications that are unnecessary for compliance with the basic conditions but instead simply interfere with the planning merits. The most likely reason for many such aberrations is that examiners (and LPAs) are fearful of developers' ever present threats of judicial review of decisions that go against them.

The examiner must also make a recommendation on whether the referendum area should be the neighbourhood area (which is the typical, default position) or a larger area. If it is recommended to extend the referendum area, reasons for that must be given in the examiner's report. The statutory rules give no indication of circumstances in which a referendum area may be larger than the neighbourhood area and, in practice, the referendum area is rarely, if ever, extended. It should be noted that this is a separate consideration to that which applies in a *Business Neighbourhood Area* – for a business neighbourhood plan – in which two referendums are held; a residents' referendum and a business referendum across the same neighbourhood area.[27]

The examiner's report must be sent to the qualifying body and the LPA. The latter must then consider each of the examiner's recommendations and decide what action it is going to take on them.

---

[26] Paragraph 10, Schedule 4B, TCPA.

[27] Paragraph 15, Schedule 4B, TCPA.

LPA's consideration of the examiner's report

If having considered the examiner's report the LPA is satisfied that the draft plan meets the basic conditions and is compatible with the Convention rights or that the draft plan would fulfil those requirements if modifications were made to it, then a referendum *must* be held on the making of a neighbourhood development plan by the LPA.[28]

There are two elements to this that are worth considering further.

First of all, the modifications that the LPA may consider necessary to make the draft plan compliant are *"not limited to those recommended by the examiner"*.[29]

However, the LPA may only consider making modifications – whether or not recommended by the examiner – that are necessary to make the draft plan compliant (with the basic conditions, Convention rights etc.) and for correcting errors.[30] The LPA may consider that the draft plan complies with the basic conditions without the need to make a modification that the examiner has recommended.

There is no obligation or statutory requirement for the authority to make an examiner-recommended modification to the draft NDP, or indeed to follow the examiner's recommendations. The decision on which, if any, modifications to make is for the LPA to make and the LPA should consider what its decision should be in respect of each of the examiner's recommendations.[31]

This is because it is the LPA that bears the statutory responsibility for making the neighbourhood plan and for all the formal decisions at every statutory stage of the NDP process. In that sense, it is the LPA that is the plan-making authority even though in the early stages of an NDP when all the real plan-making work is done it need have very little input. (Indeed, in those all important early stages of an NDP many LPAs get involved as little as possible, much to the frustration of the qualifying body which will have had no previous experience of statutory plan-making at all).

---

[28] Paragraph 12(4), Schedule 4B, TCPA.

[29] Paragraph 12(4)(5), Schedule 4B, TCPA.

[30] Paragraph 12(6), Schedule 4B, TCPA.

[31] Paragraph 12(2)(3)(4), Schedule 4B, TCPA.

The LPA's decision on what action to take in respect of the examiner's recommendations must be published (on its website) in what is known as its "decision statement", a copy of which must also be sent to the qualifying body.[32] If the LPA decides to adhere entirely to the examiner's recommendations and not to make any of its own modifications, then it must publish its decision statement within five weeks of receiving the report from the examiner unless the LPA and the qualifying body between them agree a different date.[33]

It is rare indeed for an LPA to decide to differ from an examiner's recommendation. However, where the LPA does decide not to follow the examiner's recommendations and, or, to make fresh modifications of its own, and if *"the reason for the difference is (wholly or partly) as a result of new evidence or a new fact or a different view taken by the authority as to a particular fact",*[34] then as well as the qualifying body, it must also notify the statutory consultees and anyone who made written representations under Regulation 16 of that decision and allow a six week consultation period on it. In these circumstances, the LPA must publish its final decision within five weeks of the expiry of that consultation period (unless a different date is agreed).[35]

Alternatively, the LPA may refer an issue on which it disagrees with the examiner to a further independent examination, and then it must make its decision on that issue within five weeks of receiving that examination report (again, unless otherwise agreed between the LPA and qualifying body).[36]

The LPA must also consider and make its own decision on the referendum area and whether or not to extend the neighbourhood area for the purposes of the referendum,[37] (though here too only very rarely will the LPA diverge from the examiner's report and, as we have seen, it is also

---

[32] Regulations 18 and 19, 2012 Regulations.

[33] Regulation 24A(5), 2012 Regulations as amended by the 2016 amendment Regulations.

[34] Paragraph 13(1), Schedule 4B, TCPA.

[35] Regulation 24A(5), 2012 Regulations as amended by the 2016 amendment Regulations.

[36] Regulation 24A(5), 2012 Regulations as amended by the 2016 amendment Regulations.

[37] Paragraph 12(8), Schedule 4B, TCPA.

extremely rare for the referendum area to differ from the neighbourhood area).

If the LPA considers that the draft plan meets the basic conditions (and the other regulatory requirements) then it must hold a referendum on it.[38]

This reflects the fact that if the qualifying body has produced an NDP that complies with all the statutory requirements, the LPA has a duty to put that draft plan to a referendum and subject to that, to then make the neighbourhood plan.

In reality, therefore, the LPA has no discretion on this point. It could be argued that the words *"if the authority considers"* confer a limited discretion but in fact they simply confirm that it is the LPA rather the qualifying body or the examiner that bears the statutory responsibility for the NDP. An LPA that unreasonably claimed it did not consider a draft plan compliant and on that basis refused to hold a referendum could be easily held to account, especially if the examiner had reached a different conclusion.

However, whilst the qualifying body is sent a copy of the examiner's report and the LPA's decision statement, if the LPA follows the examiner's recommendations there is no need for the qualifying body to be consulted.

At this crucial stage in the overall process, the qualifying body has no right of reply to the examiner's recommendations and no formal opportunity to make representations for the LPA's consideration prior to the latter deciding whether or not to hold a referendum.

Perhaps more significantly, the qualifying body has no right to be consulted on modifications to the draft NDP recommended by the examiner unless and in very specific circumstances,[39] the LPA decides not to follow those recommendations and even then it only needs to invite representations from the qualifying body. Otherwise the LPA may invite input from the qualifying body but it is not bound to do so.

So, in the vast majority of cases, although the qualifying body has a right to be informed, and sent copies, of the examiner's report and the LPA decision statement, it has no right to comment on, or influence, either. The qualifying body is therefore not consulted as such on the draft plan that

---

[38] Paragraph 12(4), Schedule 4B, TCPA.

[39] Under Paragraph 13(1), Schedule 4B, TCPA.

goes forward from the examination to the referendum. It is only if the LPA decides not to follow the examiner's modifications that representations from the qualifying body may be made but need not be acted upon.

Only in some further very limited circumstances has this imbalance been redressed to some extent by amending legislation,[40] with certain powers conferred on the Secretary of State to intervene.

If the LPA does not make its decision on the referendum within the prescribed five week period or it makes a decision either not based on the examiner's recommendations or which introduces modifications not recommended by the examiner, then the qualifying body may request the Secretary of State to intervene in the LPA's decision or lack of it, as the case may be.[41]

A request by the qualifying body for intervention must be in writing, setting out the reasons for the request, within six weeks of the LPA decision where that was made in time.[42]

Where the Secretary of State proposes to make directions that differ from the original NDP examiner, the qualifying body, the statutory consultees and anyone else who made representations on the draft plan must be notified of the proposed directions and the reasons for them and a further independent examination may be held.[43]

Finally, the Secretary of State will try to agree with the LPA, but in any case will decide what the outcome should be, whether or not the draft plan should go to a referendum, and if so, on what basis.[44]

The qualifying body's right to request intervention only exists where the LPA either fails to make a timely decision or decides to diverge from the examiner's recommendations. The fact remains that where, as in most cases, the LPA follows those recommendations the qualifying body cannot request intervention or even make representations. In those circumstances, the last input into, or influence on, the process by the qualifying

---

[40] Section 141, Housing and Planning Act 2016.

[41] Paragraph 13B, Schedule 4B, TCPA.

[42] Regulation 31A, 2012 Regulations as amended by the 2016 amendment Regulations.

[43] Paragraph 13B(4), Schedule 4B, TCPA.

[44] Paragraph 13B(5), Schedule 4B, TCPA.

body will effectively be at the Regulation 14 stage.

The referendum and the 'making' of the neighbourhood plan

There are detailed rules on the administration of a neighbourhood plan referendum, which is conducted by the LPA.[45] As with the examination, the LPA bears the costs of the referendum and for both functions the LPA receives a set amount of government funding for each neighbourhood plan.

Every resident on the electoral roll within the neighbourhood area is entitled to vote in the referendum, which simply asks the question of whether the policies in the NDP should be considered as part of the development plan when making local planning determinations.

If a simple majority, i.e. more than 50% of those voting, favour the plan then the LPA must make the neighbourhood plan. Unless the NDP or the referendum approving it is subject to a judicial review (which will usually be known within four to six weeks), the LPA must make, and publish on its website, the NDP within eight weeks of the referendum.[46] The detailed rules on the administration of referendums are contained in separate Regulations.[47]

In a business area, a second referendum of rateable business owners is also held. If one of the two referendums supports the NDP but the other does not, then it is for the LPA to decide whether or not to make the plan[48] and if so, it must be made within eight weeks of the last applicable referendum.[49]

Once made, the neighbourhood plan comes into force as part of the statutory development plan for the area and it must be publicised as such by the LPA on its website.[50]

---

[45] Paragraphs 14 to 16, Schedule 4B, TCPA.

[46] Regulation 18A, 2012 Regulations as amended by the 2016 amendment Regulations.

[47] The Neighbourhood Planning (Referendums) Regulations 2012 as amended.

[48] Paragraph 063, PPG on *'Neighbourhood Planning'*.

[49] Regulation 18A, 2012 Regulations as amended by the 2016 amendment Regulations.

[50] Regulation 20, 2012 Regulations as amended by the 2016 amendment Regulations.

The Neighbourhood Development Order

A *Neighbourhood Development Order* ("NDO") grants planning permission within a specified neighbourhood area either for the development described in the order or for any class of development specified.[51]

With only slight differences in the factors to be considered between the two, the NDO is subject to exactly the same statutory process as the neighbourhood plan; the qualifying body – the parish council or in unparished areas, a neighbourhood forum – initiates and promotes the order within a neighbourhood area designated by the LPA upon the application of the qualifying body.

An NDO may be made in parallel, and to work in conjunction, with an NDP so a parish council having already established an NDP can make an NDO within the existing neighbourhood area. The NDP contains planning policies. The NDO goes a step further by being, in effect, a planning permission.

The NDO is a form of permitted development order that can add new classes of locally permitted development, for example particular categories of change of use, to those already existing under the General Permitted Development Order or GPDO.[52]

It can also be more specific by granting planning permission for a particular development on a specified site, though a permission of this type is likely to be more easily and quickly obtained by a planning application, which although subject to LPA scrutiny and public consultation, is not required to navigate the statutory neighbourhood planning process.

The significance of the NDO is that it operates as a planning permission and generally no further planning application is necessary in relation to the NDO-specified development. To have that effect, though, the NDO will need to travel down an identical procedural route to any NDP.

Procedure for a Neighbourhood Development Order

As with a neighbourhood plan, once a draft order has been prepared

---

[51] Section 61E(2), TCPA.

[52] The Town and Country Planning (General Permitted Development) (England) Order 2015 as amended.

by the qualifying body it must ensure that the order is then publicised under Regulation 14 for pre-submission consultation. In practice, this may mean that the draft order is sent to the LPA for publication on its website, for consultation with the public and with the statutory consultees. Nonetheless the responsibility for this stage of publicity and consultation remains with the qualifying body which will need to consider any consultation representations and whether or not to amend the NDO in the light of them.

Following the Regulation 14 consultation, and amendment if necessary, the draft NDO must then be submitted to the LPA under Regulation 16 and, as with a neighbourhood plan, this is the point at which the qualifying body effectively loses control of the draft order and submits it for examination.

Thereupon, the LPA should check the draft order for compliance with the basic conditions and appoint an examiner to conduct the examination. The procedural requirements for this too are identical to those for a neighbourhood plan. Once the examiner's deliberations are complete, he or she will produce a report with recommendations on whether the draft order should progress to a referendum with or without modifications or not at all.

The only difference in the matters to be considered by the examiner is that the basic conditions relating to an NDO include *"having special regard to the desirability of preserving any listed building or its setting, or the character or appearance of any conservation area"*, in order to decide *"if it is appropriate to make the order"*.[53]

It is then for the LPA to consider the examiner's recommendations and decide whether or not the draft order should proceed to a referendum and if so in what form. A simple majority voting in favour of the NDO at the referendum will ensure that the order is made by the LPA and thereupon takes effect.

The effect of an NDO, whether it creates new categories of permitted development or grants permission for a particular development, is more direct and specific than the effect of an NDP which merely contains planning policies. However, in most cases a neighbourhood plan will be far more comprehensive and far reaching in its scope.

---

[53] Paragraph 8(2)(b),(c), Schedule 4B, TCPA.

Therefore, whilst the neighbourhood development order certainly has its place, most qualifying bodies will consider an NDP to be a more worthwhile return on the considerable time, cost and overall effort of the neighbourhood planning process.

The Community Right to Build Order

The *Community Right to Build Order* ("CRBO") is another, lesser known, feature of the wide-ranging Localism Act[54] and is a type of neighbourhood development order.

A CRBO grants planning permission for specified development in relation to a specified site in the specified neighbourhood area, so unlike a standard NDO it cannot create permitted development rights as such – it is a permission for a particular development and is therefore identical in effect to a detailed planning permission.

Community Organisation

The distinguishing feature of a CRBO is that it can only be applied for by a "community organisation" which must meet the detailed requirements prescribed in the legislation.[55] In essence a community organisation is one *"established for the express purpose of furthering the social, economic and environmental well-being of individuals living, or wanting to live, in a particular area"* and with a written constitution providing for any profits or assets, upon dissolution of the organisation or otherwise, to be distributed either amongst members or for other community benefit.

The community organisation must maintain at least ten members, living in different dwellings, within the "particular area" (the area for the benefit of which the organisation is established). Individuals living in the particular area must be entitled to be voting members (whether or not others can also be) and individuals who live in the particular area must hold the majority of the voting rights.[56]

---

[54] Introduced under Schedule 9, Localism Act, as Section 61Q, TCPA with detailed rules in Schedule 4C, TCPA introduced under Schedule 11, Localism Act.

[55] Paragraph 3, Schedule 4C, TCPA and Regulation 13, 2012 Regulations as amended by the 2016 amendment Regulations.

[56] Paragraph 3, Schedule 4C, TCPA.

Particular area and neighbourhood area

The particular area is not the same thing as the neighbourhood area. In its efforts, or rather the parliamentary draftsman's efforts, to assimilate the concept of the neighbourhood area (which has most significance in relation to neighbourhood plans) to CRBOs, the Act is confusing and unwieldy to say the least.

Even though the community organisation proposing the CRBO is regarded as the qualifying body for the purposes of the neighbourhood area specified in the CRBO (and the CRBO must so specify),[57] the vast majority of the detailed statutory provisions on neighbourhood areas and qualifying bodies do not apply to CRBOs or community organisations proposing CRBOs.

The legislation makes clear that a neighbourhood area specified in a CRBO may be *"any area within the LPA's area"* whether or not within the area of a parish council, and the particular area – for which the community organisation is established – must consist of or include the neighbourhood area. Furthermore, and in addition to the constitutional requirements of the organisation in relation to the particular area, at the time the CRBO is proposed more than half of the members of the organisation must live in the neighbourhood area.[58]

A community organisation applying for a CRBO could specify a neighbourhood area within an existing neighbourhood area for a neighbourhood plan, and both different to the particular area.

This is all to some extent academic in practice given that the main focus of a CRBO will be the *"specified development in relation to a specified site".*[59]

In summary, the neighbourhood area is the local planning area in which the CRBO is applied for and the particular area is the area which the community organisation proposing the CRBO is set up to benefit.

Procedure and examination

The procedure for the examination of a CRBO is identical, but with minor

---

[57] Paragraph 1(3) and Paragraph 2(1)(b), Schedule 4C, TCPA.

[58] Paragraph 4(1), Schedule 4C, TCPA.

[59] Under Paragraph 2(1)(b), Schedule 4C, TCPA.

variations that reflect the distinguishing features of a CRBO, to that for NDPs and NDOs.[60]

If the examiner's report recommends refusal of the CRBO proposal, then the LPA must refuse it.[61] If the report recommends the CRBO goes forward to a referendum, with or without modifications, then a referendum must be held.[62]

The referendum version CRBO will be subject to any modifications that the LPA considers appropriate, though the only modifications it can make must be necessary either to secure compliance with EU obligations or human rights or to correct errors.[63] This is a narrower discretion to make modifications than an LPA has in relation to a neighbourhood plan.

The LPA must decline the CRBO proposal if the specified development falls within Annex 2 of the EIA Directive[64] (generally large public projects) and is likely to have significant effects on the environment, or if the specified development is likely to have significant effects on a qualifying European site[65] and is not directly connected with or necessary to the management of that site.

The LPA may also decline to consider the proposal if another CRBO or NDO proposal relating to the same site has been submitted and is still under consideration.[66]

Just as with an NDP or NDO, a CRBO passes the referendum upon securing a simple majority of those voting, and is then made by the LPA.

List of Assets of Community Value

Another element of community empowerment introduced by the

---

[60] Paragraph 7, Schedule 4C, TCPA.

[61] Paragraph 10(2), Schedule 4C, TCPA.

[62] Paragraph 10(3), Schedule 4C, TCPA.

[63] Paragraph 10(5), Schedule 4C, TCPA.

[64] Council Directive 85/337/EEC.

[65] For the purposes of The Conservation of Habitats and Species Regulations 2010.

[66] Paragraph 4(5), Schedule 4C, TCPA.

Localism Act is the *Assets of Community Value* ("ACVs") regime, the key to which is the *'List of assets of community value'* that must be kept by every local authority.[67]

The statutory scheme begins with a community nomination for the listing of land considered by the LPA to be an ACV. Once listed, the owner of an ACV must notify the LPA of any intended sale of the land in question. A notice of intended sale invokes the statutory moratoriums, to enable a community interest group the time to express an interest in purchasing the land and then to pursue that interest to complete a purchase if it has the means to do so.

These provisions give community organisations the opportunity to bid for the purchase of land or buildings used by the community when they come up for sale; they do not confer a right to buy any property so listed.

The statutory provisions are convoluted. There are various elements to the scheme, with the Community Assets Regulations[68] adding further and all-important detail and definitions of some key terms such as the meaning of a "relevant disposal" for the purposes of the moratoriums. Here we cover the main principles.

What are community assets?

Under the heading of *'Land of community value'*, Section 88(1) of the Act provides that:

> *For the purposes of this Chapter [Chapter 3 of the Act] but subject to regulations under subsection (3), a building or other land in a local authority's area is land of community value if in the opinion of the authority –*

> *(a) an actual current use of the building or other land that is not an ancillary use furthers the social wellbeing or social interests of the local community, and*

> *(b) it is realistic to think that there can continue to be non-ancillary use of the building or other land which will further (whether or not in the*

---

[67] Section 87(1), Localism Act 2011.

[68] The Assets of Community Value (England) Regulations 2012. Different regulations apply to Wales where the "appropriate authority" for the making of the secondary legislation is the Welsh Ministers.

same way) the social wellbeing or social interests of the local community.

"Social interests" include cultural, recreational or sporting interests.[69]

Section 88(2) provides that even if land or a building is not currently in a community use, if the LPA considers that it has recently been and "*it is realistic to think that there is a time in the next five years when there could be* [a community use again]", then it may be considered for listing.

The Community Assets Regulations state that "*a residence together with land connected with that residence*" is land which is not of community value for the purposes of Section 88(3) of the Act.[70] The Regulations also make clear that land with a residential planning permission on which construction is underway but not complete is not a "residence",[71] so those circumstances alone will not prevent the land being considered an ACV.

Nomination of community assets

A community asset may be nominated for listing in response to a "community nomination" which is one made either by a parish council (or in Wales by a community council) or by "*a person that is a voluntary or community body with a local connection*".[72] A parish council, a neighbourhood forum, charities and community interest companies are all potential nominating bodies provided they have a local connection.

A community nomination must be considered by the local authority and must be accepted if the land or building nominated is in the authority's area and is of community value and, if so, must then be included on the list. If the nomination is declined the authority must give written reasons for that decision to the person who made the nomination.[73]

Whenever the local authority makes a decision to include land in, or remove land from, the list, notice to that effect must be served on every

---

[69] Section 88(6), Localism Act 2011.

[70] Paragraph 1, Schedule 1, The Assets of Community Value (England) Regulations 2012.

[71] Paragraph 2(c), Schedule 1, The Assets of Community Value (England) Regulations 2012.

[72] Section 89(2), Localism Act 2011. For the relevant definitions see Regulations 4 and 5, The Assets of Community Value (England) Regulations 2012.

[73] Section 90, Localism Act 2011.

owner and occupier of the land and the person who sought its nomination. The owner and any occupier of land listed must be informed of the effect of the listing and the right to have the listing reviewed.[74]

Review of listing

The owner of the listed asset may request a review[75] requiring the LPA to reconsider whether the listing was properly made in accordance with the statute.

The question to be asked is whether or not the use of the land or building concerned *"furthers the social wellbeing or social interests of the local community and is likely continue to do so"*. If not, then the land should be removed from the list. All the parties involved must be informed of the authority's decision on a review and the reasons for it. The procedure for reviews is set out under Schedule 2 of the Regulations. There is a right of appeal against an LPA's listing review decision.[76]

The local authority must also maintain a list of unsuccessful nominations which should include reasons why nominated land was not included in the list of assets.[77]

Effect of listing

Section 95 of the Act deals with the *'Moratorium on disposing of listed land'*. This is at the heart of the ACV provisions and means that the owner of a listed asset cannot sell or gift the property, unless it is an exempt disposal,[78] without first notifying the local authority of the intended disposition and giving any community interest group[79] (not necessarily the body who nominated the asset) the opportunity to register an interest, and then pursue that interest, to purchase the property.

---

[74] Sections 91 and 92, Localism Act 2011.

[75] Under Section 92, Localism Act 2011.

[76] Under Regulation 11, The Assets of Community Value (England) Regulations 2012.

[77] Section 93, Localism Act 2011.

[78] Prescribed under Section 95(5), Localism Act 2011 and by Schedule 3, The Assets of Community Value (England) Regulations 2012.

[79] As defined by Regulation 12, The Assets of Community Value (England) Regulations – so includes a parish council, a charity, a company limited by guarantee, an industrial and provident society and a community interest company, with a local connection.

An owner notification to the LPA of an intention to sell the land starts the six week "interim moratorium period". If at any time during that period a community interest group makes *"a written request ... to be treated as a potential bidder in relation to the land"*,[80] then the "full moratorium period" of six months (also beginning on the date of the owner's notification) comes into play to prevent the owner selling the land during that period. That gives the group that made the written request, or anyone else for that matter, the remaining time of the full moratorium period to make a serious offer to purchase the land.

If the interim moratorium period expires without a community interest group submitting a written expression of interest in the land, or in any case upon expiry of the full moratorium period, whether or not the owner is negotiating with an interested community group, the owner is then free – for a further 12 month period, "the protected period"[81] – to sell the land to whoever they choose. If the ACV is not sold within the protected period, upon expiry of that period any further intention to sell would require a new notification of intended sale and the commencement of a new interim moratorium period.

What these provisions do not do is compel the owner to accept an offer from, or to sell to, a community interest group or anyone else.

The listing of a property as an asset of community value must be registered as a Local Land Charge and appear on the Register of Local Land Charges,[82] thereby bringing it to the attention of any prospective purchaser.

The community asset provisions are intended to give local people the chance to keep land or buildings used by the community available for such community use wherever possible. Obvious examples would be an area of land proposed for housing development that is or has been used, perhaps even informally, for recreation, a village pub under threat of conversion to a private dwelling or a privately owned community leisure facility being considered for more profitable redevelopment.

Whilst the listing of any such properties as community assets will not

---

[80] Section 95(3), Localism Act 2011.

[81] Under Section 95(6), Localism Act 2011 – "the protected period" is 18 months from the date of the owner's notification of an intended sale.

[82] Section 100, Localism Act 2011.

ultimately prevent them being sold on the open market, the moratorium periods imposed by the legislation will at least give the community the time to consider whether to make a community bid, or perhaps to persuade the landowner to consider alternative proposals for the listed asset that are more favourable to local people.

Either way, the listing of a community asset may work effectively in conjunction with the policies of a neighbourhood plan, particularly where those policies militate against the landowner's more commercial aspirations.

Chapter 5: Making a Neighbourhood Development Plan

Why make a neighbourhood plan?

The simple answer is that a neighbourhood plan is part of the statutory development plan and that statutory recognition means that it can have a real and significant influence on the extent and character of development in the area it covers. That is an all-embracing influence because as well as the physical form, 'development' includes land use; the use to which land and buildings are put.

There are, of course, limits on what a neighbourhood plan can cover but its potential sphere of influence should convince anyone with a genuine interest in the area they live in that it is worthwhile making, or contributing to the making of, a neighbourhood plan.

For those not convinced that a neighbourhood plan will have a sufficiently direct effect, perhaps because the pattern of future development and land use for their area has already been set or because the area may not be particularly affected by new development, the other benefits of producing a neighbourhood plan should not be ignored. Though these secondary benefits are not in themselves sufficient reason to embark on an NDP they should certainly be taken into consideration.

Foremost amongst them is that a parish council or neighbourhood forum that produces a neighbourhood plan undoubtedly boosts its standing with the LPA, the wider community and with other organisations involved in public administration and services at a local level.

A neighbourhood plan can also be used to reflect, promote and galvanise support for community projects and agendas that are, strictly, beyond the local planning remit of the plan policies.

A neighbourhood plan can also give a community a real purpose and a reason for coming together, collaborating and socialising with common or even diffuse objectives in mind.

What are the alternatives to a neighbourhood plan and are they worth considering?

A *design statement* is a planning tool that a local council can prepare as a guide to elements of preferred design throughout or in different parts of the parish. On the other hand, a *parish plan* is generally more comprehensive than a design statement and whilst often focussed on planning it will usually cover other matters too.

Both may be useful and interesting to produce. They may even be influential from time to time but ultimately they carry little, if any, weight in planning determinations and because planning decision-makers are not bound to consider them at all, they can be ignored with impunity.

Some now rather outdated guidance on neighbourhood planning suggests that an *Area Action Plan* ("AAP") may be an alternative to a neighbourhood plan. It is not. Whilst it could cover a relatively small town or parish area, an AAP is always the work of the LPA, related to a local plan as part of a Local Development Framework. A parish council has no statutory powers or functions in relation to AAPs and even if an LPA were to propose an AAP to align with the boundary and interests of a parish council, which seems unlikely, the local council would have no control or 'ownership' of it. In any case, AAPs are now to all intents and purposes obsolete and are mentioned here for completeness only.

There are no credible alternatives to producing a neighbourhood plan; a design statement or a parish plan may have some merit but is a very pale reflection of the real thing. This is particularly so now that neighbourhood planning is well established and here to stay. Cheap imitations are now almost completely worthless!

For those unsure of the local commitment or resources to support an NDP, it may be better focussing limited resources on other forms of influence, at least until sufficient momentum can be directed towards working with the LPA to produce a neighbourhood plan. These other forms of influence are dealt with in *Chapter 7*.

Ultimately, the question for every town or parish council and prospective neighbourhood forum to consider is; *can you afford not to produce a neighbourhood plan*? Are you willing to be left out of this brave new world of localism and neighbourhood planning when all around are embracing it?

General principles

Having decided to embark on a neighbourhood plan, and before actually getting started – which many neighbourhood planning groups find to be one of the most difficult steps in the whole process – it is worth just reconsidering some first principles. What is this neighbourhood planning business really all about, how should we approach it and how should we best equip ourselves to manage it effectively and productively?

A reminder of the statutory definition[1] may be helpful at this point;

> A "neighbourhood development plan" is a plan which sets out policies (however expressed) in relation to the development and use of land in the whole or any part of a particular neighbourhood area specified in the plan.

It is worth keeping in mind that *"policies (however expressed) in relation to the development and use of land"* means *planning* policies.

The planning policies in a neighbourhood plan can only cover the neighbourhood area designated in relation to the qualifying body that applied for it, so any attempt to directly influence planning decisions beyond that area will be unsuccessful.

It is also worthwhile understanding the fundamentals of the planning system and how that system operates and is intended to operate. There is no point at all in trying to undermine or contradict statutory principles or rules on, say, permitted development, because any such efforts would be completely ineffective.

With those fundamentals acknowledged, the process of producing a neighbourhood plan should be a positive and exciting one that embraces creativity, lateral-thinking and purposeful decision-making. A neighbourhood plan should always and in every aspect be purposeful and subject – as far as possible – to the executive decisions of the qualifying body that produces it.

An NDP, in concentrating on its purpose and purposes, should aim to be a rigorous but straightforward document with only as much detail as is necessary for it to be clear, balanced and well-justified. Yes, it must be evidenced-based but it must also be capable of being easily understood

---

[1]   At Section 38A, Planning and Compulsory Purchase Act 2004 (as amended).

and interpreted – it should aim for simplicity and avoid overcomplexity.

Ultimately, as we have seen above, an NDP will be made by the LPA, which takes legal responsibility for it and therefore has to ensure that it is fully compliant. Notwithstanding that, a neighbourhood plan is the project of the local community and of the parish council (or neighbourhood forum) that produces it. It is the parish council that is the qualifying body and the plan-maker and with that goes a lot of responsibility too!

Planning the plan and organising how it will be produced is best done by reference to the different stages of its production and it makes sense to break the project down into the following five stages which are considered in detail in the pages below.

1.   Getting started – preliminary matters.

2.   Issues and options – focusing on objectives.

3.   The substance of the plan – evidence gathering and consultation.

4.   Preparing a draft plan – with planning policies that work.

5.   The statutory stages – publicity, consultation and examination.

There are of course a number of smaller steps or things that need to happen within each of these main stages. Most online guidance on neighbourhood plans simply breaks the process down by reference to the statutory steps and what needs to be achieved from them without really considering *how* the qualifying body achieves what it needs to from that process or from the neighbourhood plan itself.

Each of the aforementioned five stages requires a slightly different approach and emphasis although the qualifying body should organise the whole process with its plan-making function firmly in mind.

The five stages of a neighbourhood plan

1.   Getting started – preliminary matters

However many good reasons there are to make a neighbourhood plan, it is essential to be well organised before you start.

For all the statutory rules governing the neighbourhood plan process it is in the very early stages that many NDPs come unstuck and fail to progress. A lack of focus leads to confusion and inertia amongst those involved, often making it impossible to 'reset' with sufficient purpose. There are some essential prerequisites.

The steering group

First and foremost, you need a core group of willing volunteers to manage the project and the process associated with it. Whether you are a parish council or a neighbourhood forum, there needs to be a committed and efficient group within your organisation prepared to take responsibility for the NDP. Let's call that 'the steering group' or 'SG'.

There is no minimum or maximum size for the SG. The number of members will depend on various factors such as the scale and complexity of the plan and the available capacity of the individuals involved. What is essential is that the group as a whole is focussed and capable of communicating effectively internally and externally.

It is also essential that the SG is willing and committed to the task in hand. It should either be empowered to take executive decisions relating to the NDP on behalf of the qualifying body or be able to report efficiently to it, to enable the qualifying body itself to take decisions promptly.

Broad objectives

Secondly, there should be a clear goal or broad objectives for the NDP. As with the SG, there is no prescription for what that should be or for how objectives should be set. What is important is that your neighbourhood plan project has a clear focus – a plan for the plan!

Having an effective SG and clear objectives are obviously closely interrelated. How the SG is constituted and the objectives formulated will vary significantly from place to place.

You may be a small parish council with just a small core of active members all determined to produce a neighbourhood plan, in which case your NDP SG could simply be comprised of three or four including perhaps your chairman and clerk. Your clear goal may simply be that united desire to produce your NDP. A small parish with a compact SG is unlikely to need any more complicated objectives than that.

In a bigger parish with a diverse group of councillors with varied views on planning and related local issues, a different approach will be needed. The parish council will need to appoint an SG of willing councillors and parishioners, whilst specified objectives or topic areas will help to focus the SG and the direction of the NDP from the start.

It may be necessary to appoint working groups to cover the main issues or subject areas of your NDP such as housing, business/industrial and community development. Working groups should be comprised of parish councillors and willing parishioners who are enthusiastic about, but ideally with no vested interests in, the subject concerned. They should be mainly involved in investigating and gathering evidence on their subject areas and then reporting back to the SG with recommendations for draft planning policies.

Terms of reference

Whatever scale and level of complexity you are operating on, a written constitution or terms of reference for the SG, contained in a single document, will provide a focus for the NDP and may record how and why the decision to start the neighbourhood plan was taken.

Documentation and accurate record-keeping are essential parts of the NDP process as they provide an evidential trail that can prove invaluable should any aspect of that process come under scrutiny. The terms of reference should be the first document in that trail of evidence and one that may need to be referred to sooner than you think. It is therefore important that it is clear, not overcomplicated and formally approved by a vote of the qualifying body.

It is the qualifying body – the parish council or neighbourhood forum – that has the responsibility for producing the draft neighbourhood plan that is submitted to the LPA under Regulation 16. The terms of reference should therefore confer the necessary authority on the SG to manage any part of the process of producing the draft NDP on behalf of the qualifying body.

Costs and funding

How the NDP is to be funded needs to be considered at an early stage. Various figures have been suggested for the range of typical costs associated with producing an NDP. In the early years of neighbourhood planning, estimated typical costs of anywhere from £10,000 to £100,000 plus were talked about but it is difficult to see how a typical NDP should be anywhere near that top end figure or even half of it, though a complex plan for a significantly sized town may well cost in the upper reaches of that range.

Because there really is no 'one size fits all' approach to an NDP, there is no typical costs estimate that is reliable for all. Costs will vary according to a number of factors including size (of the neighbourhood area and its population), the number, complexity and contentiousness of local development issues and, perhaps most significantly, the volunteer resources available to the qualifying body.

In many cases, the project will expand and grow from what was originally envisaged and costs can escalate too. Ultimately it is the role of the qualifying body and any steering group to control costs by efficiently managing the project from the start.

There is no reason why a small parish concentrating on three or four main issues cannot produce an NDP for less than £10,000. On the other hand, a multi-functioning town dealing with various, and possibly some contentious, issues may have to find many times that amount in order to complete their plan.

It is important to understand what the essential inputs into a neighbourhood plan are, what they are likely to cost and who bears those costs;

- the qualifying body is responsible for the costs of promoting, preparing, producing and consulting on a draft plan prior to its first formal submission to the LPA. Those costs are likely to include some expert reports and, or, professional advice, the hire of venues for consultations and the design and printing of consultation and promotional material and the plan itself.

- the LPA meets all the costs of administering the draft plan through the statutory stages of publicity, consultation, examination and referendum, and is funded by central government to do so.

Most of the evidence, by way of expert reports and local data, needed to inform the draft plan and underpin its policies should be available from, and willingly provided by, the LPA. However, there may be items of particular local importance that will require specialist evidence or reports that the qualifying body will need to obtain and pay for.

One element of possible expenditure that can be controversial is the cost of planning consultants to provide independent advice on a neighbourhood plan. The extent to which there is a need for such advice is discussed below. The government acknowledges that independent professional advice on the plan itself will be needed in many cases. The cost of such advice is an element of expenditure that can be covered by grant.

Grant funding and applications

The government through its agent, Locality, makes available grants to contribute to the cost of an NDP and has done so from the inception of neighbourhood planning, with the grant scheme and amounts on offer being revised every couple of years or so.

The grant scheme makes available a basic grant of up to £9,000 with a further £8,000 for more complex plans that involve any of the following;

- the allocation of sites for housing;

- the inclusion of design codes (development briefs);

- a designated business neighbourhood plan;

- a cluster of three or more parishes writing a single plan;

- a neighbourhood area with a population of over 25,000.

Locality also offer technical support for any of the following;

- allocating sites for housing;

- the inclusion of design codes;

- planning to use a Neighbourhood Development Order;

- an undesignated forum needing help with designation.

The full details are available on the Locality website.[2]

Grant applications must be accompanied by a project plan and timetable for your NDP to detail the timing of particular events and milestones

---

[2] https://neighbourhoodplanning.org/about/grant-funding/.

in the process. You may only apply for grant to cover expenditure six months ahead and funds unspent after that must be returned. Locality will expect progress reports on grant-funded plans to ensure grant money is properly spent.

Further grants are now available for qualifying bodies wanting to formally review their NDP.

Use of independent consultants

Do we need to engage consultants to help us produce our neighbourhood plan? This is a question commonly asked by qualifying bodies as they embark on their NDP project and begin to consider the costs of doing so and how they are going to get started.

The question is also very relevant to an application for grant funding as it will obviously influence how much money is needed and applied for.

Whether or not there is a need for independent consultants arises in two different contexts. The first is whether there is a need for a planning consultant to advise the qualifying body on, and assist with, the neighbourhood plan itself and how to progress it through to successful adoption.

Independent experts may also have a role to play in advising the qualifying body on specialist areas that the NDP proposes to deal with, such as environmental issues, building conservation or even the use of architects to advise on design codes or development briefs for specific developments or site allocations. In most cases, the necessary expertise on such matters will be available to the qualifying body from the LPA or via Locality so the need to use independent specialists will not usually arise.

The government, Locality and most LPAs seem to take the view that in the vast majority of cases there is no need for planning consultants or independent experts to be engaged. However, it is absolutely clear and accepted by all that the reasonable costs of either are a legitimate use of grant money and should be specified on a grant application if appropriate.

There are perhaps three main reasons for the authorities' reticence about the use of consultants.

The first is that the production of a neighbourhood plan was always intended, in the spirit of localism, to be a relatively simple and straightforward level of plan-making that does not warrant professional input. Indeed, in support of this approach, early guidance on neighbourhood planning talked about draft neighbourhood plans being subject to a 'light-touch' examination – an expression that stopped being used some time ago because, quite simply, it does not reflect the reality.

Secondly, and in support of the aforementioned 'locally led and produced' approach, the government via Planning Practice Guidance, Locality by way of its technical support and online toolkits and LPAs through their websites all provide a level of information that they consider to be generally sufficient for the purposes of producing an NDP.

Thirdly, but very much related to the foregoing reasons, is that although the government, Locality and LPAs each have slightly different interests vested in neighbourhood planning, their respective approaches reflect a party line that the involvement of independent consultants may be considered to interfere with.

However, none of these reasons holds water for a neighbourhood plan that is serious about making purposeful planning policies which will make a difference. Whilst it is in the interests of government, Locality and LPAs for as many NDPs to be made as quickly and procedurally efficiently as possible, it must be right that the main objective of every qualifying body should be to produce a neighbourhood plan that works as intended to protect and promote the planning interests of the community that produces it.

An effective NDP can no longer be produced by a light-touch, party line approach that is guided simply by PPG and general online advice; it will need independent professional advice and if the qualifying body does not have that resource in-house it will have to look outside for it. Many, if not most, qualifying bodies end up engaging consultants, either to provide ongoing support throughout the process or specific advice at certain stages of it.

The examination of NDPs is no longer light-touch because it cannot afford to be; there is too much at stake. Disgruntled landowners or developers will be ready to pounce on any perceived flaw or omission by way of a legal challenge to an NDP, and examiners have to be conscious of this.

With the stakes raised and those who may seek to oppose or challenge an NDP very willing to engage professional representation, qualifying bodies unwilling to do so risk having their objectives severely compromised.

The various online guidance and resources are at best very general and at worst out-of-date and wide of the mark. In any case, such general guidance is no substitute for professional advice and representation on case-specific issues that require specific and focussed attention. Locality staff and LPA officers, particularly those with the necessary expertise, are usually far too thin on the ground to provide such support and, in any case, they are not truly independent.

Whatever stance Locality, the LPA or even for that matter the government adopts on a particular issue, it is not necessarily the correct or the only legally correct position. Very little in planning or in neighbourhood planning is entirely straightforward and just because the LPA forms one view does not mean that neighbourhood plan-makers should not proceed on a different basis. Only an expert engaged by those making the neighbourhood plan can be relied upon to advise in the best interests of that NDP and unless the qualifying body is willing to engage its own consultant and, or, legal advice it may never even know what its options are.

Of course, it makes sense for the qualifying body to make full use of any in-house and volunteer resources at its disposal but it should also be willing to consider engaging appropriate professional advice and representation where necessary. A knowledgeable planning expert who understands what the NDP seeks to achieve and can draft planning policies that will work as intended may make the difference between an effective neighbourhood plan and a useless one.

Data protection

The making of a neighbourhood plan will inevitably, at various stages, involve the collection, storage and processing of personal data. In so doing the qualifying body will need to ensure it complies with the EU General Data Protection Regulation[3] ("GDPR") and the attendant UK legislation, the Data Protection Act 2018.

Most parish councils and their clerks will already be well aware of the need for data protection compliance but is important that all NDP qualifying bodies understand what is required in the context of plan-making. General and more detailed guidance is readily available from the Information

---

[3]   The General Data Protection Regulation (EU) 2016/679.

Commissioner's Office[4] ("ICO") and other organisations.[5]

Applying for designation of the neighbourhood area

The application for designation of the neighbourhood area is the first formal step in the making of an NDP and effectively fulfils three purposes; it should establish the area to be covered by the plan, establish or confirm the standing of the applicant as a valid qualifying body, and formally notify the LPA of the applicant's intention to make an NDP.

The main principles and technicalities of area designation are dealt with above (under '*The Neighbourhood Area*', on page 58). It is worth emphasising again that where a parish council applies for the whole or part of the parish area to be designated as the neighbourhood area for its NDP, then the LPA must designate that area and has no discretion to refuse to do so.

When the LPA grants the application and designates the neighbourhood area it is effectively acknowledging the standing of the qualifying body to have the area designated. The area designation is made public on the LPA's website, the newly emerging NDP will have a name and the formal process of plan-making will be underway.

Where the applicant for area designation is not a parish council but a neighbourhood forum, then the application for area designation is even more significant and not so straightforward. In these circumstances, the standing of the neighbourhood forum in relation to the area applied for has to be established (by reference to detailed criteria[6]) before the LPA can designate the neighbourhood area and authorise the neighbourhood forum as the qualifying body. In these circumstances a single application covers the designation of the neighbourhood forum and the neighbourhood area as the two are inextricably connected.

A neighbourhood forum must comprise at least 21 people who either live or work in the neighbourhood area or are elected members of a local authority that includes all or part of the neighbourhood area.

---

[4] https://ico.org.uk/for-organisations/
guide-to-the-general-data-protection-regulation-gdpr/.

[5] E.g. https://www.local.gov.uk/our-support/general-data-protection-regulation-gdpr.

[6] Section 61F, Town and Country Planning Act 1990 (as amended) as applied to neighbourhood plans by Section 38A, Planning and Compulsory Purchase Act 2004.

Many parish councils and other neighbourhood planning groups will secure area designation as the very first step towards an NDP. It is, in any case, the formal starting point once the internal prerequisites and organisational requirements are in hand. The designation will be publicised on the LPA website under the heading of the neighbourhood plan it relates to.

2.   Issues and options

So, the SG is established, the neighbourhood area designated and the imperative of local planning issues within the constraint of general conformity understood. Where do you go from here? What next? How does the fledgling NDP begin to take shape and acquire some content, some meat on the bones of all the rhetoric and good intentions?

With the prerequisites and formalities established, the real work towards the neighbourhood plan begins. This is, for many neighbourhood planners, the most difficult part of the whole project ... getting off the ground ... deciding what your NDP should cover or how best to decide on what your NDP should cover!

As well as being often the most difficult part of the process, it is also the most important stage of the whole NDP. If the issues to be covered by your neighbourhood plan are not tested, agreed and clearly defined early on then the plan is likely to lack focus and the momentum essential to seeing the project through to completion may be lost or never even generated in the first place.

'Issues and options' is a term well known to LPAs and their forward planners as one of the first stages of a local plan which involves identifying the issues and deciding which options are to be progressed further in the consideration of how to resolve those issues.

Issues and options are of course inextricably linked to the goals or broad objectives for the NDP identified at the outset. It is how the qualifying body considers those goals are to be achieved that turns them into issues. Part of that consideration, in relation to each issue, is what the different options are.

Issues and options are tested by consultation which at this stage is most comprehensively and effectively undertaken via a questionnaire. Consultation responses need to be analysed and from that analysis, preferred options will emerge. The preferred options then need to be considered in more detail via further consultation and in the light of all available and relevant evidence in order to decide which option or options make it into the plan itself; that is the third stage – the substance of the plan.

At any consultation stage of an NDP, there are various possible methods of consultation. For example, public meetings, exhibitions, seminars, focus groups, telephone surveys, door-to-door surveys or user group surveys for particular services or developments. These may all have their place but none will be as comprehensive or arguably as reliable as a universally distributed, self-completed questionnaire.

Initial consultation/questionnaire

The initial issues and options consultation is best conducted by a self-completed questionnaire designed to elicit what your parishioners or neighbourhood area residents consider to be the main issues for your neighbourhood plan and the options that should be considered for dealing with them.

Local meetings or exhibitions are another means of testing issues and options and may be used as well but a questionnaire that can be distributed in hard copy and online is, as a means of testing public opinion, preferable for a number of reasons. It can be almost guaranteed to reach all residents (even if some choose to ignore it) who will thereby have more opportunity, and be able to take more time, to consider and respond to it.

Other advantages of a questionnaire are that the questions can be carefully drafted to elicit a range of informative responses and, perhaps most importantly, all responses submitted on a questionnaire response form can be easily collected, recorded, analysed and referred to. This is essential because as the NDP progresses through the statutory stages leading up to and including the examination it may well be necessary to refer back to consultation responses, particularly if the NDP ends up being contentious.

As the first substantive interaction between those making the plan and their constituents, the issues and options questionnaire should set out the background to the NDP and explain its significance as part of the statutory development plan. This contextual background need not be detailed, but the questionnaire – to be distributed to all those entitled to vote at the referendum – provides a good opportunity to explain the purpose and scope of the plan and to generate enthusiasm and support for it.

The questionnaire may well be the first point of contact between the qualifying body and the local public about the neighbourhood plan, so in the interests of efficiency of communication it should also serve as a marketing brochure and an explanatory note.

The detail of the questionnaire is likely to be led by, but not restricted to, the NDP goals or objectives identified by the qualifying body. The questionnaire should propose or set out the main issues, or at least the subject areas under which they fall, and test possible options via a series of questions. There must be a catch-all invitation for respondents to suggest matters not included in the questionnaire that should nonetheless be considered by the NDP.

The format of questions, the timing of the questionnaire and the period allowed for response are not prescribed by statute so may be determined by the qualifying body. Generally, the minimum consultation period – the time allowed to respond to the questionnaire – should be between six and eight weeks, which to achieve the best response rate should not significantly overlap with major holiday periods.

It is essential that the format, drafting and presentation of the questions elicits responses that can be easily understood and analysed.

Much of the standard guidance on neighbourhood plans suggests the use of multiple choice questions with numbered answers indicating the level of agreement or otherwise with the premise set by the question. All very well for marketing people and statisticians trained to process such information but useless when trying to extract real meaning and purpose from such responses.

For example, consider a question asking for an indication of agreement on a scale of 1 ('strongly agree') down to 5 ('strongly disagree') that reads, *'Do you agree that we should plan for a community leisure centre in the Parish?'*

Let us assume there are 1,000 parishioners on the electoral roll who will all be entitled to vote in the NDP referendum, and all of them know of and can access the questionnaire. We will further assume that there are 217 responses to the questionnaire – quite a good response rate to the first public consultation of an NDP – and 183 answer the above question, broken down as follows;

1 – strongly agree: 15

2 – agree: 31

3 – neither agree nor disagree: 89

4 – disagree: 41

5 – strongly disagree: 7

Those who advocate the use of such questions say that they are easy to analyse, and in a sense they are. It is obviously easy to calculate the percentages for each response and of those who agree, however strongly, with the proposition.

However, to members of an NDP qualifying body or SG who are not trained data analysts or statisticians, do these numbers lead to any clear conclusions? What purposeful decision on the preferred options for the neighbourhood plan does this numerical matrix of responses lead to?

The overwhelming majority of respondents in this example either do not want or are indifferent to the prospect of a community leisure centre and of those who have indicated a preference, a tiny majority disagree with the proposal. On that basis there would be good reason not to consider the idea of such provision any further and certainly not as a preferred option.

Yet the numbers give no real impression of the reasons for these responses or the sentiments behind them. Many of the '1' and '2' respondents may be really quite committed to such a facility, confident that it will be used by, and help to enfranchise, some of the 80% of the local population completely unrepresented in the overall response to the question.

There is nothing skewed or even that ambiguous about the above responses and not to consider the community centre further would indeed be justified on a simple statistical analysis of the democratic vote.

However, whilst NDP consultations must be fairly reflected in decision-making, neighbourhood planning is not simply a numbers game. Practical and purposeful decisions have to made, often based on a very low proportion of local support or turnout because usually only a very small number of people show any interest at all.

That is why qualitative rather than quantitative questionnaire responses are likely to be more informative and more useful than a matrix of numbers and percentages, particularly at this issues and options stage when the NDP canvas is at its most blank and should be open to ideas that will be the seeds of the evolving project.

A more useful way of phrasing and presenting the above question is:

"Would you like to see a community leisure centre in the Parish, and if so, do you have any suggestions as to where it should be located?

If you do not want a community leisure centre in the Parish, please say why not."

Arguably the need for specific, open questions inviting qualitative answers is even more acute on an increasing number of issues in neighbourhood planning such as housing that are in effect compulsory. That is because, however negative the questionnaire responses to new housing may be, in most parishes up and down the country the housing issue simply cannot be avoided. How neighbourhood plans should provide for new housing is dealt with below (*Chapter 6*) but the general approach is made clear in the NPPF.

LPAs must hand down to each parish a *Local Housing Need* ("LHN") figure for the number of new dwellings the parish must accommodate. NDPs should usually provide for a number of new dwellings based on that LHN figure.

With that in mind NDP plan-makers should use consultation questions that try to establish the type of local housing needed and where it should be located, rather than simply present a preference-rated multiple choice question which is of no use at all in this context.

To simply ask, *'Are you in favour of new housing for the Parish?'* is unlikely to serve any useful purpose, and to investigate differing levels of agreement with that proposition on a scale of '1' to '5' is even more pointless.

For all the emphasis the government puts on it, new housing is of course just one of the things that a neighbourhood plan is likely to deal with. Other general subject areas that may be covered and should at least be considered when drafting an issues and options questionnaire include industrial/employment, shops/retail, environment and green space, recreation/leisure, the historic environment and building conservation, design and local services.

Also included in an issues and options questionnaire can be whole sections or individual questions relating to specific sites, particularly where identified sites are in need of redevelopment but the type of redevelopment that may be appropriate has yet to identified or fully considered.

Drafting, refining and distributing the issues and options questionnaire will be one of the main and most important tasks facing the qualifying body and is certainly likely to be the first major plan-making input into the NDP project. It must therefore be carefully considered and prepared before it is published and put out to consultation. Because it is the initial broad stage consultation exercise there is no reason why it should not cover all reasonable proposals, suggestions and ideas from those within the steering group and the wider qualifying body, as well as from outsiders with an interest in the neighbourhood area.

It is also important to keep in mind that the initial consultation, whether it goes under the banner of issues and options and whatever form it takes (whether questionnaire, public meeting etc.) is not subject to statutory rules. It is an informal stage of the NDP process that is entirely the responsibility, and within the jurisdiction, of the qualifying body. The LPA should certainly be willing to take an interest, and if requested provide the qualifying body with advice, at this stage but an issues and options questionnaire should not be curtailed or constrained by the LPA without good reason.

Once finalised, an issues and options questionnaire must be distributed effectively, or be readily accessible, to everyone on the electoral roll in the neighbourhood area – that is everyone entitled to vote in the NDP referendum. For a business neighbourhood plan, the questionnaire should be distributed to all businesses in the neighbourhood area. A person is entitled to vote in a business NDP referendum if they are registered on the business voting register by virtue of being a non-domestic ratepayer in the referendum area.[7]

Effective distribution is in practice likely to require sufficient publicity about an online questionnaire and how to access it, and distribution of hard copies throughout the neighbourhood area or at least the provision for hard copies of the questionnaire to be collected or sent out.

It is also essential, and not perhaps as obvious as it may seem, for very clear instructions to be issued in the questionnaire itself on how it should

---

[7] See Schedule 6, Neighbourhood Planning (Referendums) (Amendment) Regulations 2014.

be completed and returned within the consultation period.

Personal data

It can be useful to collect contact information from respondents, partly to evidence that the response is from a resident parishioner, and to facilitate future contact with the respondent on the NDP. However, as we have already seen, qualifying bodies must ensure that in handling personal information they comply with the GPDR and the Data Protection Act (see above, *Data Protection*, on page 103).

Analysis of questionnaire responses

As with all NDP consultation exercises, the analysis of initial questionnaire responses should accurately and purposefully reflect local concerns and aspirations. Inevitably, the qualifying body leads that process and in its analysis of the response data will be guided partly by the objectives it has set.

The way the response data is organised has the potential to affect the outcomes of the consultation and ultimately the options that are taken forward. Whilst the qualifying body cannot be expected to have professional expertise in data analysis it should apply common sense and reasonable care in organising the exercise so that all the responses submitted are properly recorded, considered and duly reflected in any conclusions reached. This information, or at least a summary of it, should be included in the consultation statement submitted to the LPA at the Regulation 16 publicity stage.

To be reasonably efficient, the analysis of consultation responses should be organised by reference to the different options that may arise from them. That is not to say the preferred options should be in any way predetermined (obviously, they should not) but generally all possible options should be identified and the level of support, both quantitative and qualitative, for each one should be assessed and recorded. That assessment will be the basis for deciding which options are to be progressed.

The advantage of the questionnaire presenting open questions is that they invite qualitative responses and useful comments. Such comments should be assimilated for the purposes of analysis so that possible options and sub-options, or details for a particular option, begin to emerge.

From those emergent options, quantitative analysis may then be used to select preferred options. The methods of analysis and preferred option selection, and deselection, should be transparent, objective and open to review.

The qualifying body should be able to provide clear reasons why certain options are to be progressed, or preferred, whilst others are not. Those reasons should relate directly to the consultation responses and will be set out in the consultation statement.

Preferred options

For any development proposal or planning issue there will normally be several preferred or possible options identified at an early stage that are, through a process of further, more detailed consultation, whittled down to the number that will be pursued through to one or more planning policies.

On each subject area, an NDP issues and options consultation may yield several competing preferred options for further consideration or just a single one. Even in the latter case, further consultation on the details of the option may well be needed before it becomes an established proposal to be embodied in a planning policy in the neighbourhood plan.

The preferred options selected for further consideration may be proposals or site allocations for a particular development or type of development, or they may be proposals for generic planning policies. Depending on the scope of the plan there may be several preferred options on various subjects.

A preferred option should not be identified and pursued as such unless it meets the basic conditions and is realistic *and* deliverable. To consider further any option that does not meet these criteria, even if it derives from a positive questionnaire response, is a waste of precious plan-making resources.

Another point made throughout this book that bears repetition here is that it is also a waste of plan-making resources to produce NDP planning policies that add nothing to the local plan or the NPPF. Therefore, careful consideration should be given to whether it is worthwhile pursuing options that would result in NDP planning policies that are superfluous.

Ideally this filtering process should be applied when drafting the questions for the issues and options questionnaire. However, sometimes there is a clear local focus and purpose in mind when preparing the questionnaire that somehow gets lost or generalised when the response data is analysed.

The 'what will this achieve?' filter should be applied again when considering the options that go forward for further consideration. Bear in mind too that whilst selecting preferred options from the consultation responses is in a sense narrowing down the available options, it is also the stage at which the details involved with each option are opened up, investigated, consulted upon and scrutinised further. Each preferred option therefore usually generates more work than at any stage previously.

Once the qualifying body has identified its preferred options from the initial consultation, it must then decide what if any further information or details are needed to pursue them and how to present them for further consultation.

As a result of the initial consultation, it may be that on a particular issue there are no options that present themselves as viable and, or, sufficiently popular to progress. Usually, however, on any one subject there will be at least one preferred option to be progressed via further consultation, or there may be several preferred options to be taken forward.

If, for example, there are competing options for the development of a particular site, or for allocating land for a particular type of development, then there may be several preferred options and further evidence (discussed under Step 3 below) on each one will need to be presented for evaluation and more detailed public consultation. This is where emerging neighbourhood plans can get tricky – competing options usually means competing and potentially litigious developers!

When presenting competing preferred options for site allocations in an emerging NDP, it is obviously important that as far as possible there is a balanced presentation of all available evidence for each option. This means that where evidence on a particular issue – say ecological assessment – is presented on one of the options, it should be made available and properly considered for all of them.

It is worth reflecting on whether the landowner or developer behind each option would consider that you are doing so fairly. It may even be worth asking them that question directly prior to going public on the preferred options. Anyone with a vested interest in an option that they consider has been misrepresented or unreasonably dismissed could be a problem later if the draft neighbourhood plan leaves no scope for their aspirations. It may be worthwhile trying to flush out and respond to any such grievances as early as possible in the process.

We are getting a bit ahead of ourselves here. The final exercise at the issues and options or initial consultation stage is to identify the main themes and perhaps some options, maybe even preferred options, to take forward to the next stage of evidence gathering and more detailed consultation.

3.   The substance of the plan

Having completed the analysis of the initial consultation responses and drawn conclusions on what the main themes and options should be, you are ready to start formulating the substance of the plan, This part of the process is about gathering relevant evidence and allowing that evidence to influence what the plan should reflect and what it should try to achieve.

A neighbourhood plan is not simply a glossy brochure of local aspirations. It must be purposeful if it is to be at all worthwhile, and to fulfil any purpose it must be focused and have a sound evidence base.

Gathering evidence

The evidence required will, of course, vary depending on the main themes and the preferred options.

In the narrower sense, the evidence to be gathered and assessed is that required for the justification of plan objectives and the planning policies that seek to implement those objectives.

However, if we take evidence to mean the various types of information that need to be collated and presented, then that will include administrative information procedurally required as part of the plan. There are a number of specific items that fall into this category.

Procedural requirements

– *Basic Conditions Statement*
The need for conformity with the strategic policies of the local plan means that the evidence an emerging NDP must consider includes the local plan and any supporting policies, guidance and other documentation relating to the making of the local plan and the interpretation of its planning policies. This evidence should be kept to hand at every stage of the NDP process, from defining the main issues to drafting and fine-tuning the

NDP planning policies.

Conformity with the strategic policies of the local plan, with the NPPF and with EU and human rights legislation must be demonstrated in the basic conditions statement that is submitted with the draft NDP to the LPA. This document will set out the external policies that are relevant to the NDP and with which it needs to comply and, alongside each, will briefly comment on how the NDP does comply.

– *Consultation Statement*

A consultation statement also has to be prepared and submitted with your NDP if it is to pass the examination. This is a summary of all the consultation events including the initial questionnaire and therefore should be produced as a draft working document at that stage.

The consultation statement should summarise the main and salient features of each consultation including the form it took, the main questions and issues and the number of people engaged, without going into too much detail or attempting to analyse consultation evidence – that is not its purpose. It is a summary that should indicate where to find more detailed evidence and background information by reference to other documents.

– *Strategic Environmental Assessment*

Under the EU Strategic Environmental Assessment Directive[8] (the "SEA Directive") and the attendant UK Regulations[9] the qualifying body will need to consider whether the NDP will need to be subject to a *Strategic Environmental Assessment* ("SEA"). The product of an SEA is an environmental report and when submitting the NDP for examination either an environmental report, or a statement or reasons why one is not needed, is required.

An SEA is more likely to be needed if the NDP is considering allocating development sites not already covered by the local plan *Sustainability Appraisal* ("SA"), or if the neighbourhood area contains sensitive environmental assets that may be affected by NDP policies, or in any case if those policies are likely to have significant environmental effects not already addressed through the SA.

---

[8] European Directive 2001/42/EC.

[9] The Environmental Assessment of Plans and Programmes Regulations 2004 (S.I. 2004, No. 1633) ("the SEA Regulations").

The procedural requirements of an SEA are set out in the SEA Regulations but essentially the first step for the qualifying body is to prepare a screening report which will set out the elements of an emerging NDP that may trigger the need for an SEA.

The screening report can only be produced once sufficient detail about the emerging NDP is known, but should not be so late in the NDP process that it holds up progress towards the examination and referendum. If an SEA is required it should generally be produced prior to the Regulation 14 publicity so that the NDP is considered along with the accompanying SEA throughout the various statutory stages.

The screening report is sent to the SEA consultation bodies – Historic England, Natural England and the Environment Agency – for their consideration and input over a consultation period usually of five to six weeks (though the Regulations do not specify a time period). The SEA consultation bodies should, in response to the report, provide a screening opinion on whether or not they consider an SEA is required.

Under the Regulations the "responsible authority" must make a screening determination. For a neighbourhood plan this may be the LPA or the qualifying body. Usually the LPA will make the screening determination as it is set up with the procedures and resources to do so, but in any case the arrangements for making the screening determination should be agreed between the qualifying body and the LPA before the screening report is finalised. The LPA should also assist with the screening report if asked to do so.

The SEA and the screening process should not be difficult or contentious and under its general duty to assist with all aspects of a neighbourhood plan, the LPA should be willing to provide the qualifying body with any support it needs for the SEA process.

The SEA consultation bodies are also there to help and their assistance can and should be sought, if necessary, at any stage of the process. Other relevant organisations such as water companies and local wildlife trusts may also provide useful information and assistance.

There are two possible outcomes from a screening determination; if the draft NDP is 'screened in', an SEA is required. If it is 'screened out' there is no SEA needed. A notice of determination is made and accompanied by a statement of reasons if no SEA is required.

If an SEA is needed, the next stage is 'scoping' – to determine what should be addressed by the environmental report on the NDP. This is when the LPA and the consultation bodies will need to be involved and provide assistance.

Once the scope of the necessary environmental report is agreed, the qualifying body will have to engage appropriate experts to produce it. The draft environmental report should be reviewed and approved by the appropriate consultation bodies before submitting it with the NDP for examination.

It may be that, even if an environmental report is not required as a result of SEA screening, the consultation bodies make other recommendations to the qualifying body that are taken on board when producing the NDP.

The need for compliance with the SEA requirements, at least for SEA screening and for reasons to be given in support of any screening opinion, is a classic and often used procedural ground of legal challenge by developers against the making of a neighbourhood plan. However spurious the substantive arguments behind the alleged procedural flaw, it seems it is often worth a try to claim that a failure of the SEA obligations undermines the NDP.

Remember that the essence of an SEA is environmental protection and the need, when considering whether to adopt or implement a particular plan or policy, to consider "reasonable alternatives" that may be more environmentally favourable. Housing developers – the most frequent litigants against neighbourhood plans – usually struggle to assert that their preferred version of the plan or policy they are complaining about is a reasonable alternative that should have been more seriously considered under an SEA, but that will often not stop them trying.

Indeed, in three widely reported cases the developers claimed procedural breaches of an SEA based on the failure to consider reasonable alternatives.

In *BDW Trading*,[10] the policy under attack was Policy 1 of the Tattenhall Neighbourhood Plan ("TNP") which in the absence of an identified housing need figure for the neighbourhood area sought to limit the number, and location, of dwellings that could be built within the plan period.

---

[10] *BDW Trading Ltd v Cheshire West & Chester Borough Council* [2014] EWHC 1470 (Admin).

117

Three national housebuilders claimed that the reasonable alternative of simply not having Policy 1 and its limitations should have been considered instead. That option – as the claimant's argument went, the more environmentally friendly alternative – would have enabled them to build hundreds of houses on sites within their control but outside of the Policy 1 area within which the TNP sought to restrict housing.

The court agreed with the examiner of the TNP that the SEA requirements had been met and cited,[11] the evidence of the LPA's Chief Planning Officer explaining how the need to consider reasonable alternatives had been fulfilled:

> *The consultation undertaken set the framework for deciding the reasonable alternative options for the policies in the neighbourhood development plan and informed the decisions taken on what the draft policies would contain. Those options that had not commanded community support were not considered to be reasonable to take forward in the draft plan. Therefore, reasonable options were determined through the community consultation exercise.*
>
> *The outcomes of the public consultation are set out in the justification and evidence section for each of the policies in the neighbourhood development plan. These results demonstrate what would and would not be supported by the community.*

The court saw no reason to disagree that *"those options that had not commanded community support were not considered to be reasonable to take forward"* and, therefore, that *"reasonable options* [had been] *determined through the community consultation exercise"*.

The circumstances of reliance on an SEA to try to undermine the neighbourhood plan in *Gladman Developments*[12] were remarkably similar.

In the absence of still emerging strategic housing policies and housing need figures, the Winslow Neighbourhood Plan ("WNP") sought in its Policies 2 and 3 to restrict the 455 new dwellings needed in the neighbourhood area to allocated sites within a defined settlement boundary. This excluded the proposals of the claimant who maintained that the

---

[11]   At paragraph 67 of the judgment; *BDW Trading Ltd v Cheshire West & Chester Borough Council* [2014] EWHC 1470 (Admin).

[12]   *R (on the application of Gladman Developments Ltd) v Aylesbury Vale District Council* [2014] EWHC 4323 (Admin).

reasonable alternative that should have been considered under the SEA was a less restrictive policy on housing with no settlement boundary!

The court quite rightly dismissed this argument and found that the extensive consultations on the WNP undertaken by Winslow Town Council had considered the reasonable alternative, that the reasons for the settlement boundary had been explained and that there was no need for the developer's 'do nothing' option to have been specifically considered. Implicit in that reasoning is that it is difficult if not impossible to argue that the 'do nothing' or 'no policy' option could be more environmentally favourable than a planning policy that restricts development.

The challenge to the St Ives neighbourhood development plan ("St Ives NDP") and its second homes policy[13] (considered in more detail in *Chapter 6*) was entirely procedural and based largely on a claimed failure by the examiner and the LPA to consider reasonable alternatives under an SEA.

The reasonable alternative proposed as the more favourable environmental option was simply that the LPA should facilitate the building of more homes – by doing away with restrictive planning policies. The developer's argument was that some of the dwellings that would result from that would be owned by local people – the purpose behind the second homes restriction in the NDP – even if most of them would continue to be snapped up by second homers. Again unsurprisingly, the court emphatically dismissed that argument.

These cases demonstrate that whilst the SEA requirements do need to be meaningfully addressed and reasonable alternatives assessed through the NDP consultation process – and that assessment explained in the consultation statement – the assessment only needs to be proportionate to the neighbourhood plan and its policies. Alternatives that are clearly not reasonable because they are obviously not more environmentally favourable need not be considered beyond that.

– *Appropriate assessment under the EU Habitats Directive*
Most neighbourhood plan-makers will not be familiar with the Habitats Directive[14] or how and when it may be relevant to an NDP, so it is worth dealing with the background first.

---

[13]   *R (on the application of RLT Built Environment Limited) v The Cornwall Council and St Ives Town Council* [2016] EWHC 2817 (Admin).

[14]   Council Directive 92/43/EEC.

Since a now widely discussed decision of the Court of Justice of the European Union ("CJEU") in the *People Over Wind*[15] case, that we consider in a little more detail below, when an "appropriate assessment" is required and what it should consist of has become a hot topic in planning circles.

The starting point for consideration of the SEA Directive or the EIA Directive is the nature of the plan or project itself and what impact it may have over the area it will affect, whether or not that area is of particular sensitivity. The Habitats Directive, on the other hand, only requires an appropriate assessment (meaning an appropriate environmental assessment) if a designated site is affected, so it is essentially site-specific in its effect.

So whilst the SEA Directive, for development plans, and the EIA Directive,[16] for development projects, deal with the general requirement for an environmental assessment whenever a certain level of environmental impact is predicted, the Habitats Directive, which applies to both plans and projects, focuses on sites of particular environmental sensitivity, such as Special Areas of Conservation.

Article 6(3) of the Habitats Directive provides that:

> *Any plan or project not directly connected with or necessary to the management of the site but likely to have a significant effect thereon, either individually or in combination with other plans or projects, shall be subject to appropriate assessment of its implications for the site in view of the site's conservation objectives. In the light of the conclusions of the assessment of the implications for the site and subject to the provisions of paragraph 4, the competent national authorities shall agree to the plan or project only after having ascertained that it will not adversely affect the integrity of the site concerned and , if appropriate, after having obtained the opinion of the general public.*

The Habitats Directive has effect in UK law under The Conservation of Habitats and Species Regulations 2017, known as 'the Habitats Regulations'. The 2017 Regulations replace and consolidate the earlier 2010 version[17] with an important new regulation introduced in respect of neighbourhood

---

[15] *People Over Wind & Sweetman v Coillte Teoranta* (C-323/17).

[16] Directive 2011/92/EU as amended by Directive 2014/52/EU. The EIA Directive and its amendments are now consolidated under Directive 2014/52/EU.

[17] With the 2017 Regulation 105 replacing 'old' Regulation 102 and Regulation 107 replacing Regulation 103.

plans in the light of the CJEU judgment in *People Over Wind*.

Just as with the SEA and EIA, the Habitats Regulations take effect in rela-tion to any private or public sector-proposed project, plan or programme, so that includes proposed development, and development plans (covered in 'Chapter 8 – Land Use Plans' of the Habitats Regulations).

Another similarity is that the detail required of the environmental assess-ment or report required under the SEA/EIA regime and an appropriate assessment under the Habitats Regulations is not prescribed by the respective regulations but defined by 'scoping' which is undertaken on a case by case basis to establish exactly what any assessment needs to cover and report on.

The practical effect of this is that where, for a particular project or plan, an EIA *and* an appropriate assessment under the Habitats Regulations are required they may well be, and in all likelihood will be, one and the same thing – an environmental assessment and report covering all the issues identified at the scoping stage.

Regulation 105 of the Habitats Regulations

Under the heading *'Land use plans – Assessment of implications for European sites and European offshore marine sites'*, Regulation 105 pro-vides that:

> *(1) Where a land use plan -*
>
> > *(a) is likely to have a significant effect on a European site or a European offshore marine site (either alone or in combination with other plans or projects), and*
> >
> > *(b) is not directly connected with or necessary to the management of the site,*
>
> *the plan-making authority for that plan must, before the plan is given effect, make an appropriate assessment of the implications for the site in view of that site's conservation objectives.*

Under Regulation 105(2)-(4), the plan-making authority must also:

– for the purposes of the assessment consult the appropriate nature conservation body and have regard to any representations made;

- if they consider it appropriate, consult the general public, and;

- in the light of the assessment, and subject to any overriding public interest (see Regulation 107), give effect to the plan only after concluding that it will not adversely affect the integrity of the designated site.

Under Regulation 107, "*If the plan-making authority is satisfied that, there being no alternative solutions, the land use plan must be given effect for imperative reasons of overriding public interest* [human health, public safety, beneficial consequences of primary importance to the environment; or other imperative reasons] ... *it may give effect to the land use plan notwithstanding a negative assessment of the implications for* [the designated site or sites]".

In the circumstances of an overriding public interest for giving effect to a plan notwithstanding a negative environmental assessment, the plan-making body may make a request for information or guidance from the Secretary of State who in turn may seek, and share with the plan-making body, the opinion of the European Commission on the plan.[18]

Where the plan-making body intends to give effect to a plan notwithstanding a negative assessment, it must notify the Secretary of State and allow a period of 21 days to give the Secretary of State the opportunity to issue a direction to temporarily or indefinitely stop the plan taking effect.[19]

Application of the Habitats Regulations to neighbourhood planning prior to People Over Wind

In an attempt to relieve a neighbourhood plan qualifying body from becoming mired in the Habitats Regulations unnecessarily, Schedule 2 of the Neighbourhood Planning Regulations[20] was introduced:

In relation to the examination of neighbourhood development plans the following basic condition is prescribed ... The making of the neighbourhood development plan is not likely to have a significant effect on a European site [as defined in the Habitats Regulations] *(either*

---

[18] Regulation 105(2)-(4).

[19] Regulation 105(2)-(4).

[20] The Neighbourhood Planning (General) Regulations 2012 – when brought into force Schedule 2 referred to the 2010 Habitats Regulations.

alone or in combination with other plans or projects).

This is a strange statutory provision. The words *"the following basic condition is prescribed"* seem rather meaningless in the context in which they appear and at best present a confusing picture. There are five basic conditions, one of which is compliance with EU obligations. The provision under Schedule 2 does not add another basic condition and neither is it an exemption to the requirements of EU Directives or the Habitats Regulations to which it expressly refers.

What Schedule 2 amounts to is guidance to NDP examiners in the form of a rather weak presumption, that in most cases the making of a neighbourhood plan is in itself unlikely to have a significant effect on a designated site. In effect what Schedule 2 is saying to NDP examiners is 'in case you are concerned that the NDP you are examining could be regarded as *likely to have a significant effect on a European site*, don't be, as the mere making of an NDP is unlikely to have such an effect'.

From a practical perspective, and with a firm note of caution, this is simply common sense in that in most cases simply making a neighbourhood plan (or any development plan, for that matter) is unlikely to have a significant effect on a designated European site even if such a site or sites is within the plan area. This is partly because a neighbourhood plan is only supposed to add detail to the strategic policies of a local plan under which account should already have been taken of any European sites.

However, Schedule 2 does not, and cannot, obviate the need for due consideration of whether a draft NDP may be likely to have a significant effect, perhaps because it is allocating sites for development in close proximity to designated European sites and, or, the draft plan seeks to introduce policies that would undermine the protection or conservation objectives of such sites.

The foregoing provisions of the Habitats Regulations and Schedule 2 of the Neighbourhood Planning Regulations amounted to the statutory position prior to the CJEU decision, of April 2017, in *People Over Wind*. We consider below (*'Post-POW changes to the Habitats Regulations and the NPPF'*) how that has changed as a result of the CJEU judgment.

People Over Wind ("POW")

Whether we like it or not this case is of relevance to those making neighbourhood plans as, notwithstanding the wider political landscape, it has necessitated renewed interest in the Habitats Directive – even though many policy and decision-makers in the UK cannot wait to see the back of it.

One of the basic conditions of an NDP is that is must comply with EU law and for the time being at least EU law still has direct effect in the UK. Even when that time has passed the implementing UK legislation will still be effective unless and until it is revoked. So, yes, *POW* is important for qualifying bodies.

Whilst in a guide to neighbourhood planning we need not dig too deep into the legal intricacies of a case such as this, the principles involved and the reaction to *POW* are instructive and qualifying bodies need to understand the implications of both for NDP plan-making.

The case arose from the proposal to lay cables connecting the already permitted Cullenagh Wind Farm to the grid. This activity, the necessary undertaking of a utilities company in providing services, is in Ireland as it is throughout the UK, permitted development subject to certain exceptions. Under Irish planning rules, one of those exceptions is where an appropriate assessment is required under the Habitats Directive – in those cases planning permission is necessary.

As the project had potential effects on two Special Areas of Conservation ("SACs"), under the Habitats Directive it had to be screened in order to decide if an appropriate assessment was required. By virtue of what were described as 'protective measures' intended to reduce any harmful effects on the key SAC objectives, the project was screened out, meaning that neither an appropriate assessment nor planning permission was required.

That was notwithstanding that the screening report itself said that in the absence of protective measures there was the potential for damage to the protected habitat and clearly explained what the negative impact of the development would be and exactly how it would be caused. In short, the negative impact identified was the silting up of watercourses that would prevent the reproduction of a subspecies on the verge of extinction – the Nore pearl mussel – of which only 300 individuals were left in existence.

Furthermore, the protective measures on which the developer sought to rely were yet to be detailed and agreed with the competent authority when the project was screened out.

The screening decision was, perhaps unsurprisingly, challenged in the Irish

High Court which referred the matter to the CJEU for its interpretation on the relevant part of the Habitats Directive in Article 6(3).

The CJEU ruled that measures to avoid or reduce the harmful effects of a project on a designated site should not be taken account of at the screening stage; such measures had to be considered as part of a full assessment – an appropriate assessment.

To anyone who understands the purpose behind the Habitats Directive, the reasoning of the CJEU for its decision appears so obvious as to be self-evident, including that:

> *- the need for protective measures indicates the project is likely to have a significant effect on the designated site (particularly if the proposed protective measures do not work) and consequently an appropriate assessment should be carried out;*

> *- a full and precise analysis of the measures capable of avoiding or reducing any significant effects cannot be undertaken at the screening stage, but only by an appropriate assessment – a full assessment, and that;*

> *- taking account of such measures at the screening stage risks undermining the whole purpose of the Habitats Directive.*

As well as being the only sensible interpretation of the Habitats Regulations, the CJEU decision in *POW* is simply common sense. Yet, much of the comment and general reaction to the case in the UK could lead one to assume that the decision blocks any development anywhere near a protected site. The real effect of *POW*, as we shall see, is far less draconian.

Before we consider the reaction to, and the real effects and extent of, *POW* it is worth remembering that the Habitats Directive applies to any project of whatever nature that may have effects on designated sites, whether proposed development, an emerging development plan or a project or programme of an entirely different type. Here we are principally concerned with planning and more specifically with plan-making.

Reaction to POW

The adverse reaction and furore generated by *POW*, particularly amongst those planning professionals who act mainly for developers, is interesting in itself and tends to reflect the culture of planning in the UK generally

– a culture that neighbourhood planners have to be aware of and conversant with.

Some have expressed irritation at Mr Sweetman, who brought the legal challenge, seemingly because as a well-organised environmentalist he has dared to venture into what his critics seem to believe should be the sole preserve of developers – using the courts to challenge planning decisions that go against them.

What Mr Sweetman has in common with many large developers, in particular the big supermarkets and all the major housebuilders, is that he is indeed a serial litigant. Unlike those developers, however, he is not motivated by profit but by matters firmly in the public interest. What also distinguishes him is that he has been serially successful in his litigious efforts, and particularly on the points he argues before the CJEU. Those who act for environmental groups as well as developers, and can see the bigger picture, would argue that Mr Sweetman should be congratulated rather than mocked.

However, against the background of an increasingly permissive UK planning regime, EU Directives that clearly are, and need to be, regulatory in order to achieve their purpose are seen as an irritation by developers. This problem is compounded by the underlying political tensions with the EU and in particular the undoubted reluctance of lower tier courts (beyond which most planning cases do not proceed) to apply the EU and the attendant UK legislation as purposefully as it should be applied. Rarely, if ever, in UK planning cases are questions of interpretation of EU law referred to the CJEU.

The critics of the *POW* judgment prolifically cite the 2004 case of *Hart*,[21] for example, in which the judge described the suggestion that mitigation measures should be considered as part of a full environmental assessment (exactly the issue in *POW*) as "ludicrous". It is difficult to imagine the Supreme Court, if ever asked to consider the issue, taking such a dismissive view of the relevant legislation.

Also widely applauded is the pragmatic approach of the post-*POW* decision of the High Court in *Langton*[22] despite the fact that, being a case about badger culling licences issued by Natural England, it has little

---

[21] *R (Hart DC) v SSCLG* [2008] 2 P. & C. R. 16.

[22] *R (Langton) v Secretary of State* [2018] EWHC 2190 (Admin).

relevance to planning or plan-making. Even so, the decision that conditions of the licence intended to prevent harmful impacts on a designated site need not be subject to appropriate assessment just because *"they are integral features of the project"* is somewhat questionable.

What the facts in *Langton* do very well demonstrate, however, is that it is not only developers, but the authorities and even the agency charged with protecting and conserving nature in England, that all engage in the exercise of avoiding having to undertake a full environmental assessment.

Environmental groups know only too well how compliant planning authorities usually are in screening out projects whose true environmental impacts are not known, thus enabling the developer to avoid the full and proper assessment necessary. Screening in a proposed development and then being involved in scoping and assessing it is considered by under-resourced LPAs to be as much of a burden as it is by developers – far easier for the LPA to screen out, safe in the knowledge that is what the developer wants anyway.

That is the reality, and there is no doubt that in all too many cases the purpose of the protective legislation is undermined and the environment suffers as a result. It is also the culture within which the adverse reaction to the CJEU decision in *POW* finds a receptive audience.

The complaints that the *POW* judgment is confused and confusing about the type of measures that cannot be taken into consideration at the screening stage, and that it creates impractical obstacles for developers, themselves seem rather misplaced when the details of the case are considered.

The terms of the request by the Irish High Court for a preliminary ruling on the interpretation of Article 6(3) were *"Whether, or in what circumstances, mitigation measures can be considered when carrying out screening for appropriate assessment under Article 6(3) of the Habitats Directive?"*

In saying that *"it is not appropriate, at the screening stage, to take account of the measures intended to avoid or reduce the harmful effects of the plan or project ..."* the court could not have been clearer or more to the point.

Objectively, the application of the court's interpretation to the facts is entirely reasonable. To argue that proposed but untested protective measures should, at the screening stage, be taken to mean that an appropriate assessment was not necessary entirely misses the point of an appropriate assessment.

Another criticism is that the court did not adequately define the meaning and significance of 'mitigation measures'. The screening report in *POW* referred to protective measures, whilst the High Court referred to mitigation, yet neither term features in Article 6 of the Directive.

The CJEU recognised this, and in applying an obvious logic, said that both terms *"should be understood as denoting measures that are intended to avoid or reduce the harmful effects of the envisaged project on the site concerned."* When looking at the purpose behind the Directive, it is difficult to understand why anyone should have a problem with this. For measures that may be described as 'protective', 'mitigation', 'conservation', 'preventive', 'compensatory' or 'integral', instead read 'measures intended to avoid or reduce the harmful effects of the envisaged project'. Simple, easy to understand and to apply.

What this does all mean of course is that any measures intended to avoid or reduce the harmful effects will, or at least should, not be taken account of at the screening stage to avoid an appropriate assessment but rather that there are likely to be significant effects and therefore an appropriate assessment is required.

There is no doubt that most developers consider an appropriate assessment to be an impractical hurdle and an unreasonable burden, and also an opportunity for environmental groups to get involved and raise objections. Yes, an appropriate assessment of a development project or plan will mean more work for the developer or plan-maker and for the LPA. However, an appropriate assessment means just that. There is no prescription about what it must contain other than it should be full and thorough. If those involved spent half as much time diligently scoping rather than trying to contrive a screened out decision, then in most cases an appropriate assessment in itself need be neither a great obstacle nor a particular burden.

There will be some cases, of course, where an appropriate assessment leads to the conclusion that compensatory measures may be required to offset an adverse impact or even that due to the likely impact, the project in question should not go ahead at all in the proposed form. Better that, surely, than a proposal that proceeds in the absence of a full assessment on the basis of a flawed screening report?

Such is the fuss over *POW* that some may indeed wonder what the effect of appropriate assessment would have been on many of the projects that previously avoided them.

However, those who suggest the *POW* decision now reflects an inconsistency in the approach to assessment required under the Habitats Directive from that under the EIA Directive do have a point.

Article 4(5)(b) of the amended EIA Directive[23] says that *"where proposed by the developer ... any features of the project and/or measures envisaged to avoid or prevent what might otherwise have been significant adverse effects on the environment"* may be considered at the screening stage to decide that an EIA is not required.

Given that the purpose of the EIA Directive is to provide a more efficient and effective regime of environmental assessment to combat new and emerging environmental threats, and that it specifically attempts to deal with the conflicts of interest that can arise within the "competent" (meaning the regulatory) authority, Article 4(5)(b) seems counterproductive. The principles enunciated by the CJEU in *POW* are far more compelling; *"proposed measures envisaged to avoid or prevent what might otherwise be significant adverse effects"* should, logically, be subject to a full assessment to test whether or not they will avoid or prevent such effects.

Nonetheless, it does seem to be the case that where a project is caught by both directives, the developer may need to engage in a full assessment under the Habitats Directive that he could possibly avoid under the EIA rules. This has little bearing on plan-makers however as development plans come under the SEA regime rather than EIA.

Post-POW changes to the Habitats Regulations and the NPPF

In what appears to be a direct response to *POW*, the 2017 Habitats Regulations introduced an entirely new provision, Regulation 106, under the heading of *'Assessment of implications for European site: neighbourhood development plans'*:

> *106(1) A qualifying body which submits a proposal for a neighbourhood development plan must provide such information as the competent authority may reasonably require for the purposes of the assessment under regulation 105 or to enable it to determine*

---

[23] Directive 2014/52/EU.

whether that assessment is required.

Furthermore, Regulation 106(3) makes clear that *"where the competent authority decides to revoke or modify a neighbourhood development plan after it has been made, it must for that purpose make an appropriate assessment of the implications for any European site likely to be significantly affected in view of that site's conservation objectives..."*.

Under the all-embracing definition of "competent authority"[24], in respect of a neighbourhood plan, that will invariably be the LPA.

Whilst Regulation 106 is a useful reminder to any qualifying body, it is questionable whether it really adds anything to the responsibilities of neighbourhood plan-makers under Regulations 15 and 16[25] that set out the requirements for LPA publicity of a plan proposal and the information the qualifying body must send to the LPA in respect of that. Furthermore, both the qualifying body and the LPA should be keen to ensure that the draft NDP complies with the basic conditions, of which one is compliance with relevant EU law.

In any case, further amendments to the Habitats Regulations were introduced that changed Schedule 2 of the Neighbourhood Planning Regulations to read as follows:

> *In relation to the examination of neighbourhood development plans the following basic condition is prescribed for the purpose of paragraph 8(2)(g) of Schedule 4B to the 1990 Act;*
>
> > *The making of the neighbourhood development plan does not breach the requirements of Chapter 8 of Part 6 of the Conservation of Habitats and Species Regulations 2017* [that is Regulations 105 – 111 of the Habitats Regulations].[26]

This seems merely to put the rather strange presumption of the old Schedule 2 in a different way. In any case, the effect is that if a proposed neighbourhood plan is likely to have significant adverse impacts on a European site, then it must undergo an appropriate assessment in

---

[24] Under Regulation 7.

[25] Neighbourhood Planning (General) Regulations 2012.

[26] As amended by Regulation 3, The Conservation of Habitats and Species and Planning (Various Amendments) (England and Wales) Regulations 2018.

accordance with the Habitats Regulations and provided it does so and reasonably complies with any such assessment then it complies with the basic condition of compliance with EU law.

Perhaps more significant than the amendments to regulations is the revision to the NPPF prompted by *POW*. The *POW* judgment was one of two things that necessitated significant revisions to the NPPF within weeks of its publication in July 2018. (The other – formula for assessing housing need in light of 2018 household growth predictions – is dealt with in *Chapter 6* at page 159). Both changes had to be considered via a departmental Technical Consultation.[27]

The original (July 2018) Paragraph 177 NPPF read:

> *The presumption in favour of sustainable development does not apply where development requiring appropriate assessment because of its potential impact on a habitats site is being planned or determined.*

In its proposed revision of Paragraph 177, the Technical Consultation acknowledged that the effect of the *POW* ruling *"is that appropriate assessment of habitats impacts is required in plan-making and decision-making whenever there is a potential impact on a habitats site, regardless of any mitigation measures proposed."*

It was also acknowledged that *"the judgment means that* [under the existing Paragraph 177] *sites with suitable mitigation are now excluded from the application of the presumption, which was not the intention of the policy."*

In order *"to make clear that the presumption is disapplied only where an appropriate assessment has concluded that there is no suitable mitigation strategy in place"*, the now revised Paragraph 177 reads:

> *The presumption in favour of sustainable development does not apply where the plan or project is likely to have a significant effect on a habitats site (either alone or in combination with other plans or projects), unless an appropriate assessment has concluded that the plan or project will not adversely affect the integrity of the habitats site.*

This is of course a thoroughly sensible revision that certainly clarifies the

---

[27] Ministry of Housing, Communities and Local Government – Technical consultation on updates to national planning policy and guidance, October 2018.

position. The irony is that the pre-revision Paragraph 177 did not have the intended effect anyway, irrespective of *POW*, because it did not allow for an appropriate assessment that concludes in favour of development!

This oversight – presupposing that an appropriate assessment will always have a negative outcome for the proposal in question – seems to underpin much of the misplaced criticism of the *POW* judgment and the culture of pre-emptive screening out that goes with it.

An appropriate assessment does not prejudge anything but considers the evidence on all the properly scoped issues, including proposed mitigation, to inform a decision on whether a project or plan should go ahead and if so, on what basis and with what conditions. To screen out avoids that process, quite reasonably where there is no potential impact, but to contrive screening out to avoid the possibility of a negative outcome completely defeats the purpose of proper environmental assessment.

So what is the effect of POW on neighbourhood plans?

First of all, we need to consider again the revised Paragraph 177 NPPF, and the presumption in favour of sustainable development that it refers to at Paragraph 11, NPPF, and in particular the presumption 'for plan-making'.

For neighbourhood plan-making only the first part of the presumption applies (as the second limb deals with strategic policies) and that says that *"plans should positively seek opportunities to meet the development needs of their area, and be sufficiently flexible to adapt to rapid change"*.

Notwithstanding Paragraph 177, it is difficult to see how this general advice within the presumption should be changed or varied by the decision in *POW*, even if the neighbourhood plan does require an appropriate assessment. Subject to any such appropriate assessment, the NDPs should still *"positively seek opportunities to meet the development needs of their area etc."*

Secondly, the new Regulation 106 of the Habitats Regulations and the new Schedule 2 of the Neighbourhood Planning Regulations both suggest that there may well be circumstances in which an appropriate assessment will be needed to ensure that a draft NDP complies with the basic conditions.

Obviously what *POW* tells us is that if we have to consider measures intended to avoid or reduce the harmful effects of the envisaged plan, then the NDP requires an appropriate assessment.

The questions that qualifying bodies need to ask are these:

1.   Are there any European sites within the neighbourhood area or in sufficient proximity to the neighbourhood area so that they could be affected by NDP policies?

2.   If there are European sites within the neighbourhood area or in sufficient proximity to it, does the draft NDP allocate any development sites within a European site or significantly closer to such a site than any existing development of the type proposed or does the draft NDP otherwise promote any such new development?

3.   If the answer to question 2 is 'yes', are there any potential adverse environmental impacts arising from the draft NDP policies relating to the development sites in question or development otherwise proposed by the NDP?

If all three questions are answered affirmatively then the making of a neighbourhood plan may be likely to have a significant effect that will trigger the need for an appropriate assessment.

Notwithstanding Schedule 2, if there are potential impacts on European sites from the making of the NDP, whether or not possible mitigation measures are being considered, then the draft NDP should be subject to appropriate assessment.

Ultimately, the LPA should advise the qualifying body on this issue because, as we have already seen, any legal challenge to the making of the NDP or any decisions relating to it will be against the LPA. LPAs are likely to adopt a cautious view in the light of *POW* and require draft NDPs to undergo appropriate assessment even when it may not be strictly necessary.

Whenever an appropriate assessment is required the qualifying body should work with the LPA to produce a scoping report that will inform suitably qualified experts in the production of the necessary environmental assessments and reports that, ultimately, will be submitted along with the draft neighbourhood plan for examination.

Evidence from detailed consultations

Once preferred options have been selected from the analysis of initial consultation responses, further detailed public consultation will usually be needed particularly if the options are potentially contentious or if there are competing options. The nature and extent of any such consultations will depend on the subject matter.

A typical example is a consultation on which competing sites should be allocated for housing in the neighbourhood area.

The projected number of new dwellings to be delivered should be determined objectively by an assessment of Local Housing Need ("LHN") undertaken by the LPA and notified to the qualifying body for the purposes of the neighbourhood plan.[28]

The potential housing sites that come forward for consideration to meet the LHN will usually be those the LPA is already aware of as a result of a 'call for sites' exercise and any others submitted for consideration as part of the NDP process. The consideration of competing sites for housing allocations is almost inevitably contentious so care must be taken not only to present them fairly and accurately for public consultation but also to objectively consider all reasonable representations and consultation responses.

This process of detailed consultation, for any NDP allocations or policies but particularly for housing sites must be rigorous, reasonable, objective and transparent. It therefore goes without saying that it must also be carefully recorded so that decisions taken by the qualifying body, and the evidence behind those decisions, can be easily understood at the examination.

As we have seen already, a summary of every consultation must be included in the consultation statement submitted by the qualifying body to the LPA.

Shaping the plan and its policies

Once preferred options have been selected and detailed consultations are underway for any options that require it, then the outline of the plan and the type of policies it needs to include will start to take shape.

The process of shaping the plan towards its first draft will comprise various inputs; the original objectives of the NDP and the different subject or policy areas that relate to those objectives, documentary evidence from third party sources (such as expert evidence on ecology, transport

---

[28] Paragraph 65, NPPF.

or historic features), LPA advice and evidence on particular issues such as LHN and the responses and other evidence that comes from the various public consultations undertaken for the NDP.

That process will from time to time lead to additional questions or issues that will need to be resolved, sometimes by further consultations. The process should not be overcomplicated, but it can be involved and any difficult or contentious issues need to be dealt with. If the NDP is to pass the examination with planning policies that are purposeful and workable, that desired outcome and how it will be achieved should be kept in mind throughout.

The qualifying body should get to grips with, and be well briefed on, any contentious issues as early in the process as possible; if not dealt with they can come back to bite at a later stage when, as we have seen, the qualifying body may have little or no control on the decisions taken.

Whilst the balanced consideration of all the evidence and accurate recording of consultations as part of the due process is essential, it is important to remember that the plan and its policies should be led by decisions of the qualifying body taken in the best interests of the neighbourhood area and its residents. The requirements of due process are important, and may even compromise some elements of the plan, but they should not crowd out the purpose behind the plan or the legitimate aspirations of the community.

Arguably the main responsibility of the qualifying body is to ensure, as far as possible, that those legitimate aspirations are not only reflected but promoted in the NDP. To discharge this responsibility will often involve making difficult decisions in the face of LPA and developer pressure.

4.   Preparing a draft plan

First draft

When all the consultation exercises are concluded and the assessment of evidence on all the subject areas of the emerging plan is complete, you are ready to begin drafting the plan itself.

Setting out the plan and how it is drafted may seem a minor and insignificant exercise, but it is in fact far more important than that. A neighbourhood plan will be the most significant document most parish councils ever produce. At the very least it will be a part of the statutory development plan and publicly available on the LPA website. It should stand up technically but must also be coherent and well presented, professionally if possible, to maximise its impact. How the first draft is initially conceived will be crucial to achieving this.

There is no standard form or template for an NDP but a thorough introduction to the neighbourhood area and its characteristics is a good starting point. Further background information is also needed, on the area generally and on specific issues or parts of the area, to explain the imperatives behind the plan.

Whilst the consultation statement and appendices will detail the process and consultations undertaken, the plan itself should provide an overview of the whole project – a summary of how the community engaged with the plan and over what time period.

In addition to the main purpose of a neighbourhood plan – effective planning policies – it can and should express planning related community aspirations that may be beyond the strict scope of the NDP's planning policies. Much hoped for highways improvements or new schools are strategic issues that a neighbourhood plan cannot set dedicated planning policies for or be too prescriptive about. However, it is perfectly reasonable for the NDP to identify such aspirations and explain how they could be brought forward and supported by the local community. This type of information will be informative for third parties and in particular for developers and for the LPA – it may even guide the LPA in its policy making or on its Community Infrastructure Levy Charging Schedule and more generally on infrastructure requirements in the area.

The main sections of your neighbourhood plan will cover the policy subject areas. The subject area, whether it be housing, the environment, retail provision etc., should be introduced in the context of the neighbourhood area, followed by an explanation of the policy objectives and how the NDP will achieve those objectives. Further to that will be the policy itself, usually highlighted or emphasised in some way for quick reference.

Planning policies with a purpose

As the essence of a neighbourhood plan and the main reason for its existence, it follows that each of its planning policies must have a clear purpose and be effective in achieving that purpose. This cannot be over-emphasised; a neighbourhood plan without effective planning policies is simply not worthwhile.

What also bears repetition as it is often misunderstood is that the examination is only required to test the plan's compliance with the basic conditions, not the efficacy of neighbourhood plan policies or the extent to which they are likely to meet their objectives. To put it very bluntly, very few if any neighbourhood plan examiners or the LPAs they are engaged by are particularly concerned whether the objectives of the NDP will be met when planning determinations are made.

There are all too many NDPs already made that do not heed these concerns and which contain planning policies that simply do not work as intended. With this in mind, great care needs to be taken when considering other NDPs as precedents for an emerging one.

Current local plan policies are another misleading precedent for NDP policies, mainly because they are intended to operate at a strategic level or at least above the local level, and are therefore less likely to impose detailed requirements or restrictions. Read in isolation, contemporary local plan policies often appear very permissive and the extent to which they are restrictive is only implied from a knowledge of other parts of the local plan or certain defined terms within it. Trying to replicate such policies in a neighbourhood plan is unlikely to produce effective results.

Every neighbourhood plan policy should be clear and easily understood. The purpose or objective of the policy should be clear from the supporting text and based on evidence collected during the NDP process. The policy may be worded permissively, or restrictively subject to certain requirements being met. An NDP policy should not conflict with the strategic objectives of the local plan but it may impose detailed requirements not referred to elsewhere.

Professional expertise should be sought when drafting your neighbourhood plan policies. Going to the effort and expense of preparing a neighbourhood plan without taking professional advice on the drafting of its planning policies is a misguided false economy, rather like a hard working business owner doing his own bookkeeping but refusing to employ an accountant to prepare and audit his accounts.

There are two reasons why this book contains no examples of or templates for an NDP or for individual NDP policies. The first is that every neighbourhood plan will be different – with different objectives and background – so that no template could be a helpful or reliable guide to a new and emerging NDP. Secondly, every neighbourhood plan and all supporting information is, as it has to be, publicly available on the website of the LPA that made it. To get an idea of what an NDP looks like and how others have dealt with issues of concern to them, the starting point is to look at the website of your own LPA.

Professional and independent review

It is inescapably the case that neighbourhood planning and the process of having a neighbourhood plan made and in effect are not as straight-forward as originally envisaged or intended. Planning is increasingly contentious, LPAs are under pressure to issue planning permissions and the stakes, particularly for certain types of development, are high.

Against this background many LPAs offer an independent review of draft neighbourhood plans prior to examination. It will generally be in the LPA's interests to have NDPs in their area pass the examination and some therefore recommend that an examiner known to them reviews the plan first. This may be a worthwhile exercise but it is not truly independent and the implications of that should be borne in mind.

Again, the distinction between compliance with the basic conditions for the examination, and the efficiency of the neighbourhood plan in achieving its objectives, should be remembered. The qualifying body should always be willing to engage its own professional expertise to advise on, and review, its draft plan prior to Regulation 14 submission and throughout the statutory stages that follow that.

5.   The statutory stages

The details of the statutory process are dealt with in detail in *Chapter 4*. Here we deal with the practical implications for the qualifying body of the somewhat confusing legislative provisions that between Regulations 14 and 16 quickly transfer responsibility for, and control of, the draft NDP to the LPA and then in turn to the examiner, with only cursory further recourse, if that, to the qualifying body.

Regulation 14 – pre-submission consultation and publicity

As we have seen, when the draft plan is publicised for six weeks under Regulation 14 the qualifying body is still in control of the plan and how this consultation and publicity – under Regulation 14 – may affect it.

That said, if changes are needed to the draft plan as a result of the six week Regulation 14 consultation period, it is likely that the 'new' amended plan will have to go through another six week period of Regulation 14 publicity in order to consult on the changes.

In order to avoid the costs, delays and uncertainty associated with a Regulation 14 re-run, the qualifying body should undertake informal consultation with the relevant consultation bodies first to flush out and resolve any issues before the statutory process begins. The consultation bodies themselves should be keen to provide their input and advise on their specialist areas. The LPA should also be willing to assist at this point.

If important issues cannot be resolved with the agreement of the consultation bodies and the LPA prior to Regulation 14 publicity, the qualifying body should seek its own independent professional advice and should know exactly where it stands before engaging in the statutory process.

Having sailed through the Regulation 14 stage, the draft plan will be ready for submission to the LPA under Regulation 16, effectively the submission of the plan for examination.

Regulation 16 – publicising a proposal

In submitting the plan to the LPA under Regulation 16 the qualifying body must ensure the plan proposals comply with the Regulation 15 requirements which include the presentation of a basic conditions statement and a consultation statement along with the draft plan.

It has already been emphasised that because the qualifying body effectively loses ownership of the draft NDP at this point, it must ensure that the submission version of the NDP not only complies with the Regulations but is also in a form – with effective and purposeful planning policies – that the qualifying body is happy with. The subsequent examination will only remedy flaws in compliance. It will not turn a poorly drafted and ineffective NDP into one that works as intended.

Examination and the examiner's report on the examination

As we have seen in the preceding chapter, the examination and the consideration of the examiner's report on the examination will in most cases exclude the qualifying body entirely. Any decisions on the examiner's report are taken by the LPA as it has the legal responsibility for bringing the draft NDP into force via the referendum.

In the majority of cases the only involvement of the qualifying body at this critical stage will be some influence over the LPA's choice of examiner, as the qualifying body must consent to that choice. The LPA usually invites the qualifying body to choose from a shortlist of candidates. In most cases there will be no obvious reason to choose one examiner over another but as it is has the opportunity, the qualifying body should try to make a reasoned selection from the information available and may even request an examiner not on the LPA's shortlist.

The chosen examiner will often have examined other NDPs within the LPA area and will have established a good working relationship with the LPA. Whilst this is almost inevitable it may undermine the principle of independence and is one of several factors that can contrive to shut the qualifying body out of the examination process.

If the examiner decides to hold the examination by way of a hearing, which is unusual because most examiners prefer to make their deliberations in private without the pressure of the public gaze or a predetermined timetable, then the qualifying body may be invited to attend.

A hearing is held *"in any case where the examiner considers that the consideration of oral representations is necessary to ensure adequate examination of the issue or a person has a fair chance to put a case".*[29] It follows from this that any such issue or issues should be identified, and notified by the examiner to all relevant parties in advance of the hearing.

The hearing must be in public and the qualifying body, the LPA and any person considered entitled to put their case at the hearing must be given the opportunity of making oral representations. The examiner determines the procedure for the making of representations and any questioning of the party making them.[30]

Generally, the examiner should undertake any questioning at the examination, except where he or she considers that *"questioning by another is necessary to ensure adequate examination of a particular issue, or that a person has a fair chance to put a case".*[31]

Where a hearing is held, the qualifying body should be well prepared for it.

---

[29] Paragraph 9(2)(a), Schedule 4B, TCPA.

[30] Paragraph 9(5), Schedule 4B, TCPA.

[31] Paragraph 9(6), Schedule 4B, TCPA.

A hearing will only be held because the examiner considers an issue to be of significance or because a party with an interest in the neighbourhood plan has, in their written representations, persuaded the examiner that they should have a chance to make oral representations. In either case the qualifying body should carefully consider its case for the hearing and whether it needs professional representation.

An examination hearing usually only results from pressure brought to bear by a landowner or developer looking to change or object to a significant element of the draft NDP such as a policy allocating land for housing, specifically such a policy that does not include the land of the objector concerned. If the draft NDP submitted for examination is to pass the examination, then the qualifying body may need to be willing to robustly resist any such objections, and a good showing at the hearing will be critical to that.

The other circumstances in which the qualifying body may be involved in the examination process is if, in response to the examiner's report, the LPA does not issue its decision statement within the prescribed time period, or decides not to follow one or more of the examiner's recommendations, or decides to make modifications of its own that are not recommended by the examiner. The qualifying body may then request the intervention of the Secretary of State.[32]

A request for intervention under Regulation 31A must be made in writing by the qualifying body, giving reasons for the request, by the prescribed date; six weeks from the date of the LPA's decision statement.[33] If the intervention is on the basis that the LPA has failed to issue a decision notice in time, then there is no prescribed date for the intervention request by the qualifying body.

Once a valid intervention request has been made it is then for the LPA to provide the Secretary of State with the relevant documentation including a copy of the examiner's report.[34] The Secretary of State may appoint an inspector to consider the request and in response to it may issue a direction to the LPA, accompanied by reasons, that differs to that of

---

[32] Regulation 31A, 2012 Regulations as amended by the 2016 amendment Regulations.

[33] Regulation 31A(2)(3)(4), 2012 Regulations as amended by the 2016 amendment Regulations.

[34] Regulation 31B, 2012 Regulations as amended by the 2016 amendment Regulations.

the examiner.[35] If so, then the qualifying body, any person who made representations to the examination and any consultation bodies must be notified of that direction[36] which must then be followed by the LPA.

Therefore, there are limited circumstances in which the qualifying body may seek to overturn a decision (or lack of a decision) of the LPA in its response to the examiner's report, but the qualifying body cannot challenge the examiner's report directly.

Potential pitfalls with Regulation 16 and the examination process

It is important to emphasise again that when the proposed NDP is presented to the LPA for publicity and consultation under Regulation 16, the qualifying body is effectively submitting its proposed NDP for examination and thereafter has very little, if any, control over it.

Whilst under Regulation 14 the qualifying body carries out the consultation and has the opportunity to amend the draft NDP in the light of representations made, once submitted to the LPA under Regulation 16 that opportunity has passed. It is only at or during the Regulation 14 consultation stage that the NDP and any amendments to it remain within the control of the qualifying body.

When submitting a plan proposal under Regulation 16, the qualifying body must include a basic conditions statement explaining how the draft NDP complies with the basic conditions. Under its statutory duty to advise and assist qualifying bodies[37] the LPA should advise on compliance with the basic conditions throughout the process and certainly well before Regulation 14 consultation. However, the willingness of LPAs to discharge this duty efficiently varies enormously.

Furthermore, there is no requirement for representations made in response to the Regulation 16 consultation to be published or for the qualifying body to be made aware of them.

Therefore, even if the draft NDP, the basic conditions statement or any Regulation 16 representations reveal to the LPA flaws in the NDP proposal

---

[35] Regulation 31D, 2012 Regulations as amended by the 2016 amendment Regulations.

[36] Regulation 31C, 2012 Regulations as amended by the 2016 amendment Regulations.

[37] Paragraph 3, Schedule 4B, TCPA.

that may offend the basic conditions, there is no requirement for the LPA to make the qualifying body aware of those flaws or for it to be given any opportunity to address them.

Neither will the LPA itself necessarily seek to address any flaws at this stage as to do so it is likely to require a 'new' draft plan that would (but only with the agreement of the qualifying body) have to go back to the Regulation 14 stage. As the LPA bears the responsibility for, and the costs of, the Regulation 16 publicity and consultation, it will usually be reluctant to repeat or re-run any part of the process.

Instead, the LPA may be more inclined to submit a flawed draft plan for examination where it will be for the examiner to identify, and recommend modifications to address, any flaws or failures to comply with the basic conditions. However, the examiner-recommended modifications may not be the solution that the qualifying body would have preferred or chosen if it had been given the opportunity to resolve the issue prior to examination, and as we have also seen the qualifying body has no right to question or challenge the examiner's recommendations directly.

The qualifying body, solely responsible for the draft plan and required to consult on it at every turn is, at the all-important Regulation 16 stage, reduced to an interested observer – a mere bystander with no meaningful influence or real control over what happens next.

The significance of this is often overlooked. Something fundamental is absent from Regulations 16 and 17; the opportunity for the qualifying body to take account of Regulation 16 representations and LPA advice on compliance with the basic conditions, and then make any necessary amendments before submitting its draft NDP, if necessary in amended form, for examination. That opportunity does not exist.

However, there is another problem here. As well as representations from generally supportive statutory consultees that may highlight a failure to fulfil the basic conditions, Regulation 16 representations also include objections from anyone opposed to the draft plan. The lack of opportunity to respond to those puts the qualifying body and its draft neighbourhood plan at a real disadvantage.

Such objections automatically, via Regulation 17, become submissions to the examiner for consideration at the examination and unless the examiner decides to hold a hearing which is extremely rare, the qualifying body has no right of reply. This is a serious problem for the qualifying body.

Most Regulation 16 representations are substantive objections focussed on having particular policies and, or, site allocations of the draft NDP struck out.

Regulation 16 objections are rarely made by parishioners who dislike the draft NDP, because they have the opportunity to vote against it in the referendum. On the other hand, locals who support the draft NDP and those involved in the preparation of it tend to assume that it is a complete and self-contained statement rendering further representations unnecessary. They will vote in favour of it at the referendum.

Objections typically come from landowners and developers disgruntled that their land is not allocated for development. The corporate house-builders, already collaborating and often holding option agreements with landowners at an early plan-making stage, are well resourced and financially motivated. Their professionally prepared objections, submitted as Regulation 16 representations, will be forceful and usually carry a thinly veiled threat of legal challenge if the objection is not upheld. To give way to the objection often means neutralising essential policies of the NDP or abandoning them altogether.

Objectors have another key advantage. In practice the submission draft plan may have been finalised at least several months before the deadline for making representations under Regulation 16. Objections are therefore likely to be more up-to-date in terms of planning policy and guidance than the draft NDP and will appear more persuasive to the examiner because of that.

With no knowledge of the objections submitted, the qualifying body cannot address them. Even if the LPA informs the qualifying body of Regulation 16 objections to the NDP, there is no right for the qualifying body to make its own representations and if it does attempt to address objections via its own written representations, the examiner can simply refuse to consider them.

The one thing that any examiner and the LPA that has engaged them will want to avoid is any threat of a legal challenge from a litigious corporate housebuilder. Therefore, no matter how much local support a particular NDP policy or housing allocation may have, if the examiner can be persuaded by a developer that it may fail to comply with one of the basic conditions, then the examination report is likely to recommend that the NDP policy or allocation in question be struck out. That is often what the objecting developer is seeking because it provides the opportunity for their site to be considered afresh.

Developer objections that simply emphasise the relative merits of one site over another should not be considered by the examiner because the sole function of the examination is to assess whether the draft plan meets the basic conditions. However, many NDP examiners are relatively new recruits and though professionally qualified, often lack the experience and technical expertise to adjudicate confidently on contentious or difficult issues. If in doubt, they tend to err on the side of caution, which in practice means siding with the developer.

If the issue under consideration is whether to strike out an NDP site allocation because a large housebuilder claims to have a better site, then even though that argument has nothing to do with the basic conditions, in all too many cases the examiner will be pressured to favour the developer's case. The housebuilder has deep pockets and (applying a law of averages approach) will think nothing of issuing a legal challenge, whereas in practice the disappointed qualifying body will have no recourse at all.

The qualifying body must be especially wary here. Not only is the examiner likely to be sensitive to and particularly cautious about developer-led objections but the modifications recommended to address such perceived compliance issues are often swingeing and quite brutal such as the deletion from the draft neighbourhood plan of whole planning policies. It is often the policies that are the most significant and fundamental to the plan that are axed in this way.

Even at the stage when the LPA considers what decisions to take in respect of the examiner's report and its recommendations, the qualifying body still has no right to influence or seek to change the LPA decision or decisions except in very limited circumstances (considered in *Chapter 4* on page 80).

Some NDP examiners do stand up to developers and it is those cases that often, when the developer appeals the LPA decision based on the examiner's report, go on to the Planning Court and sometimes result in reported case law.

It is also the case that developers who do lodge legal challenges to draft NDPs often fail in their judicial review. But for all those cases, the ones that do attract media attention and should encourage all NDP examiners to be more robust, there are many more where a developer's invalid objection nevertheless sways the examiner and usurps the essence of the neighbourhood plan produced by the qualifying body.

All too often a parish council that has several spent years and many thousands of pounds producing a neighbourhood plan, as it is encouraged to do, is left with no remedy against commercially motivated objections intended to undermine its work and the whole purpose of its NDP.

To stand any chance of avoiding this fate the qualifying body must fully understand how the statutory procedure operates from Regulation 14 onwards so that the aforementioned pitfalls can be anticipated and guarded against as much as possible.

Referendum

As we have already seen above (under *'The referendum and the 'making' of the neighbourhood plan'* – see page 82) once the LPA has decided to progress the draft NDP, still formally known as a 'plan proposal' at this stage, to a referendum the responsibility for arranging all aspects of that lies with the LPA.

The qualifying body has no formal duties or responsibilities at this stage although it may well decide to informally publicise the referendum and to actively campaign for local support for the NDP, particularly if the draft plan is contentious or a low turnout is expected.

Typically, the turnout for an NDP referendum is low, often only around 20% or so, and at this crucial referendum stage every effort should be made to maximise voter interest and to capitalise on that for the future application of the NDP and its planning policies. On the other hand, and providing a majority vote in favour of the draft NDP is achieved, the qualifying body should not be discouraged by a low referendum turnout.

The neighbourhood plan in force

Having achieved a majority vote of support at the referendum, the LPA must decide to make the neighbourhood plan and in so doing will convert the draft plan or plan proposal so long in preparation into a neighbourhood development plan that becomes part of the statutory development plan and must be publicised as such on the LPA website.

Of course, in the unlikely event that less than 51% of those voting at the referendum support the draft plan, then it progresses no further. From a practical perspective if it is to be rekindled, efforts should be made to address the unpopular elements of it and a suitably amended version must go back at least to the Regulation 14 stage.

Having a neighbourhood development plan made and in force is a real achievement of which everyone involved should be proud. The life of the neighbourhood plan now enters a new phase. It is now part of the statutory development plan. How will it be regarded, interpreted, used and applied in practice? Until that starts to happen the NDP is not really tested.

Monitoring

The most obvious way of monitoring a newly made neighbourhood plan is to simply consider how often and how purposefully it is applied in local planning determinations.

Is the NDP referred to by planning officers in their consideration of local planning applications and if so, how is it applied? How are development proposals assessed against the NDP policies? Which NDP policies are regularly invoked? Are there NDP policies that should be considered in the determination of planning applications but for some reason are being ignored, or not interpreted in the way they are intended to be?

There seems little point in producing a neighbourhood plan if this basic level of monitoring – or put more simply, local interest – is not engaged in. The whole point of making any development plan is for it to guide decisions on development in its area. If the qualifying body shows no interest in those decisions, then it will not know how its NDP is being applied and this begs the question as to whether it was worthwhile producing it in the first place.

Neighbourhood planning is, just like the wider planning system of which it is a component part, a regime of plan-making and decision-taking, or in the terminology used in *Chapter 2*, of forward planning and development control. Without the former, the latter has no basis and without the latter the former is completely pointless.

Therefore, the qualifying body of a made neighbourhood development plan must take an interest in planning generally and local planning decisions in particular. The various ways of doing so are covered in the next chapter.

That said, in these still relatively early years of neighbourhood planning it may have to be acknowledged that the monitoring of planning deci-sion-making described above will in many cases draw quite depressing conclusions. Although things are changing quickly, even now many LPAs remain ambivalent about neighbourhood planning and reluctant to recognise the significance of neighbourhood plans for planning deter-minations. Parish councils and qualifying bodies must therefore be not only vigilant but determined in promoting and monitoring their NDPs once they are made.

Monitoring of an NDP in force must also be undertaken in a more tech-nical sense by keeping abreast of national planning guidance (in the form of the NPPF and PPG), local plan policies and any Supplementary Planning Documents ("SPDs"). This is to make sure that NDP policies conform and do not conflict with strategic local plan policies, and comply with other NPPF guidance. Where an NDP has fallen behind or out of compliance with the local plan or the NPPF, then it should be reviewed and updated to avoid obsolescence.

Review

As Planning Practice Guidance[38] reminds us, a neighbourhood plan must set out the period for which it is to have effect[39] and NDP policies remain in force until the plan policy is replaced. However, even in the very early years of the plan period of a neighbourhood plan, its policies only truly remain in force provided they can be considered up-to-date for NPPF purposes.

So, whilst there is no formal requirement to review or update a neigh-bourhood plan,[40] the need for even a relatively recently made NDP to be regularly reviewed has become imperative. Whilst it used to be considered that a review every five years was appropriate in most cases, this is now unlikely to be sufficient.

It stands to reason that any development plan must keep up-to-date with changing circumstances and attendant planning policies and guid-ance but a qualifying body should have particular regard to Section 38, Planning and Compulsory Purchase Act 2004 ("PCPA") and Paragraph 14, NPPF.

---

[38] Paragraph 084, PPG on *'Neighbourhood planning'*.

[39] Section 38B(1)(a), Planning and Compulsory Purchase Act 2004.

[40] Again, see Paragraph 084, PPG on *'Neighbourhood planning'*.

Section 38, Planning and Compulsory Purchase Act 2004 ("PCPA")

We have already seen the fundamental importance of Section 38(6), PCPA, which lays down the guiding principle for the interrelationship between the development plan and planning determinations, and which is known as the primacy of the development plan.

From a practical perspective for neighbourhood planners, the immediately preceding subsection, Section 38(5), is almost as important. It provides that:

> *If to any extent a policy contained in a development plan for an area conflicts with another policy in the development plan the conflict must be resolved in favour of the policy which is contained in the last document to become part of the development plan.*

This means that an NDP policy may be rendered obsolete and meaningless if a local plan with a conflicting policy is adopted the following month or even the following week.

Such potentially harsh effects should be rare, not least because a local plan should contain mainly strategic policies and an NDP non-strategic policies, in accordance with the NPPF. However, Section 38(5) contains a salutary warning for the timing of any neighbourhood plan in relation to the adoption of a local plan. An NDP should be made as soon as possible after the local plan to which it should relate.

In practice, of course, the precise timing of the making of an NDP cannot be engineered by the qualifying body so regular review of a neighbourhood plan in force will be necessary to ensure the necessary compliance and the effectiveness that only comes with that.

Paragraph 14, National Planning Policy Framework

Paragraph 14 NPPF is perhaps the most explicit imperative for why an NDP should be kept up-to-date.

Paragraph 14 is, in effect, the government's retort to a qualifying body that objects to a planning application for housing on the basis that it conflicts with the neighbourhood plan for the area and therefore rebuts the presumption in favour of sustainable development. As we examine in more detail in the next chapter, Paragraph 14 introduces new and much more rigorous tests for how a neighbourhood plan can be considered up-to-date for NPPF purposes – tests that will often be too stringent for a team of volunteers (which is essentially what a qualifying body is) to be able to comply with. It is another measure of just how keen the government is to be seen to be driving massive new housebuilding (whether or not that is truly sustainable, or deliverable).

Ordinarily, a planning policy in an NDP, that must be NPPF-compliant to have been made, would stand as the test of sustainable development. However, for housing applications, that is no longer considered sufficient.

For a housing policy or allocation in a made NDP to rebut the presumption in favour of sustainable development in the case of a non-compliant or conflicting housing application, a further four requirements must be satisfied. Two of those relate to matters entirely beyond the control of the qualifying body; the amount of deliverable housing sites 'provided by' the LPA, and the rate of actual housing delivery (which is solely within the control of developers and usually at the mercy of market conditions).

Nonetheless, Paragraph 14 also stipulates that for an NDP housing policy or allocation to be a reason for the refusal of a conflicting housing application, there are a further two requirements of the neighbourhood plan itself. First, it *"must have become part of the development plan two years or less"* before the date the planning application is determined and secondly, the NDP *"must contain policies and allocations to meet its identified housing requirement"*.

Additionally, for the NDP to be considered up-to-date under Paragraph 14, the LPA must have *"at least a three year supply of deliverable housing sites (against its five year housing supply requirement, including the appropriate buffer as set out in paragraph 73)"* and the LPA's *"housing delivery must have been at least 45% of that required over the previous three years"*. The NDP qualifying body obviously has no control at all over these requirements.

Paragraph 14 creates obvious problems for a neighbourhood plan and its qualifying body which the latter can do little if anything about. Briefly, for a detailed discussion follows in *Chapter 6*, the problems include the following:

–   an NDP must contain housing policies and allocations – so it appears that an NDP must now contain housing allocations for its housing policies to be effective;

- whether or not the NDP – that has already passed an examination – contains policies and allocations to meet its identified housing requirement will fall to be determined again by the planning decision-maker without any recourse necessarily to the qualifying body;

- the identified housing requirement is not always clear and is not set by the qualifying body, but the LPA;

- there may be some uncertainty over the exact point at which the NDP becomes part of the development plan,[41] and;

- housing developers will be able to use all these factors to their advantage and in any case will be able to influence the timing of the determination of their applications to take them beyond the two years currency of the NDP.

It must be remembered that to be able to rely on the NDP, all of the Paragraph 14 requirements must be met. If any one of them is not, the NDP – even though part of the statutory development plan – may be worthless in resisting a housing proposal that is in conflict with it.

So, if having reviewed its NDP and for whatever reason the qualifying body decides to update it, how does it go about doing so?

Modification

The legislation provides for the expedited modification of a neighbourhood plan by the LPA, with the consent of the qualifying body, simply to correct an error.[42]

Beyond that, modification is the culmination of the process of monitoring and review. Monitoring local planning decisions and emerging planning policies and guidance should indicate when a review of the NDP is necessary and any such review should consider what, if any, modification of the plan is needed to restore the effectiveness of the plan. The question then to be asked is; *By what process is a neighbourhood plan modified?*

---

[41] See Section 3, Neighbourhood Planning Act 2017.

[42] Section 61M(4), TCPA.

The provisions of the Neighbourhood Planning Act 2017[43] and attendant Regulations[44] go some way to answering that by applying the procedure for the making of a neighbourhood plan to any proposal by the qualifying body to modify an existing plan. The all important stages (discussed above in *Chapters 4* and *5*) at Regulations 14, 15, 16, 17 and 18 now apply in almost exactly the same way to a proposal to modify.

Furthermore, in a provision that replicates the LPA's statutory duty to assist in the making of an NDP, *"the LPA must give such advice or assistance to a qualifying body as, in all the circumstances, they consider appropriate for the purpose of, or in connection with, facilitating the making of a proposal for the modification of a neighbourhood development plan for a neighbourhood area within their area".*[45]

PPG summarises[46] the three different types of modification that can be made to an NDP or NDO and the process that applies to each:

Minor (non-material) modifications are those which would not materially affect the policies in the plan or permission granted by the order. These may include correcting errors, such as a reference to a supporting document, and would not require examination or a referendum. (Minor modifications may be made by the LPA simply with the consent of the qualifying body).[47]

Material modifications which do not change the nature of the plan or order would require examination but not a referendum. This might, for example, entail the addition of a design code that builds on a pre-existing design policy, or the addition of a site or sites which, subject to the decision of the independent examiner, are not so significant or substantial as to change the nature of the plan.

Material modifications which do change the nature of the plan or

---

[43] Section 4 and Schedule 1, Neighbourhood Planning Act 2017 – Schedule 1 imports a new Schedule A2, 'Modification of Neighbourhood Development Plans' into the Planning and Compulsory Purchase Act 2004.

[44] The Neighbourhood Planning (General) and Development Management Procedure (Amendment) Regulations 2017.

[45] Paragraph 3, Schedule A2, Planning and Compulsory Purchase Act 2004.

[46] Paragraph 106, PPG on *'Neighbourhood planning'*.

[47] Paragraph 084a, PPG on *'Neighbourhood planning'*.

order would require examination and a referendum. This might, for example, involve allocating significant new sites for development.

If the qualifying body proposes modifications that do materially affect the policies in the plan, then at the Regulation 14 pre-submission publicity and consultation stage when the modified plan is submitted to the LPA, the qualifying body must state whether they believe that the modifications are so significant or substantial as to change the nature of the plan and give reasons for that. When sending the modified plan to the examiner for examination, the LPA must give its view, with reasons, on the same issue, and also provide the examiner with a copy of the original plan.[48]

After considering such representations and the reasons for them, from the qualifying body and the LPA, the examiner must *"then determine whether the modifications contained in the draft plan are so significant or substantial as to change the nature of the neighbourhood development plan which the draft plan would replace".*[49]

PPG suggests that if the proposed modifications are in the form of a design code or other matters supplementary to an existing NDP policy, then they may well be considered not to change the nature of the plan even though they are material changes to it.[50]

If the examiner determines that the modifications would change the nature of the plan then he or she must notify the LPA and the qualifying body of that determination[51] and the qualifying body has the opportunity to withdraw the proposal at that stage.[52]

If after a determination that the proposed modifications change the nature of the plan the qualifying body notifies the examiner it wishes to proceed with the modifications, then an examination, examiner's report, LPA decision on such and, ultimately, a referendum will follow exactly as if the proposed modifications were for the making of a new plan.[53]

---

[48] Paragraph 085, PPG on *'Neighbourhood planning'*.

[49] Paragraph 10(1), Schedule A2, Planning and Compulsory Purchase Act 2004.

[50] Paragraph 086, PPG on *'Neighbourhood planning'*.

[51] Paragraph 10(3), Schedule A2, Planning and Compulsory Purchase Act 2004.

[52] Paragraph 10(4), Schedule A2, Planning and Compulsory Purchase Act 2004.

[53] Paragraph 10(5), Schedule A2, Planning and Compulsory Purchase Act 2004 which effectively applies Paragraph 8, Schedule 4B, TCPA in these circumstances.

If the examiner determines that the proposed modifications are not so significant or substantial as to change the nature of the plan, then the proposal proceeds to an expedited examination procedure that simply tests compliance with the basic conditions.[54]

The LPA may decline to consider a "repeat proposal" for modifications if in the previous two years and based on essentially the same proposal, the LPA has refused to make a modified plan either because it failed to comply with the basic conditions or that the examiner recommended it should not be made.[55]

There are also detailed provisions under the 2017 Act for modifications to neighbourhood areas and for any consequential modifications to NDPs and NDOs.[56]

Modifications with a purpose

A final word on modifications is that if the qualifying body is going to the trouble of proposing to the LPA anything other than corrections or non-material modifications, then it should ensure a comprehensive approach is taken so as to include modifications that may be desirable in addition to those that are, for updating purposes, necessary.

---

[54] Under Paragraphs 11 to 14, Schedule A2, Planning and Compulsory Purchase Act 2004.

[55] Paragraph 5, Schedule A2, Planning and Compulsory Purchase Act 2004.

[56] Section 5, Neighbourhood Planning Act 2017.

Chapter 6: Neighbourhood Plans and Housing

As we have seen already, a neighbourhood plan may cover as many or as few local planning related matters as the qualifying body decides. There is no requirement or prescription for any particular subjects or a certain number of subjects to be addressed and the subject areas covered by NDPs will inevitably vary depending on local objectives and aspirations. In this respect housing is no different from any other local planning topic.

However, whilst there is no strict requirement for a neighbourhood plan to contain policies on housing, there are now very real imperatives for most NDPs to do so. It is important to understand the background to those imperatives, both in terms of the broad policy objectives and the national planning policy strictures (in the form of the NPPF and the online PPG) that are intended to ensure those objectives are fulfilled. Therefore, housing warrants its own dedicated chapter in this book.

Qualifying bodies should also take note that most of the legal challenges against neighbourhood plans come from housing developers whose proposals have been obstructed by an NDP; whether by allocations policies that have not included their site or by generic policies to which their proposed development is contrary. In many of the reported cases, the decision went against the developer and upheld the policies of the made or emerging neighbourhood plan.[1]

However, the current NPPF, first introduced in July 2018 and revised in February 2019, has a much stricter focus on the need for local and neighbourhood plans to be right up-to-date in their policies for housing delivery. Therefore, whilst some important principles for neighbourhood plans in relation to housing have been confirmed by case law, regard must be had to the NPPF guidance to ensure that NDP policies on housing will be effective.

---

[1] See *BDW Trading Ltd v Cheshire West & Chester Borough Council* [2014] EWHC 1470 (Admin), *R (on the application of Gladman Developments Ltd) v Aylesbury Vale District Council* [2014] EWHC 4323 (Admin) and *Crane v Secretary of State for Communities and Local Government* [2015] EWHC 425 (Admin).

The background to government policy and the 'housing crisis'

Put simply, current government policy is to build 300,000 houses a year.

This objective is, by any reckoning, a crude policy statement that belies not only the true characteristics of the housing crisis, such as it is, but also how to effectively address that crisis.

There are commentators, academics and experts who recognise that the nature of the housing crisis and the means of solving it are far more nuanced than simply building as many houses as possible anywhere and everywhere. Nonetheless that continues to be the general approach supported by a broad political and media consensus heavily influenced by the very effective lobbying of developers and the construction industry.

That broad consensus also maintains that the main cause of the crisis is an inefficient, overcomplicated and obstructive planning system. Others would say the real crisis is characterised by the homeless, the rough sleepers, the families moved around by their local authority from one bed and breakfast to another and the very poor living standards in squalid private sector accommodation at the mercy of rogue landlords. Few of these folk will ever be able to afford the 3, 4 or 5-bedroom family homes that most developers seek planning permissions for, often on greenfield sites. Many of these underhoused would not even qualify for the type of affordable housing that developers can be required to provide through planning agreements.

Notwithstanding the hundreds of thousands of empty homes in the UK,[2] the hundreds of thousands of unimplemented residential planning permissions[3] (many of which are simply allowed to lapse) and (on any one night) the 25 million or so unoccupied bedrooms in underoccupied dwellings in England alone,[4] the government continues to maintain that the planning system is to blame for an under supply of new housing and it is this above all else that the NPPF seeks to address.

---

[2] In March 2019 there were reported to be over 216,000 empty or 'long-term vacant' homes in the UK; http://www.theguardian.com/society/2019/mar/11/empty-homes-england-rises-property.

[3] In February 2018 it was reported that planning permissions for 423,000 houses throughout the UK were unimplemented; https://www.telegraph.co.uk/property/news/uk-has-backlog-423000-new-homes-planning-permission-waiting/.

[4] http://www.if.org.uk/wp-content/uploads/2011/10/IF_housingrel_defin_LE2.pdf.

Whilst it is not the purpose of this book to campaign against the generally erroneous characterisation of the housing crisis, it is impossible to objectively assess the NPPF and its housing policies for the purpose of neighbourhood planning without understanding the significant anomalies and contradictions of the NPPF approach.

The first of those is how the target of 300,000 new homes a year is arrived at. The root source of the government's new housing target is the national census from which future projected growth in households is extrapolated. The census encourages aspirational responses and uses other predicted factors such as future immigration that usually result in exaggerated and therefore unreliable figures that are subsequently reduced downwards. The recent trend is that the household growth figures predicted by the census are overestimates.

The 2016-based figures for net increase in households (published in September 2018) were significantly lower than previously projected, causing a reassessment of the 'new' NPPF published in July 2018 which then had to be revised (though not as might logically be expected – see below, page 167).

Given that in early 2020, a year after the revisions to the latest NPPF, the government maintains that the "*planning system fails to keep pace ... and fails to deliver enough homes ...*",[5] what will come as perhaps the greatest surprise to many are the government's own figures for the number of residential permissions issued. These statistics[6] are the hard evidence of the output of the planning system and whatever ministers may say, the truth of the matter is that in 2018 and 2019, planning permissions were issued for 383,300 and 371,800 new homes respectively; a 25% uplift on the government's already inflated target of 300,000!

Of course, once a planning permission is issued there is still much to do. The developer will usually have to complete the acquisition of the site, and then ensure that planning conditions are discharged. They will also have to build and properly service the houses for which permission has

---

[5] https://www.gov.uk/government/publications/planning-for-the-future.

[6] MHCLG Planning Statistical Release 27 June 2019 https://assets.publishing.service. gov.uk/government/uploads/system/uploads/attachment_data/file/812867/Planning_ Applications_January_to_March_2019_-_statistical_release.pdf.

MHCLG Planning Statistical Release 25 March 2020 https://assets.publishing.service. gov.uk/government/uploads/system/uploads/attachment_data/file/875032/Planning_ Application_Statistics_October_to_December_2019.pdf.

been granted. Some developers will simply decide not to implement and build out a planning permission they hold or will fail to secure the funding to do so, and others may go bust in the meantime ... but it is simply not true to say the planning system fails to deliver enough homes.

Whether or not it is flaws in the planning system that are really the main cause of the housing crisis, it is inescapable that the one issue above all others driving the government's continued support for neighbourhood planning is housing supply and the need to maximise it. The government's own assessment is that more residential planning permissions are granted in areas covered by a neighbourhood plan.

Yet ironically, the allocation of housing sites is increasingly contentious and a potential stumbling block for many neighbourhood plans. Whilst the opportunity for local people to have a say in where new housing goes is one of the main reasons for many NDPs coming into existence, allocating one site for housing over another has the potential to undermine an NDP and prevent it from reflecting the aspirations and objectives of those making it. That is because most challenges to draft neighbourhood plans come from housing developers whose sites have not been allocated. When such challenges succeed the NDP is usually either neutralised because key policies are struck out, or abandoned altogether. Qualifying bodies therefore need to understand throughout the plan-making process how, and to what extent, their NDP should provide for new housing.

An overview of NPPF policies on housing and housing delivery

The NPPF attempts to formulate national planning policies that will deliver the government target of 300,000 new houses annually. Ostensibly it does that by saying that the supply of land for housing should be sufficient to meet objectively assessed housing need – plus some. That is of course perfectly logical. If only it were that straightforward.

Not only is the devil in the detail but also in the inevitable time lag inherent in the forward planning process which usually means that by the time the plan in question is adopted, the evidence on which it is purportedly based is no longer up-to-date. This is a perennial problem – one that most politicians simply fail to grasp or accept. Most national planning policies intended to simplify or speed up the planning process usually do exactly the opposite. So, is the current NPPF published in February 2019 any different?

Whether or not the NPPF simplifies or complicates the supply of housing through the planning system, there is another elephant in the room – a fundamental truth that national policy makers fail to acknowledge and which threatens to undermine much of the NPPF approach to housing – that is that planning authorities and plan-makers do not build or supply houses – they merely plan where they should go.

Assessing housing need – the standard methodology

The standard methodology[7] is to be used by LPAs to determine how many new houses they need to provide planning permissions for in their local plan area. LPAs may use an alternative approach to the standard methodology but only in exceptional circumstances, and if they do they can expect it to be scrutinised more closely at the examination[8] of the local plan in question.

The first two steps of the standard methodology for assessing the number of new houses needed in any LPA area are straightforward.

First, the figure for household growth projections for each local authority area – published by the Office for National Statistics ("ONS") – is the baseline figure from which the LPA takes an annual housing need figure; if the ONS projection for an area is 1,000 new households over a 10 year projected period, the LPA housing need figure is 100 per annum – the baseline figure.

Step 2 then adjusts the baseline figure by putting the ONS affordability ratio for the area into the standard methodology formula to give an affordability adjustment factor that is then applied to the baseline housing need figure. This gives a new annual housing need figure adjusted for affordability. Under the formula, more new housing is needed in areas where housing is less affordable than in an area with a median level of affordability.

Step 3 of the standard methodology then applies a cap to the affordability adjusted figure. Where the LPA's strategic housing policies are less than

---

[7]   Paragraph 60, NPPF and Paragraph 004, PPG on '*Housing and economic needs assessment*'.

[8]   Paragraph 003, PPG on '*Housing and economic needs assessment*'.

five years old, the local housing need figure is capped at 40% above the Step 1 baseline figure. This seems to be a rather arbitrary moderation, albeit one which recognises that LPAs may struggle to find enough land for the affordability factor increase in what has already been assessed as the number of houses needed. For LPAs whose housing policies are not up-to-date, the 40% cap applies to whichever is the higher of the baseline figure or the figure set out in their most recent strategic policies.

The resultant figure represents the LPA's annual housing need and the LPA must plan accordingly by making strategic planning policies that allocate sufficient sites for the number of new dwellings assessed to be needed.

What should strategic housing policies provide for?

According to the NPPF, the LPA must make strategic planning policies to provide for its annual housing need, as assessed by the standard methodology, and by attendant allocations of housing land.[9]

LPAs are of course free to plan for more housing than the annual housing need figure and are encouraged to do so in growth areas or where strategic infrastructure improvements are likely to make more housing deliverable. Some LPAs will also agree to provide more housing to accommodate a neighbouring area's housing requirement.[10]

The NPPF goes on to say that planning policies should reflect and provide for the different types of housing needed in the area[11] and for appropriate levels of affordable housing. Major housing or mixed developments should, subject to certain exemptions, provide at least 10% of their housing as affordable housing.[12] Residential developments that are not major developments (that is, with no more than 10 dwellings) other than in designated rural areas (where policies may set out a lower threshold of five units or fewer)[13] are not subject to the requirement to provide affordable housing.

---

[9] Paragraphs 65 and 67, NPPF.

[10] See Paragraph 010, PPG on *'Housing and economic needs assessment'*.

[11] Paragraph 61, NPPF.

[12] Paragraph 64, NPPF.

[13] Paragraphs 62 and 63, NPPF.

In the section entitled *'Identifying land for homes'*, the NPPF sets out exactly how planning policies should be prepared and formulated to provide for the housing required.

This is summed up in one of the most significant paragraphs in the NPPF for neighbourhood plan-makers – Paragraph 65:

> *Strategic policy-making authorities should establish a housing requirement figure for their whole area, which shows the extent to which their identified housing need (and any needs that cannot be met within neighbouring areas) can be met over the plan period. Within this overall requirement, strategic policies should also set out a housing requirement for designated neighbourhood areas which reflects the overall strategy for the pattern and scale of development and any relevant allocations. Once the strategic policies have been adopted, these figures should not need retesting at the neighbour-hood plan Examination, unless there has been a significant change in circumstances that affects the requirement.*

However, the NPPF acknowledges that LPAs will not always be able to set out a housing requirement for designated neighbourhood areas either because a neighbourhood area is designated at a late stage in the strategic policy making process or after strategic policies have been adopted or because strategic policies for housing are out-of-date.[14]

In these circumstances and if requested to do so by the NDP qualifying body, the LPA should provide an indicative figure for the neighbourhood area housing requirement.[15] According to Paragraph 66, NPPF:

> *This figure should take into account factors such as the latest evidence of local housing need, the population of the neighbourhood area and the most recently available planning strategy of the local planning authority.*

This suggests that no single factor will be determinative and in such cases it may be that the qualifying body can have some influence with the LPA over the figure arrived at.

---

[14] Paragraph 66, NPPF, Footnote 31.

[15] Paragraph 66, NPPF.

Also noteworthy is that, whilst the standard method[16] (described above) for assessing housing need for the local authority area is an objective process that produces an exact figure, there is no equivalent method or formula for determining a neighbourhood area's housing need. The relevant factors (under Paragraph 66) are a useful guide for LPAs who nonetheless are left with considerable discretion to determine what, in many neighbourhood areas, will be an essential input into the neighbourhood plan process.

Identifying 'deliverable' housing sites is now a key and integral part of strategic and local policy making. The NPPF emphasises in more detail than ever before what 'deliverable sites' actually means and how plan-makers, particularly LPAs and their local plans but also qualifying bodies and their neighbourhood plans, should ensure that allocated sites are deliverable.

This emphasis is summarised at Paragraph 67, NPPF:

> *Strategic policy-making authorities should have a clear understanding of the land available in their area through the preparation of a strategic housing land availability assessment. From this, planning policies should identify a sufficient supply and mix of sites, taking into account their availability, suitability and likely economic viability. Planning policies should identify a supply of: a) specific, deliverable sites for years one to five of the plan period; b) specific, developable sites or broad locations for growth, for years 6-10 and, where possible, for years 11-15 of the plan.*

Paragraph 68, NPPF recognises the importance of small and medium-sized sites because it says they are often built out relatively quickly and therefore LPAs should identify, through the development plan and brownfield registers, land to accommodate at least 10% of their housing requirement on sites no larger than one hectare, unless there are strong reasons why this 10% target cannot be achieved. Neighbourhood plans are also encouraged to consider small and medium-sized sites for housing in their area.[17]

However, the NPPF states clearly that the supply of large numbers of new homes can often be best achieved through planning for larger scale

---

[16] Paragraph 60, NPPF and Paragraph 004, PPG on *'Housing and economic needs assessment'*.

[17] Paragraph 68, NPPF.

development, such as new settlements or significant extensions to existing villages and towns, provided they are well located and designed, and supported by the necessary infrastructure and facilities.[18]

Delivery of housing sites – a five year supply

Under the heading of *'Maintaining supply and delivery'* the NPPF, at Paragraph 73, goes on to explain that:

> *Strategic policies should include a trajectory illustrating the expected rate of housing delivery over the plan period, and all plans should consider whether it is appropriate to set out the anticipated rate of development for specific sites. Local planning authorities should identify and update annually a supply of specific deliverable sites sufficient to provide a minimum of five years' worth of housing against their housing requirement set out in adopted strategic policies, or against their local housing need where the strategic policies are more than five years old.*

The essence of Paragraph 73 is that the LPA must identify and update annually a supply of specific deliverable sites sufficient to provide a minimum of five years' worth of housing; in other words the LPA must, every year, identify all the sites with planning permission that it expects to be delivered and which will therefore contribute to the need for housing locally. This is what is referred to in Paragraph 74 and elsewhere in the NPPF and PPG as the LPA's annual position statement, and it is simply that – a statement of what the LPA considers to be the deliverable housing sites in its area at that particular time.

According to Paragraph 73, the source that the annual position statement is updating is either, where the local plan was adopted less than five years prior to the July 2018 version of the NPPF, the strategic policies therein or, where strategic policies are more than five years old, the LPA's local housing need according to the standard methodology (discussed above on page 159).

The second part, and further requirement, of Paragraph 73 is that *"The supply of specific deliverable sites* [for the five year period] *should in addition include a buffer (moved forward from later in the plan period)"*. The

---

[18] Paragraph 72, NPPF.

buffer, expressed in percentages of the number of dwellings provided by the sites comprising the LPA's annual housing land requirement, should be at least 5% (to ensure choice and competition in the market for land), 10% (if the LPA wants to demonstrate a five year supply of deliverable sites through an annual position statement or recently adopted plan, to account for any fluctuations in the market during that year) or 20% (where there has been significant under delivery of housing over the previous three years, to improve the prospect of achieving the planned supply).

Paragraph 74, NPPF, confirms how an LPA should demonstrate its five year supply of housing sites:

A five year supply of deliverable housing sites, with the appropriate buffer, can be demonstrated where it has been established in a recently adopted plan, or in a subsequent annual position statement which:

a) has been produced through engagement with developers and others who have an impact on delivery, and been considered by the Secretary of State; and

b) incorporates the recommendation of the Secretary of State, where the position on specific sites could not be agreed during the engagement process.

What is meant by 'deliverable' and 'developable' sites is clearly fundamental. These terms are defined in the Glossary to the NPPF:

Deliverable: *To be considered deliverable, sites for housing should be available now, offer a suitable location for development now, and be achievable with a realistic prospect that housing will be delivered on the site within five years. In particular:*

a) sites which do not involve major development and have planning permission, and all sites with detailed planning permission, should be considered deliverable until permission expires, unless there is clear evidence that homes will not be delivered within five years (for example because they are no longer viable, there is no longer a demand for the type of units or sites have long term phasing plans).

b) where a site has outline planning permission for major development, has been allocated in a development plan, has a grant of permission in principle, or is identified on a brownfield register, it should only be considered deliverable where there is clear evidence that housing completions will begin on site within five years.

Developable: *To be considered developable, sites should be in a suitable location for housing development with a reasonable prospect that they will be available and could be viably developed at the point envisaged.*

Having identified sites to maintain the supply of housing, LPAs must monitor and encourage delivery of housing on those sites. Where, according to the Housing Delivery Test, delivery is below 85% of the housing requirement over the previous three years, the LPA should produce an action plan to address the causes, and identify actions to increase delivery in future years,[19] though the only such measure suggested in the NPPF is a shorter time limit for implementing permissions (imposed by planning condition).[20]

Making sense of the NPPF approach to housing delivery

Many of those involved in the making of a neighbourhood plan, whether as a parish councillor or clerk, a member of an NDP working group or simply an interested member of the local community, will have limited technical knowledge of planning or plan-making. For others, planning is an entirely new subject. Yet, all of you – as plan-makers – are the people the NPPF is directly addressing in what is arguably its principal aim; encouraging the supply of land to provide at least 300,000 houses a year for the next 20 years or so.[21]

We will therefore assume that those making a neighbourhood plan and particularly those new to planning will want to understand how the overriding imperative for housing land delivery is intended to be put into practice. It is therefore worth recapping on how the NPPF sets out to increase housing delivery and consider whether it is likely to succeed in

---

[19] Paragraph 75 and Footnote 39, NPPF.

[20] Paragraph 76, NPPF.

[21] Section 5, NPPF – *'Delivering a sufficient supply of homes'*.

that objective.[22]

Matching delivery to need is unarguably the correct approach but only if that need is properly and objectively evidenced. The household growth projections used tend to be exaggerated in that the projections often exceed the actual growth in population or the need for a particular type of dwelling. There are as many different opinions, blogs and commentaries on this subject as there are ways of interpreting the statistics in the first place and the reader is free to choose which they prefer.

However, what is irrefutable is that after publishing the 2018 NPPF, the government acknowledged that using the standard method to calculate housing need, based on the 2016 household growth projections, cut the number of homes needed from 269,000 to 213,000[23] (by any reckoning a significantly lower figure than the 300,000 target). However, after going to consultation on this the government nonetheless concluded that the standard method for calculating housing need should remain unchanged and that it should keep the 2014 household growth projections (rather than the more current 2016 projections) as its baseline. This is confirmed in Planning Practice Guidance.[24]

In other words, and what is also irrefutable is that, the NPPF-prescribed method for assessing housing need is not based on the current version of the statistical source the government chooses to use. In short, the NPPF standard methodology is not based on the latest (or best) evidence of actual housing need.

So why should the planning system be strained to breaking point in an effort to issue at least 300,000 residential planning permissions a year when even the ONS data suggests that we may actually only need around 213,000 houses per annum in order to meet demand? The answer, or at least the policy-based explanation for this, is 'historic under-delivery'.

That is why the current NPPF concentrates more than ever before, and in some detail, on perceived under-delivery and what should be done about

---

[22] One baseline measure for future comparison is that in the 2016/17 financial year, 217,350 new homes were completed, the second highest level since 1992. (https://www.telegraph.co.uk/business/2017/11/16/government-celebrates-building-217000-homes-year-hitting-target/). This was widely celebrated and of course was achieved well before the current NPPF was even published.

[23] 'Government unveils major reforms to NPPF' – The Planner, 1 November 2018.

[24] Paragraph 004, PPG on '*Housing and economic needs assessment*'.

it. The NPPF purports to deal with this issue in several ways; by making it an express requirement for LPAs to have a five year supply of deliverable sites: by imposing a definition of what is meant by deliverable; by making even recent plans effectively out-of-date in various circumstances so that the policies therein are given less weight or ignored by decision-takers; by imposing the buffer to compensate for shortfalls in delivery; and by encouraging LPAs to impose a shorter time-limiting conditions on planning permissions for housing sites.

The NPPF starting point for monitoring delivery is that the LPA must demonstrate a five year supply of sites providing the number of houses to meet the area requirement plus the buffer, and as we have seen the LPA must demonstrate its five year supply either through an annual position statement or a recently adopted plan.[25]

However, even on the face of it, this is where the NPPF starts to get muddled. Consider Footnote 38, to Paragraph 73 NPPF which reads as follows:

> *For the purposes of paragraphs 73b and 74 a plan adopted between 1 May and 31 October will be considered 'recently adopted' until 31 October of the following year; and a plan adopted between 1 November and 30 April will be considered recently adopted until 31 October in the same year.*

Even if we overlook the fact that a plan adopted between 1 November and 31 December cannot logically *be considered recently adopted until 31 October in the same year,* how can it make sense for a plan adopted on 1 May to be considered recently adopted for a period of 18 months, whilst a plan adopted a day earlier on 30 April, loses its currency after just six months?

Either way, under this test all local plans quickly lose their currency and cease to be 'recently adopted' within a matter of months. This is somewhat inconsistent with the general NPPF requirement that local plans and strategic policies should be reviewed every five years.[26] Nonetheless, for the purposes of demonstrating a five year supply of deliverable sites plus the buffer, most LPAs most of the time will have to rely on an annual position statement.

---

[25] Paragraph 74, NPPF.

[26] Paragraph: 062, PPG on *'Plan-making'*.

This is highly significant because an annual position statement is not planning policy or part of the development plan. It is merely a record – a statement listing the housing sites with planning permissions in the LPA area that make up its five year supply. One wonders then why an annual position statement must be *"produced through engagement with developers and ... [be] considered by the Secretary of State"* and even be subject to *"the recommendation of the Secretary of State, where the position on specific sites could not be agreed during the engagement process"*?

In any event, it seems that an annual position statement may supersede or supplant the strategic policies of a local plan that is less than a year old (in some cases) and which has gone through the full scrutiny of public consultation and an examination. Remember, all that an annual position statement is supposed to do is to demonstrate – or not as the case may be – that the LPA has issued deliverable planning permissions for a five year supply of housing. It is not a planning policy or even a statement of planning policy yet – it seems that an annual position statement may regarded as more authoritative evidence of whether or not there is a five year supply than allocations in the strategic planning policies of an adopted local plan.

So, what are LPAs supposed to engage with developers or seek the consideration of the Secretary of State about, when producing their annual position statement? The answer to that is deliverability.

It is difficult to see what the NPPF's definition of deliverable sites really adds to the blatantly obvious. Much of the definition of deliverable is a tautology; any site with a detailed planning permission must inevitably be considered deliverable unless and until that permission expires. Such sites will obviously, therefore, be considered deliverable unless there is clear evidence – in other words, until it is clear – that they will not be delivered!

Furthermore, naming the sites with detailed planning permissions that have not expired or where a start has been made[27] is the only obvious way for the LPA to identify deliverable sites.

However – and this is where the engagement with developers comes

---

[27] A material start (made by a relatively simple building operation such as excavating a services trench) within the standard three year time period will implement a permission and keep it alive indefinitely, though there is generally no obligation to build out the development permitted. Therefore, a material start will allow the developer to keep his options open and he may still abandon the site and decide not to 'deliver' houses on it.

in – the LPA has no control over when it may be told that the developer no longer intends to build out or deliver a particular site. Only when the developer decides and communicates that will the LPA have 'clear evidence' the site will not be delivered. It appears that this is the type of information the LPA should elicit from developers when producing its annual position statement.

The problem is that the annual position statement – with the aforesaid developer and Secretary of State input – may decimate the LPA's planned five year supply of sites[28] and, or, completely undermine its performance in the Housing Delivery Test without any blame at all attaching to the LPA in such circumstances. The effect of that is to render the LPA's strategic housing policies non-compliant with the NPPF, leaving a policy vacuum and a local plan that in the key policy area of housing, is effectively useless. So much for the plan-led system.

The fundamental and underlying problem here is that neither the planning system nor its plan-makers can control delivery or deliverability and certainly not by any of the means the NPPF seeks to attribute to them.

It is developers who deliver houses and no matter how many planning permissions they hold, it is developers who decide if and when they will build houses. Furthermore, developers only build houses on any particular site if and when it is as profitable to do so as they would like it to be. Unless a particular site with planning permission promises to be as profitable as the developer hopes and expects, he will be willing to let that permission lapse entirely if more favourable planning policies bring more profitable alternative sites elsewhere within his scope. It is not difficult to see, therefore, how developers' engagement with an LPA's annual position statement could be motivated by a desire to secure more profitable planning permissions.

Under-delivery is not caused by the planning system – by definition it describes the failure to develop a site with the benefit of a planning permission that has already been granted. Under-delivery is primarily a factor of market forces.

For these reasons, reducing the time period for implementation of a

---

[28] Although the provision of a buffer may be intended to avoid or compensate for such effects, for the buffer to have its intended effect, the buffer sites must also be deliverable yet if a market downturn has caused the non-deliverability of the primary sites the effectiveness of the buffer will also be open to question.

permission by amending the standard time-limiting planning condition is unlikely to improve deliverability and may in fact worsen it by forcing developers to abandon certain sites with permissions earlier than they currently have to.

It is certainly the case that focussing planners' minds towards a five year supply of deliverable sites is likely to have the intended effect in many cases, at least for as long as the housing market remains buoyant. However, none of the policies in, or measures proposed by, the NPPF will ensure deliverability.

Furthermore, by putting so much pressure on deliverability, any shortfalls in the delivery of strategic (local plan) allocations or the five year supply of sites may quite quickly mount up and will threaten to cause a policy vacuum, because in line with the NPPF rationale developers will argue that those strategic policies are either out-of-date or otherwise not in accordance with the NPPF. That then brings into play the presumption in favour of sustainable development for decision-taking which we consider again below.

This major concern with the NPPF and its policies on housing – the some-what unrealistic approach to the currency of local plans and their strategic planning policies – is only exacerbated when we consider typical plan periods and the lengthy adoption process.

Most local plans, and neighbourhood plans for that matter, represent a 'plan period' of 15 to 20 years (which will be indicated on the cover of the plan itself). The process of the examination, through which every local plan and NDP must pass, will itself usually take at least several months and often significantly longer than that – a couple of years or so is not uncommon for a local plan examination, particularly if there are legal challenges or other complications involved. This leads to another poten-tially confusing anomaly which is that most plans are now only adopted some time after the beginning of the plan period they expressly provide for. LPA forward planning officers are used to this lengthy process and its inevitable time lag but for many neighbourhood plan makers it will appear confusing and disorientating to say the least.

One only needs to look at the dates of the various assessments and other evidential documents supporting a current local plan to get an idea of how long it typically took an LPA to produce a local plan under the pre-vious national guidance. That was before the various complicating factors introduced by the current NPPF.

The main factor in delays to the plan-making process (other than a reduction in local authority resources) is increased complexity. Complexity inevitably prolongs rather than abbreviates the plan-making process. The current NPPF and the attendant PPG is more voluminous and complex than at any time since neighbourhood planning was introduced – and it requires LPAs to get to grips with a number of new or relatively new concepts; the standard methodology, the five year supply, the buffer, the Housing Delivery Test and under-delivery action plans[29] to name but a few.

An LPA is also required to regularly review its local plan. Planning Practice Guidance makes clear that local plans should be reviewed and, if necessary, updated every five years. In the section on *'Plan-making'* under the heading of *'Plan reviews'* it provides the following summary:

> *To be effective plans need to be kept up-to-date. The National Planning Policy Framework states policies in local plans and spatial development strategies, should be reviewed to assess whether they need updating at least once every 5 years, and should then be updated as necessary.*

> *Under regulation 10A of The Town and Country Planning (Local Planning) (England) Regulations 2012 (as amended) local planning authorities must review local plans, and Statements of Community Involvement at least once every 5 years from their adoption date to ensure that policies remain relevant and effectively address the needs of the local community. Most plans are likely to require updating in whole or in part at least every 5 years. Reviews should be proportionate to the issues in hand. Plans may be found sound conditional upon a plan update in whole or in part within 5 years of the date of adoption. Where a review was undertaken prior to publication of the Framework (27 July 2018) but within the last 5 years, then that plan will continue to constitute the up-to-date plan policies unless there have been significant changes as outlined below.*

> *There will be occasions where there are significant changes in circumstances which may mean it is necessary to review the relevant strategic policies earlier than the statutory minimum of 5 years, for example, where new cross-boundary matters arise. Local housing need will be considered to have changed significantly where a plan has been adopted prior to the standard*

---

[29] Paragraph 75, NPPF.

> *method being implemented, on the basis of a number that is significantly below the number generated using the standard method, or has been subject to a cap where the plan has been adopted using the standard method. This is to ensure that all housing need is planned for a quickly as reasonably possible.*[30]

Although the PPG gives examples of when local plans may need a review and updating more frequently than every five years, it makes no suggestion as to how such updates may be expedited. Nor does it offer any acknowledgement of the difficulties of doing so.

Whilst the LPA can review specific policies on an individual basis, the PPG confirms that *"updates to the plan or certain policies within it must follow the plan-making procedure; including preparation, publication, and Examination by the Planning Inspectorate on behalf of the Secretary of State."*[31]

Notwithstanding the due process of the normal plan-making procedure, and ignoring the fact that it is somewhat ambitious to expect new planning policies with statutory force to be adopted even within a couple of years, the current NPPF describes circumstances in which key, and often contentious, strategic planning policies may be obsolete within a few months.

So we end up in the rather anomalous position that an NPPF, the main function of which is to provide guidance to plan-makers in their making of a statutory development plan that the public, including developers, can rely on as such, and which ultimately seeks to enhance the efficiency of the planning process, has – in the crucial policy area of housing at least – only added more complexity; more tests of, and obstacles to, an LPA's plan-making powers and more potential for strategic planning policies to be undermined.

The consequences of out-of-date housing policies

To understand the consequences when a failure of plan-making occurs

---

[30] Paragraph 062, PPG on *'Plan-making'* – see also Paragraph 065, PPG – for examples of matters that may prompt an LPA to update its local plan.

[31] Paragraph 069, PPG on *'Plan-making'*.

under the NPPF – whether it be a two year old housing policy that falls foul of 'under-delivery' (or for that matter a policy on retail provision that has not been revised when it should have been) – we need to revisit Paragraph 11; the presumption in favour of sustainable development.

*For **decision-taking** the presumption means;*

c) approving development proposals that accord with an up-to-date development plan without delay; or;

d) where there are no relevant development plan policies, or the policies which are most important for determining the application are out-of-date, granting permission unless:

> *i. the application of policies in this Framework that protect areas or assets of particular importance provides a clear reason for refusing the development proposed; or;*

> *ii. any adverse impacts of doing so would significantly and demonstrably outweigh the benefits, when assessed against the policies in this Framework taken as a whole.*

Before we consider again the application of the presumption, it is important to note that the NPPF expressly makes clear that out-of-date policies include:

... for applications involving the provision of housing, situations where the local planning authority cannot demonstrate a five year supply of deliverable housing sites (with the appropriate buffer, as set out in paragraph 73); or where the Housing Delivery Test indicates that the delivery of housing was substantially below (less than 75% of) the housing requirement over the previous three years.[32]

In essence, how the presumption operates for decision-taking is quite clear. Where there are no relevant policies, or the policies which are most important for determining the application are out-of-date, permission should be granted unless either of the two strict exceptions applies.

---

[32] Footnote 7 to Paragraph 11, NPPF (page 6) which provides confirmation if it were needed that although neither a failure to demonstrate a five year supply or a failure of the Housing Delivery Test is a planning policy as such, they seem to become planning policies for the purposes of Paragraph 11 or at least facts which supplant and override planning policies.

The first limb exception applies only to designated areas or assets of particular landscape or historic importance that are protected by NPPF policies. Such areas or assets include the Green Belt,[33] National Parks, Areas of Outstanding Natural Beauty (AONBs), Sites of Special Scientific Interest (SSSIs) and European-designated sites[34] and World Heritage Sites, Conservation Areas and Listed Buildings.[35] The policy in question must provide a clear reason for refusing the development proposed.

For permission to be refused under the second limb, it needs to be shown that any adverse impacts of the proposed development *"would signifi-cantly and demonstrably"* outweigh the benefits of it. That too is a strict test.

Generally speaking and in most cases it will be difficult to invoke either of these exceptions to the presumption in favour of development. Both of the exceptions rely on matters of judgement and it will take obvious and significant adverse impacts to override the presumption and tip the balance against granting permission. For objectors and concerned third parties looking for permission to be refused it will usually be essential to rely on clear and up-to-date planning policies and avoid the presumption altogether.

So where a strategic local plan housing policy has fallen foul of the NPPF criteria so that little if any weight still attaches to it, the presumption in favour of sustainable development for decision-taking is likely to apply to applications for housing development on unallocated sites; either sites previously identified but omitted from strategic allocation policies (usually known as 'omission sites') or speculative applications on 'windfall' sites. Either way, these sites will not have been fully tested by the local plan process and such applications will often come as a surprise to local people.

In many cases, such applications may not involve protected areas or assets, or adverse impacts that significantly and demonstrably outweigh the benefits in terms of planning policy, but that is not to say the impact on the area will not be considered adverse or damaging by local people.

The likely practical effect, therefore, of the failure of a strategic hous-ing policy on a parish or neighbourhood area affected by a speculative

---

[33] NPPF, Chapter 13 – *'Protecting Green Belt land'*.

[34] NPPF, Chapter 15 – *'Conserving and enhancing the natural environment'*.

[35] NPPF, Chapter 16 – *'Conserving and enhancing the historic environment'*.

housing proposal, is that the presumption in favour of sustainable development will lead to the approval of that housing development whether or not that accords with the wishes, and any plan-making intentions, of local people.

A significant case[36] heard in the High Court towards the end of 2019 demonstrates some of the issues considered above and in particular the swingeing effect of NPPF guidance on strategic housing allocations in a local plan.

The big buffer eating into the Green Belt

This legal challenge to the adoption, by Guildford Borough Council, of its local plan[37] was brought by two parish councils[38] and an individual objector and centred around two main issues; the LPA's Objectively Assessed Housing Need figure ("OAN") and whether there were genuinely "exceptional circumstances" justifying the removal of the proposed housing sites from the Green Belt.

The interested parties to the case were the owners and developers of the housing sites under challenge and the Second Defendant was the Secretary of State for Housing Communities and Local Government whom the judge noted was *"taking a more active role than is common".*[39]

On both the main issues this case is a rather salutary lesson for parish councils and we will briefly look at the second point first.

Paragraph 136 of the NPPF reads as follows:

> *Green Belt boundaries should only be altered where exceptional circumstances are fully evidenced and justified, through the preparation or updating of plans.*

Both of the claimant parish councils were primarily concerned that Green Belt sites within their respective parishes were being removed from the

---

[36] *Compton Parish Council & Ors v Guildford Borough Council & Anor* [2019] EWHC 3242 (Admin).

[37] Local Plan: Strategy and Sites (2015-2034) - adopted in April 2019.

[38] Compton Parish Council and Ockham Parish Council.

[39] Paragraph 5, Judgment; *Compton Parish Council & Ors v Guildford Borough Council & Anor* [2019] EWHC 3242 (Admin).

Green Belt in less than exceptional circumstances – simply to make way for housing, housing they claimed was not necessary. The housing site in Compton Parish is Blackwell Farm; a more classic example of prime Green Belt land – immediately adjacent to, but very clearly demarcated from, the intensively developed city edge – is hard to imagine.

However, somewhat unfortunately for the parish councils it was held that for Paragraph 136 purposes, *"general planning needs, such as ordinary housing, are not precluded from its scope; indeed, meeting such needs is often part of the judgment that "exceptional circumstances" exist; the phrase is not limited to some unusual form of housing, nor to a particular intensity of need."*[40] In other words, ordinary housing is capable of amounting to "exceptional circumstances" justifying the removal of land from the Green Belt.

Furthermore, whether or not something that is capable of amounting to exceptional circumstances does, in a particular case, amount to exceptional circumstances is a matter purely for the planning decision-maker and *"was not in law capable of being one ... likely to require some caution and judicial restraint"*.[41]

Those hoping that Paragraph 136 of the NPPF amounts to as robust a protection of the Green Belt as one could reasonably expect a national planning policy to provide, will need to think again in the light of this judgment. The Secretary of State was, of course, one of those opposing the claims of the parish councils and, as we have seen, the judge was clearly very mindful of that!

The background to the Green Belt removal problem was a housing need figure for the local plan area over the plan period of 14,602. A 2016 version of the emerging local plan had put the OAN at 12,426 but when the lower 2018 household growth projections were published, the OAN was reduced to 10,678.

However, the OAN of 14,602 that the parish councils were challenging, and that had been used at the examination of the local plan to justify the Green Belt removals, therefore included a buffer[42] of almost 4,000 dwellings – or more than 36% of the objectively assessed figure. As we

---

[40] Paragraph 72, Judgment.

[41] Paragraph 69, Judgment.

[42] See Paragraph 73, NPPF.

have seen above, Paragraph 73, NPPF recommends a buffer of between 5 and 20% depending on the circumstances. It is hardly surprising that the parish councils in this case considered that planning for housing so much in excess of the objectively assessed need was worthy of legal challenge.

The way the judge dealt with the level of the buffer was to say that: "*I can see that a different approach to the quantity of headroom might have commended itself, but that* [too] *was plainly a matter of planning judgment*".[43]

It should be illustrative but not encouraging for neighbourhood planners to understand that on both the main issues, the court held that the decisions taken by the inspector examining Guildford's local plan were simply matters of planning judgement even though those judgements – and indeed the judgment of the court – seem to pay little attention to the wording of the respective NPPF paragraphs[44] or the most obvious purposes behind them.

Part of the problem in this case seems to be that strategic housing sites were allocated in the emerging local plan in the absence of sufficiently advanced neighbourhood plans, and before it became a requirement under the 2019 NPPF for the LPA to present a parish council with a local housing need figure.[45]

The decision in this case is a real blow to the neighbourhood planning aspirations of the two parish councils involved and to the many thousands of local objectors to the proposed housing sites in question. It frankly flies in the face of localism and serves to demonstrate why the culture change considered in the final chapter of this book is long overdue.

We now need to consider how neighbourhood plans and those making them should deal with the increasingly complicated subject of housing.

How should neighbourhood plans deal with housing?

Given the potential difficulties, the first question a qualifying body may well ask is: '*Do we need to deal with housing at all?*'

---

[43] Paragraph 99, Judgment.

[44] Paragraphs 73 and 136, NPPF.

[45] See Paragraphs 65 and 66, NPPF.

The short answer is, no – there is no strict requirement for an NDP to say anything about, or contain any planning policies on, housing locally. Indeed, there are circumstances, and no doubt many neighbourhood areas where such circumstances apply, in which it would be rather pointless and somewhat irrelevant for the neighbourhood plan to deal with housing at all. An example would be where the LPA has made clear that the neighbourhood area is not required to provide any housing sites for the foreseeable plan period and where other strategic policies protect the area from speculative housing development.

However, a more considered response to the question of whether the NDP should cover housing should take into account two possibilities; the first is whether Paragraph 14, NPPF could be relevant to the NDP in question, and the second is whether there are any housing related issues – other than housing supply and site allocations – that the NDP should look to address in local planning policies.

Paragraph 14, NPPF

Paragraph 14 deals with the presumption in favour of sustainable development where there is a neighbourhood plan in place.

> *In situations where the presumption (at paragraph 11d) applies to applications involving the provision of housing, the adverse impact of allowing development that conflicts with the neighbourhood plan is likely to significantly and demonstrably outweigh the benefits, provided all of the following apply;*
>
> > *a) the neighbourhood plan became part of the development plan two years or less before the date on which the decision is made;*
> >
> > *b) the neighbourhood plan contains policies and allocations to meet its identified housing requirement;*
> >
> > *c) the local planning authority has at least a three year supply of deliverable housing sites (against its five year housing supply requirement, including the appropriate buffer as set out in paragraph 73); and*
> >
> > *d) the local planning authority's housing delivery was at least 45% of that required over the previous three years [as assessed by the Housing Delivery Test].*

In the light of this chapter's foregoing assessment of the NPPF approach to housing supply and delivery, the potential significance of Paragraph 14 to qualifying bodies and their neighbourhood plans should be apparent. If your neighbourhood area is intended or expected to take any of the LPA's assessed housing need, then the circumstances in which Paragraph 14 becomes relevant and how it would apply should be carefully considered. Such is the apparent significance of Paragraph 14, it is worth examining it in a little more detail.

In essence, in respect of applications for new housing in any area covered by a neighbourhood plan the presumption in favour of granting permission will be rebutted or disapplied subject to four strict provisos. It seems the intended purpose of Paragraph 14 is, where there is an appeal or legal challenge by a housing developer against refusal of a housing application, to give a neighbourhood area (with an up-to-date NDP with its own housing policies) some extra protection against unwanted housing where the LPA's strategic housing policies are out-of-date.

The reference to the presumption (at Paragraph 11d) makes it clear that we are talking about the presumption in relation to *decision-taking*. Furthermore, as Paragraph 14 requires there to be an NDP that has become a part of the development plan, its reference to Paragraph 11d must be read as meaning where *"there are no relevant* [strategic/local plan] *policies, or the* [strategic/local plan] *policies which are most important for determining the application are out-of-date"*. This may be stating the obvious but the point is that, if there *are* relevant and up-to-date strategic policies, in accordance with the NPPF, for determining the application then there are no Paragraph 11d circumstances to invoke the presumption or any consideration of Paragraph 14.

The type of applications with which Paragraph 14 is concerned are those involving the provision of housing. The development need not be solely residential but may be mixed use of any kind provided there is an element of housing proposed.

For the presumption to be rebutted under Paragraph 14, the development applied for must conflict with the neighbourhood plan. That is quite a stern test but ultimately a matter of judgement. An application that is not deemed to comply with an NDP or that is not made pursuant to it, may not necessarily conflict with it.

We now need to look at the provisos to Paragraph 14, all four of which must apply if the presumption in favour of a permission is to be rebutted.

First, the neighbourhood plan must have become part of the development plan two years or less before the date on which the decision is made.

On the face of it this is entirely straightforward but we must remember that in this area of planning generally, and here in particular, timing is everything – and the date of relevant events for these purposes is anything but straightforward. For a start, when does an NDP become part of the development plan?

According to the relevant legislation *"the development plan* [includes any] *neighbourhood development plans which have been made in relation to* [the] *area"*.[46] The logical consequence is that an NDP becomes part of the development plan on the date it is made by the LPA.

However, the same legislation also states that an NDP *"also forms part of the development plan for that area"*[47] when it is approved by a referendum but before it is made by the LPA – in other words before the LPA has got round to issuing the formal decision to make the plan (though it then ceases to be part of the development plan if the LPA subsequently decides not to make it).[48]

The difference between the date of the referendum and the date the LPA makes the plan could be merely days or it could be weeks but it may prove crucial to the application of Paragraph 14, as will the date on which the determination of the application is made. Where there is an attempt to invoke Paragraph 14 on appeal, it will of course be the date of the appeal decision that is relevant, and the NDP will have to be less than two years old at that point – that may be many months or even a year or two after the application was refused.

The second proviso is that the neighbourhood plan contains policies and allocations to meet its identified housing requirement.

This in itself seems quite clear but as we have seen the identified housing requirement for a neighbourhood plan is not – unlike the LPA area housing requirement – subject to a specific formula or definite criteria. Indeed, the LPA cannot be compelled to specify a housing requirement figure for a neighbourhood area, in which case, as we have seen, it should give the

---

[46] Section 38(3) of the Planning and Compulsory Purchase Act 2004.

[47] Section 38(3A) of the Planning and Compulsory Purchase Act 2004.

[48] Section 38(3B) of the Planning and Compulsory Purchase Act 2004.

qualifying body an indicative figure.[49]

Notwithstanding these potential difficulties, PPG[50] makes very clear that the proviso at Paragraph 14(b) is to be strictly applied:

> ... the *'policies and allocations' in the* [neighbourhood] *plan should meet the identified housing requirement in full, whether it is derived from the housing figure for the neighbourhood area set out in the relevant strategic policies, an indicative figure provided by the local planning authority, or where it has exceptionally been determined by the neighbourhood planning body.*

Nonetheless where the NDP contains housing policies and allocations that are in accordance with a specified housing requirement for the neighbourhood area, this second proviso to Paragraph 14 should be met.

Thirdly for any reliance on Paragraph 14, the LPA must have at least a three year supply of deliverable housing sites (measured in the same way as its five year housing supply requirement), including the appropriate buffer.

The fourth proviso is that the LPA's housing delivery was at least 45% of that required over the previous three years (as assessed by the Housing Delivery Test).

So, whilst the last two conditions for Paragraph 14 to be brought into play are ostensibly within the control of the LPA, because they relate to deliverability, these two factors are actually in the hands of developers. They are certainly not within the scope of the qualifying body to influence, however attentive to, and up-to-date with, local housing needs its NDP may be.

There is no doubt that Paragraph 14 will motivate NDPs and their makers to include housing policies and allocations to meet any housing requirement identified for the neighbourhood area, and indeed for the very limited period of time specified by Paragraph 14(b), that is exactly how best to proof a neighbourhood plan against speculative housing development.

That said, due to the various requirements needed to bring Paragraph 14 into play there may be relatively few cases in which it renders even an

---

[49] Paragraph 66, NPPF.

[50] Paragraph 097, PPG on *'Neighbourhood planning'*.

up-to-date neighbourhood plan the trump card its makers might expect it to be.

We reflect on this further in the 'practical advice' below but what Paragraph 14 does serve to emphasise for qualifying bodies is the importance of the timing of a neighbourhood plan in relation to the adoption of the higher level strategic policies of a local plan.

Timing of the neighbourhood plan in relation to the local plan

Although, the timing of an NDP also has a wider and more general significance, it is particularly relevant to whether or not the neighbourhood plan has any influence on planning applications for unwanted or inappropriate housing developments and, therefore, we deal with it here.

The starting point for any such consideration is Paragraph 009 of PPG on *'Neighbourhood planning'*:

Can a neighbourhood plan come forward before an up-to-date local plan or spatial development strategy is in place?

Neighbourhood plans, when brought into force, become part of the development plan for the neighbourhood area. They can be developed before or at the same time as the local planning authority is producing its local plan (or, where applicable, a spatial development strategy is being prepared by an elected Mayor or combined authority).

A draft neighbourhood plan or Order must be in general conformity with the strategic policies of the development plan in force if it is to meet the basic condition. Although a draft neighbourhood plan or Order is not tested against the policies in an emerging local plan the reasoning and evidence informing the local plan process is likely to be relevant to the consideration of the basic conditions against which a neighbourhood plan is tested. For example, up-to-date housing need evidence is relevant to the question of whether a housing supply policy in a neighbourhood plan or Order contributes to the achievement of sustainable development.

Where a neighbourhood plan is brought forward before an up-to-date local plan is in place the qualifying body and the local planning authority should discuss and aim to agree the relationship between policies in:

- *the emerging neighbourhood plan*

- *the emerging local plan (or spatial development strategy)*

- *the adopted development plan*

with appropriate regard to national policy and guidance.

The local planning authority should take a proactive and positive approach, working collaboratively with a qualifying body particularly sharing evidence and seeking to resolve any issues to ensure the draft neighbourhood plan has the greatest chance of success at independent Examination.

The local planning authority should work with the qualifying body so that complementary neighbourhood and local plan policies are produced. It is important to minimise any conflicts between policies in the neighbourhood plan and those in the emerging local plan, including housing supply policies. This is because section 38(5) of the Planning and Compulsory Purchase Act 2004 requires that the conflict must be resolved in favour of the policy which is contained in the last document to become part of the development plan.

Strategic policies should set out a housing requirement figure for designated neighbourhood areas from their overall housing requirement (paragraph 65 of the revised National Planning Policy Framework). Where this is not possible the local planning authority should provide an indicative figure, if requested to do so by the neighbourhood planning body, which will need to be tested at the neighbourhood plan Examination. Neighbourhood plans should consider providing indicative delivery timetables, and allocating reserve sites to ensure that emerging evidence of housing need is addressed. This can help minimise potential conflicts and ensure that policies in the neighbourhood plan are not overridden by a new local plan.

Paragraph 009, for good reason, provides a long answer to what appears to be a simple question: *can a neighbourhood plan come forward before an up-to-date local plan or spatial development strategy is in place?*

The short answer is 'yes', a neighbourhood plan can come forward – and be adopted – before an up-to-date local plan is adopted but the real question, which is more complicated, is whether that is the right approach in all the circumstances.

Aside from restating a couple of touchstone principles of neighbourhood planning, namely conformity with strategic policies and the all-important effect of Section 38(5), Planning and Compulsory Purchase Act 2004,[51] perhaps the best advice offered by Paragraph 009 PPG is that the LPA and the qualifying body should discuss between them, and collaborate on, the interaction between NDP and local plan. This is because, apart from anything else, there are a whole range of factors that influence the timing of the NDP in relation to the local plan and in any given set of circumstances there is probably no one right answer as to which plan should come first.

So, the qualifying body should always aim to liaise with the LPA in any event, and not just when a neighbourhood plan is brought forward before adoption of an up-to-date local plan, although in those circumstances collaboration is particularly important.

However, the qualifying body should always keep in mind that although the PPG says that the LPA *"should take a proactive and positive approach, working collaboratively with a qualifying body, particularly sharing evidence and seeking to resolve any issues to ensure the draft neighbourhood plan has the greatest chance of success at independent examination"*, there are many LPAs that do not work as positively or collaboratively with qualifying bodies as they should and in practice there is very little that can compel them to do so.

The LPA may be less than helpful or not collaborative for any number of reasons; often it is a lack of resources but equally it may be that local politics is pushing the LPA in a different direction to the one the qualifying body wants to take with its neighbourhood plan. It is naïve and unrealistic of those making a neighbourhood plan not to anticipate and be attentive to this widespread problem.

This brings us back to another touchstone principle that recurs throughout the book; a neighbourhood plan is the project of the local community and of the qualifying body making it, and the neighbourhood plan that

---

[51] If to any extent a policy contained in a development plan for an area conflicts with another policy in the development plan the conflict must be resolved in favour of the policy which is contained in the last document to be adopted, approved or published (as the case may be).

becomes part of the development plan should reflect that. Too many compromises may neutralise an NDP to the extent that casts a shadow over the whole effort of preparing and producing it. Above all else, the qualifying body may need to remind itself that it is independent from the LPA, and that sometimes it may be necessary to exert that independence.

Practical advice to qualifying bodies on how neighbourhood plans should address strategic policies on housing supply

By now it will be very clear that where a neighbourhood plan does need to address strategic housing policies, how it does so will involve a number of potentially quite complicated factors, many of which are not within the control of the qualifying body. There will be those NDPs that are free of such considerations, perhaps because the neighbourhood area is not due to take any more of the LPA's housing requirement.

Where the NDP does need to involve itself with housing supply, however, there is no one size fits all approach to be recommended. Instead, it is a matter of ensuring that all the relevant factors and influences have been considered, including;

- strategic/local plan housing policies and allocations and whether those strategic policies are up-to-date or soon to be reviewed or replaced;

- whether the LPA has a five year supply with a buffer, and passes the Housing Delivery Test;

- the neighbourhood area housing requirement figure or indicative figure;

- any recently determined, recently submitted but not yet determined or due to be submitted housing applications in the neighbourhood area and their potential impact on the other factors here;

- if up-to-date strategic policies have yet to be adopted, the effect of the presumption for decision-taking at Paragraph 11, NPPF, and;

- following from that, the effect of Paragraph 14, NPPF and how to invoke that;

- the timing of the neighbourhood plan in relation to the local plan (as usefully explained in Paragraph 009 PPG);

- last but not least, from a due process of public consultation what conclusions can be drawn about what local people want – in terms of the numbers of, and locations for, new houses in the neighbourhood area.

It will be virtually impossible for the qualifying body to properly understand all these elements without at least some discussion, and ideally purposeful engagement, with the LPA. The qualifying body must try to do just that. If the LPA is reluctant to collaborate in the way that it should then the qualifying body should obtain as much information as it can and then consider its position, perhaps with the aid of independent professional advice.

With or without the help of the LPA, the qualifying body should try to ascertain whether its objectives for the neighbourhood area align with the LPA's intended course of action in respect of its strategic policies and also the extent to which the LPA supports the NDP. If the LPA is not expressly supportive of all the NDP housing allocations, particularly in the face of strong developer objections, that can undermine the NDP at examination and result in key NDP policies and allocations being struck out. The qualifying body has little or no opportunity to respond to this at the examination stage.

Of course, there will be a greater significance riding on the aforementioned factors where there is competition for local housing allocations because it is those cases that are far more likely to become contentious. Ultimately the LPA may be unconcerned about which sites within a neighbourhood area provide its five year housing supply, knowing that even if sufficient allocations are not made in strategic or NDP policies, it can either produce a Supplementary Planning Document ("SPD") to provide further allocations or it can allow the default of the presumption – for decision-taking – to take effect in response to speculative applications.

Having weighed up all the relevant factors and circumstances, the qualifying body will be able to decide the approach it wants to take. If there is clear local support for the allocation of specific housing sites to meet the neighbourhood area housing requirement then it is likely to make sense to give effect to that through NDP housing policies and allocations.

Assuming that such an NDP will survive its examination intact, the qualifying body must then decide on a strategy for the timing of it being made that maximises the currency and effectiveness of the NDP policies and allocations.

Generally, it is logical and procedurally simpler for an emerging NDP to be running in parallel with emerging strategic policies and to come into force just after adoption of the new local plan. This also means that any conflict with the local plan should be resolved in favour of the (later) NDP policy[52]. Although the making of the NDP may lag behind adoption of the local plan, decision-takers can still accord weight to an emerging neighbourhood plan,[53] with more weight to be given to one that has passed the examination stage.[54]

However, if the adoption of a new local plan looks too far ahead for comfort or if the strategic housing policies (for any of the reasons considered above) of even a relatively recent local plan are likely to be considered out-of-date, then the imperative may be to try to secure the protection of Paragraph 14, NPPF, against the operation of the presumption, by bringing the NDP into force sooner rather than later. However, in practice this may not be easy to achieve because it will need the cooperation of the LPA which should arguably be more concerned with updating its strategic policies to avoid the operation of Paragraph 14 in the first place!

Another problem with this approach is that even if an NDP satisfies the relevant Paragraph 14 provisos, the protection against the presumption in favour of an unwanted housing development is still dependent on the LPA having a three year housing supply and passing the Housing Delivery Test.

Furthermore, for a qualifying body to try to bring its NDP forward in order to invoke Paragraph 14, it will be reacting to a very particular set of circumstances such as an already submitted or anticipated major housing application in conflict with its emerging neighbourhood plan. If such

---

[52] Section 38(5), Planning and Compulsory Purchase Act 2004.

[53] Paragraph 48, NPPF, says that: *"Local planning authorities may give weight to relevant policies in emerging plans according to: a) the stage of preparation of the emerging plan (the more advanced its preparation, the greater the weight that may be given); b) the extent to which there are unresolved objections to relevant policies (the less significant the unresolved objections, the greater the weight that may be given); and c) the degree of consistency of the relevant policies in the emerging plan to this Framework (the closer the policies in the emerging plan to the policies in the Framework, the greater the weight that may be given)"*.

[54] Section 70(2), Town and Country Planning Act 1990 (as amended).

a strategy is to succeed a careful balance will have to be struck in the timing of the NDP becoming part of the development plan; it must be soon enough to be effective but on the other hand, not too soon that its currency has expired by the time the planning application it needs to be in place for is determined.

As we can see, trying to predict and assess in detail all the potential factors that may influence, or be influenced by, exactly when a neighbourhood plan takes effect and becomes part of the development plan, is a minefield. Even if it is possible for a qualifying body to say exactly when it wants or expects its plan to go to referendum or to be made by the LPA, the inherent uncertainties of the plan-making process and its timing mean that more often than not predicted timescales are not met.

Ultimately, the best advice for qualifying bodies is to ensure that clear and robust substantive housing policies and allocations that meet the stated needs and objectives of local people are brought into force by a neighbourhood plan made as soon as possible after the local plan is adopted, and with the full support of the LPA if possible. Only if there are particular circumstances with obvious imperatives for pre-empting the adoption of a new local plan or revised strategic policies, along with a clear strategy for doing so, is that course of action likely to be worthwhile.

Neighbourhood plan site allocations

It must be emphasised again that for all the NPPF guidance encouraging neighbourhood plans to plan positively for the homes 'needed' in their neighbourhood area, there is no compulsion on an NDP to do so (there is of course no compulsion to produce an NDP at all), so a neighbourhood plan could avoid the subject of housing completely.

However, most qualifying bodies will be keen to ascertain from the LPA the LHN figure for their neighbourhood area so that the emerging NDP can take account of it and begin to plan for that housing requirement if that is the intention.

It may be that the LHN for the neighbourhood area is intended to be met or partially met by detailed or outline permissions already granted, by strategic allocations (in the local plan) or by any combination of such permissions and allocations and a windfall allowance.[55] Only if the unmet LHN figure for a neighbourhood area is very low is it likely that a windfall allowance alone would be relied upon.

So, if the LHN for the neighbourhood area is unfulfilled or partially unfulfilled then the outstanding balance must be planned for. In other words, it should be possible to see from the current development plan (local plan, and NDP if there is one) how the whole of the LHN for the area is to be met.

As we have seen above, whilst it is not mandatory for a neighbourhood plan to do this, it is mandatory for the LPA to do so.[56] Therefore, if an NDP does not plan for any unmet LHN for its neighbourhood area, then the LPA will have to, either by reviewing and updating its local plan or by producing an SPD and allocating new housing sites by one of those means. This may also be the default position where one or more of the housing allocations in a draft neighbourhood plan is struck out at the examination of the NDP.

Either way, it will take the matter of site allocation out of the hands of the qualifying body and its neighbourhood plan. As we have also seen from the foregoing consideration of the NPPF, ultimately any part of the LHN that remains unmet by existing permissions and policy commitments will bring the presumption in favour of sustainable development at Paragraph 11, NPPF, into play.

If the qualifying body, and local people via NDP consultations, want the emerging NDP to influence any aspect of new housing in the neighbourhood area, then they need to decide how best to do that. The most direct means of doing so is by allocating sites for housing in the neighbourhood plan and, if possible, allocating sites for enough housing to fulfil any unmet LHN.

The general approach to this, and to other matters for substantive NDP policies, is dealt with in *Chapter 5*. The starting point for the qualifying body when considering local site allocations to address any unmet LHN,

---

[55] A windfall site is one that is not planned or allocated by the LPA but materialises from what may be described as a speculative planning application (whether or not it is compliant with planning policy). A windfall allowance is a predicted number - based on previous years' actual windfalls - of windfall sites likely to come forward during the plan period.

[56] Paragraph 67, NPPF.

is to consider which sites in the neighbourhood area may be suitable and deliverable for housing or for additional housing. It may be necessary to undertake an exercise usually associated with the plan-making function of LPAs, a call for sites. However, in many cases the qualifying body will be well aware from the LPA, or from the local plan process, of a number of potential housing sites.

Once potential housing sites within the neighbourhood area have been identified, the qualifying body will need – possibly with the help of professional advice – to assess their preliminary suitability in order to ensure that there are no fundamental obstacles to developability. To progress a particular site via the necessary public consultation, only to find that the site was always a non-starter due to, say, unacceptable flood risk, would obviously be a demoralising waste of time and money.

Having identified a sound shortlist of potentially developable sites, the qualifying body should then prepare the public consultations needed to assess those sites fully. The consultations should explain the background – being the need for the neighbourhood plan to seek to address any unmet LHN. The potential number of dwellings from each of the shortlisted sites should be made clear, and to what extent the sites are competing against one another to become an allocated site in the statutory development plan should also be understood so that local people know the basis of the consultation in which they are participating.

Through a rigorous and carefully considered process of public consultation, potential housing sites should be assessed, ranked and ultimately selected for allocation via a positively worded NDP planning policy. Other housing issues may be addressed as an element of site-specific allocations or by generic housing policies – that is, policies that seek to address any housing applications that may come forward, whether or not pursuant to site allocations – in the NDP.

Other housing issues

We need to remind ourselves that almost the entirety of this chapter up to this point has dealt with the *number* of homes that are needed, supplied and delivered. That is because the role of the planning system in fixing the housing crisis is seen as revolving primarily around numbers, or more specifically the annual target of 300,000 new homes. The NPPF reflects this and, of course, what the NPPF reflects must, in turn, be carried through into strategic planning policies and then down to neighbourhood plan level.

So, notwithstanding the arguably unsatisfactory consequences the top-down approach to granting planning permissions for housing in the UK is essentially and primarily a numbers game.

The NPPF does say that:

> *Within this context* [the numbers game], *the size, type and tenure of housing needed for different groups in the community should be assessed and reflected in planning policies (including, but not limited to, those who require affordable housing, families with children, older people, students, people with disabilities, service families, travellers, people who rent their homes and people wishing to commission or build their own homes).*[57]

However, this self-evidently common sense guidance is merely that. It does not carry the force or prescribe the same level of detail for strategic policy makers as the NPPF guidance on the numbers of homes that must be delivered. Whilst strategic planners must plan for a certain number of houses in their area, there is no such obligation for their strategic planning policies to stipulate with anything like the same detail or precision the types of dwelling that should be provided.

Whilst this rather unbalanced approach to housing supply undoubtedly creates and perpetuates problems, the intention is that the size, type and tenure of housing needed for different groups may be determined locally by non-strategic local plan or neighbourhood plan policies, and such policies may indeed attempt to do just that.

Typically, though, non-strategic local plan policies dealing with the size and type of housing tend to be rather general, partly because it is difficult to be uniformly prescriptive across the whole of a local plan area. The precise mix of housing needed can in most cases be better provided for by neighbourhood plans.

This is where neighbourhood plans can and should carry real influence; by addressing the types of housing needed, and just as importantly the types of housing *not* needed, in the neighbourhood area. There are various ways in which an NDP can do this.

---

[57] Paragraph 61, NPPF.

Size, type and tenure

Once the LPA has issued a local housing need figure or indicative figure for the neighbourhood area in accordance with the NPPF, so that the qualifying body understands how many new dwellings the area must accommodate, there is no reason why the neighbourhood plan should not contain planning policies prescribing size, type or tenure of those dwellings (unless such matters are definitively set out in strategic policies).

It is unusual for details of size, type and tenure to be strictly prescribed by generic local plan policies though strategic site allocation policies may do so and may be more difficult to vary via an NDP. It must also be remembered that the thresholds for, and the proportion of, affordable dwellings are matters of national policy (Paragraphs 63 and 65, NPPF) that developers will not, generally, build in excess of. A neighbourhood plan policy that insists on any greater level of affordable housing provision through a general policy is unlikely to survive the examination without being either struck out or significantly modified.

However, where there is an evidenced need for affordable housing in a particular area, an NDP that seeks to allocate sites and facilitate affordable housing to meet that need should be encouraged. Indeed, in May 2019 the government introduced a three year Discounted Market Homes Project to encourage – through additional grant funding of between £10,000 and £50,000 per scheme and technical support – community groups to bring forward discounted market homes through neighbourhood plans.[58]

The size, type and design of dwellings are all matters suitable for neighbourhood plan policies and whether or not such policies evolve will depend on the sufficiency of the local evidence to support them. Design and, to an extent, type of house are matters that are often guided by the character of an area and the cues to be taken from that.

The size of a dwelling is usually described for planning policy purposes by reference to the number of bedrooms, and as the marketability of new homes and the profitability of building them are highly sensitive to this factor, a neighbourhood plan that tries to influence it – perhaps by stipulating a high proportion of smaller two or three bedroom houses – must be based on clear evidence of greater local need for homes of a

---

[58] https://www.gov.uk/government/news/
malthouse-launches-85-million-fund-to-help-communities-deliver-discounted-homes.

particular size.

This level of detail may be imposed as a secondary element in a site allocation policy, or as a generic policy for any planning applications for housing that come forward. An example of the latter could read as follows:

Where proposals for residential development of eight dwellings or more comply with other policies of this plan, planning permission will be granted provided the development delivers a mix of homes in the following proportions;

2 bedroom homes: 30–40%;

3 bedroom homes: 30–40%;

4+ bedroom homes: 20–30%.

Types of housing 'not needed'; the example of St Ives and second homes

One area in which neighbourhood plans have been particularly influential, pioneering even, is in attempting to address local housing issues.

Perhaps the best example is where neighbourhood plans have tried to deal with the proliferation of second homes in certain parts of the country. The influx of second (or in some cases third or fourth) home owners has an obviously inflationary effect on house prices that drives many local people, including key workers, out of the market and often, therefore, out of the area.

This is a well publicised problem that has attracted widespread attention in the mainstream media as well as more focussed analysis in planning and legal journals. The main media focus has been on the St Ives Area Neighbourhood Development Plan 2015 – 2030 (the "St Ives NDP") and its attempt to deal with the issue.[59]

For a number of reasons, the St Ives NDP remains the best example for further consideration. This is partly because of the prominence of the town as a popular resort for second home owners, and the united

---

[59] See for example, 'There goes the neighbourhood', The Law Society Gazette, 16 May 2016 or at https://www.lawgazette.co.uk/practice-points/planning-blocking-second-homes-in-st-ives/5055252.article.

acknowledgement of the problem between St Ives Town Council, as the qualifying body for the neighbourhood plan, and Cornwall Council as the LPA. The proposed policy solution is therefore arguably the most sophisticated to date and came forward in an NDP that emerged via a neighbourhood planning regime that had matured somewhat since the early years of its inception. Notwithstanding all that, its 'second homes policy' still precipitated a judicial review of the St Ives NDP plan which is another reason for the media interest. The legal case[60] is instructive in itself and we shall return to that.

The starting point for any neighbourhood plan policy is evidence of the need for it. The evidence of the need for the second homes policy established by St Ives Town Council was that the proportion of dwellings in the area not occupied by a resident household increased by 67% between 2001 and 2011;[61] and that continuing trend was undermining the social fabric of the community.

Consequently, the St Ives NDP contains the following policy;

H2 Principal Residence Requirement

Due to the impact upon the local housing market of the continued uncontrolled growth of dwellings used for holiday accommodation (as second or holiday homes) new open market housing, excluding replacement dwellings, will only be supported where there is a restriction to ensure its occupancy as a Principal Residence.

Sufficient guarantee must be provided of such occupancy restriction through the imposition of a planning condition or legal agreement. New unrestricted second homes will not be supported at any time.

Principal Residences are defined as those occupied as the residents' sole or main residence, where the residents spend the majority of their time when not working away from home.

The condition or obligation on new open market homes will require that they are occupied only as the primary (principal) residence of those persons entitled to occupy them. Occupiers of homes with a

---

[60] *R (on the application of RLT Built Environment Limited) v The Cornwall Council and St Ives Town Council* [2016] EWHC 2817 (Admin).

[61] Page 25, St Ives Area Neighbourhood Development Plan 2015 – 2030.

Principal Residence condition will be required to keep proof that they are meeting the obligation or condition, and be obliged to provide this proof if/when [the] Council requests this information. Proof of Principal Residence is via verifiable evidence which could include, for example (but not limited to) residents being registered on the local electoral register and being registered for and attending local services (such as healthcare, schools etc).

This policy is a marked and purposeful improvement on its predecessors in other neighbourhood plans principally because it defines the type of occupation that new open market housing will be restricted to; that of a Principal Residence. It also makes clear that the restriction will be put in place via a legal agreement or planning condition and sets out the types of evidence that may be used to determine whether occupation complies with that restriction.

Taken from a planning permission for a single new open market dwelling issued in 2019, the planning condition used by the LPA, Cornwall Council, to secure the principal residence restriction reads as follows:

The dwelling hereby permitted shall not be occupied otherwise than by a person as his or her Only or Principal Home. For the avoidance of doubt the dwelling shall not be occupied as a second home or holiday letting accommodation.

The Occupant will supply to the Local Planning Authority (within 14 days of the Local Planning Authority's written request to do so) such information as the Authority may reasonably require in order to determine whether this condition is being complied with.

Reason: To safeguard the sustainability of the settlements in the St Ives NDP area, whose communities are being eroded through the amount of properties which are not occupied on a permanent basis and to ensure that the resulting accommodation is occupied by persons in compliance with policy H2 of the St Ives Neighbourhood Plan 2015 – 2030.

Informative

This condition shall not preclude periods of occupation by visiting guests but those visiting guests will not individually or cumulatively contribute towards the occupation of the property as a Principal Home. The condition will require that the dwelling(s) is/are occupied only as the primary (principal) residence of those persons entitled to occupy them. Occupiers of homes with a Principal Residence condition will be required to keep proof that they are meeting the condition, and be obliged to provide this proof if/when the Local Planning Authority requests this information. Proof of Principal Residence is via verifiable evidence which could include, for example (but not limited to) residents being registered on the local electoral register and being registered for and attending local services (such as healthcare, schools etc.).

Questions with Policy H2 and the application of the above condition nonetheless remain. The policy makes no real attempt to prevent ownership of more than one home (because it would be impossible to do so) provided the St Ives dwelling is the principal one. So, in the case of, say, a semi-retired couple who split their time roughly equally between their St Ives home and one elsewhere, how would Policy H2 be interpreted and enforced? What would be determinative evidence of principal residence occupation? It may be possible to register for local services in St Ives but spend the majority of the year resident elsewhere, perhaps in the already well established family home. In short, it may be possible to fulfil some of the suggested evidential criteria of principal residence whilst to all intents and purposes occupying the St Ives dwelling as a second home.

The real problem is that whatever evidence is sought of the local property being a principal residence, almost by definition it needs to be considered by reference to another residence elsewhere and whilst St Ives Town Council and Cornwall Council may be able to gather reliable evidence of the former it will be more difficult and time consuming to do so in respect of the latter. It is by no means impossible for the councils to undertake the necessary investigations but do they have the resources to do so? Taking planning enforcement action against a breach of a condition imposed under Policy H2 is unlikely to be straightforward.

In principle, the principal residence condition is no different from other occupancy conditions such as holiday occupancy, agricultural occupancy, or business manager occupation of a tied dwelling; and all, if justified in planning terms, are entirely reasonable planning tools. For the LPA, however (it is of course the LPA rather than the NDP qualifying body that takes enforcement action) breach of a principal residence condition is likely to be far more difficult to prove and to enforce against.

An indication of these difficulties is apparent in that the policy uses the term "Principal Residence" whilst the condition refers to "Principal Home".

Both are referred to as if they are defined terms though neither term is actually defined in either the policy or the condition (or in planning legislation). Whilst on the face of it, the meaning of 'principal' is fairly obvious, in the context of second homes it is anything but and that is revealed by the overly wordy 'Informative' to the condition.

However, reservations over the planning efficacy of Policy H2 were nothing to do with the legal challenge against it. The grounds of the judicial review application were procedural – essentially technicalities. It was claimed that neither the examination inspector, nor Cornwall Council in its decision to make the St Ives NDP pursuant to the referendum (with an 83% vote in favour of the plan), had even considered whether the Policy complied with the SEA Directive and Regulations or with Article 8 of the ECHR. Compliance with both is one of the basic conditions that a neighbourhood plan must fulfil.

Insofar as the claimant suggested any substantive non-compliance with either the SEA Regulations or the ECHR, the reasoning on both counts was weak to say the least; that a reasonable alternative (under the SEA requirements) to Policy H2 that should have been considered as more favourable to the environment was simply to facilitate the building of more open market housing so that almost inevitably some of it may end up in the hands of local people! The non-compliance with Article 8 was said simply to be that Policy H2 somehow breached the right to respect for an individual's private and family life and his home. Unsurprisingly, the court gave very short shrift to such arguments and found on the evidence that the grounds of legal challenge were not made out because the examination inspector and Cornwall Council *had* duly considered the EU requirements in question.

What is interesting from the perspective of a qualifying body is the motivation of the claimant who challenged the St Ives NDP on what were essentially technicalities with what can only be described as weak substantive arguments behind them. Even if the court had upheld the challenge, it does not follow that Policy H2 would necessarily have been struck out or modified at all.

One thing that Policy H2 looks set to stop or at least severely curtail is the construction of individualistic, premium dwellings of the type often built for wealthy incomers as second homes. In a place like St Ives such properties are an important source of work for local firms of architects and the developers they work with, and Policy H2 will undoubtedly put a dampener on such business due to the restriction it imposes. There was, therefore, an obvious motivation for the legal challenge to the St Ives NDP.

Furthermore, even if ultimately weak on its merits, a well presented legal challenge to the decision of an LPA can sometimes persuade the authority to agree to reverse or change its decision rather than risk the considerable costs incurred by an unsuccessful defence of the claim.

It is therefore easy to understand why the legal challenge to the St Ives NDP was considered worthwhile even though it failed.

There are a number of very useful conclusions to be drawn from Policy H2 and the various publicity and attention it has attracted.

The first is that the problem of second homes, and other local issues elsewhere that are capable of being influenced by planning, are absolutely ripe for consideration and inclusion in a neighbourhood plan.

Secondly, the commercial significance of such issues means that any attempt to impose a planning solution will inevitably be controversial, and often contentious. This means that the qualifying body should anticipate the possibility of a legal challenge to a neighbourhood plan that includes such a policy-based solution. Furthermore, that in itself is likely to make the LPA and the NDP examiner cautious about it (because as we have seen, the legal claim is actually against the decision of the LPA). In the St Ives case Cornwall Council and the examiner were supportive of the policy and the plan, but not all LPAs or examiners are so robust.

Thirdly, such a purposeful and potentially contentious neighbourhood plan policy must be based on clear, sound and irrefutable evidence. There must be evidence of the underlying need for the policy and there should be strong evidential support for the effectiveness and reasonableness of the proposed policy-based solution; will the policy address the problem in a way that complies with the basic conditions?

Fourthly, and just as importantly, the policy and any supporting elements to it must be carefully worked out. How the policy will work in practice must be thoroughly considered and drafted accordingly. The policy must be effective in achieving its stated aims and if it involves the imposition of a planning condition on all relevant permissions (as St Ives' Policy H2 does), the condition must be clear, workable and enforceable.

Finally, and notwithstanding the aforementioned prerequisites, the neighbourhood plan policy solution may not be perfect, and it is unlikely to be without imperfect or even unintended consequences. It is, of course, such imperfections that disgruntled developers, and often the media too, will pick up on. However, provided a policy-based solution fulfils the afore-mentioned practical and procedural requirements so that it stands a good chance of surviving the examination of the NDP, then that policy should nonetheless be pursued. This is particularly so if it has widespread local support and provides a solution to a problem that others fail to address.

The St Ives NDP really is a case in point and an exemplar of what neighbourhood planning can achieve. For sure, its Policy H2 is not a technically perfect planning solution and there may well be some unintended consequences from it, but it will undoubtedly be at least partially successful in doing what it set out to do which is curbing the proliferation of second homes.

What is arguably even more important is that, perfect or not, Policy H2 from inception to execution is the work of local people motivated to solve a local problem; a problem that no one else was getting to grips with. Of course – as the critics so gleefully point out – it may have an adverse impact on the local economy. However, what those critics fail to grasp is that local people were well aware of that but clearly considered it to be the lesser of two evils and went ahead with the innovative neighbourhood plan policy anyway.

A cautionary tale - the Southbourne case

Whilst it would have been appropriate to conclude this chapter on the encouraging note of the St Ives NDP, the 2019 Court of Appeal decision in the Southbourne case[62] – as we shall refer to it here, because it involves the Southbourne Parish Neighbourhood Plan ("SPNP") – unfortunately must have the final say in any practical guide on how neighbourhood plans should deal with housing.

Although the case went to the Court of Appeal on a single and quite fundamental point of law, for a number of reasons it has even wider significance for neighbourhood plan makers as it touches on many of the issues raised, not only in this chapter, but throughout the book. The case therefore serves as a cautionary note for anyone expecting, as they should, that their neighbourhood plan policies should be respected and applied by decision-makers.

---

[62] *Chichester District Council v SSHLG* [2019] EWCA Civ 1640.

Background and development plan policies

The background is an outline planning application by the second respondent to the appeal, Beechcroft Land Ltd, for 34 dwellings on a greenfield site – an old orchard – on the edge of the village of Southbourne, to the west of Chichester in West Sussex.

The application invoked the relevant policy matrix from the Chichester Local Plan ("CLP") and the SPNP, both of which were less than two years old – and on the face of it very much up-to-date in NPPF terms – when the LPA, Chichester District Council ("CDC") determined the application in February 2017.

The CLP at *Policy 2: Development Strategy and Settlement Hierarchy* sets out a settlement hierarchy that identifies "Settlement Hubs", including Southbourne, *"to meet identified local needs"*. Each "Settlement Hub" is defined by a "Settlement Boundary", that can be reviewed and amended by the relevant neighbourhood plan. Within the "Settlement Boundary", there is a presumption in favour of the types of development specified in CLP Policy 2 and in relevant NDPs.

Policy 2 also refers to CLP *Policy 20: Southbourne Strategic Development*;

> *Land at Southbourne will be allocated for development in the Southbourne Neighbourhood Plan including any amendments to the Settlement Boundary. Development which is required to be planned for will include:*
>
> * *300 homes;*
>
> * *Supporting local facilities and community uses; and*
>
> * *Open space and green infrastructure.*

In addition to this 'strategic' housing development of 300 units, under CLP Policy 5, *"small scale housing sites"* must be identified in the SPNP (or failing that a site allocations DPD) for 50 dwellings to meet local needs in Southbourne Parish, outside of Southbourne Village.

However, Policy 2 makes clear that *"Development in the Rest of the Plan Area outside the settlements listed ... is restricted to that which requires a countryside location or meets an essential local rural need or supports rural diversification"*.

This is also echoed in CLP *Policy 45: Development in the Countryside*;

> *Within the countryside, outside Settlement Boundaries, development will be granted where it requires a countryside location and meets the essential, small scale, and local need which cannot be met within or immediately adjacent to existing settlements.*

Anyone who knows this increasingly overcrowded and congested part of the south coast, once pleasantly but now uncomfortably squeezed between what is now the South Downs National Park to the north and the various designated areas of the coastal harbours and marshes to the south, will realise that 350 additional dwellings is a lot for this small parish to find. This is especially so when local people – as in most cases – would prefer to see new development integrated within existing settlements in order to avoid coalescence between built-up areas.

The neighbourhood plan

The SPNP nonetheless rises to this challenge admirably. It is generally a very good example of a neighbourhood plan and subject to an important proviso that we shall return to, the policies of the SPNP that are relevant to this case are reasonably well drafted and appropriately detailed with carefully set out supporting evidence underpinning clear and purposeful objectives. Furthermore and equally importantly, the SPNP is not only in conformity with the strategic objectives of the CLP – it would not have passed its examination if it were not – but it goes further than many neighbourhood plans in expressly demonstrating that conformity within the wording of its policies and their supporting paragraphs.

By way of example is SPNP *Policy 1: Development within the Settlement Boundaries*;

> *The Neighbourhood Plan will support development proposals located inside the Settlement Boundaries of Southbourne/Prinsted ... [etc] ... as shown on the Policies Map, provided they accord with other provisions of the Neighbourhood Plan and development plan.*

As the supporting paragraphs make clear, the purpose of this policy is *"to encourage future development ... to the established settlements"* and *"to protect the essential countryside character of the defined settlement gaps"*. In order to accommodate the amount of development for which the CLP expresses a need, Southbourne's settlement boundary was amended as shown on the SPNP Policies Map.

SPNP *Policy 2: Housing Site Allocations* is so straightforward that it can be summarised even more succinctly. It allocates four sites for housing, clearly shown on the Policies Map, with a specified number of units for each site that in total fulfils entirely the overall CLP housing requirement for the parish of 350 (comprising strategic development of 300 dwellings and an "indicative housing number" of 50).

Whilst it is certainly true that the relevant policies of the CLP are a little cumbersome and unwieldy, the policy matrix for determining an outline application for 34 new dwellings outside the Southbourne settlement boundary and not on any of the housing sites allocated in the SPNP is easy for anyone with a basic grasp of planning principles to understand. The Beechcroft application for development, that does not require a countryside location (for CLP Policy 2 purposes) and outside of a settlement boundary, was not in compliance with any part of the development plan and was also very clearly contrary to the overall development plan strategy.

LPA refusal of the application

Accordingly, by reference to the NPPF, the CLP and the SPNP, CDC refused the application, giving two comprehensive reasons for refusal, by its decision notice of February 2017. The first reason was that;

> *The site lies outside of the settlement boundary for Southbourne and in the designated countryside wherein the policies of the development plan state that development will only be permitted where it meets an essential, small scale and local need which cannot be met within or immediately adjacent to the existing settlement. The proposed development does not meet the criteria of policy 45 and is contrary to the Development Strategy and Settlement Hierarchy for the Plan area which identifies where sustainable development, infrastructure and facilities will be accommodated in terms of scale, function and character. The proposed development is therefore contrary to policies 1, 2, 5, 20 and 45 of the Chichester Local Plan: Key Policies 2014-2029. Furthermore, the site is not allocated for development in the Southbourne Neighbourhood Plan 2014-2029, contrary to policies 1 and 2 of the made Southbourne Neighbourhood Plan 2014-2029. The Council is able to demonstrate that it has a 5 year housing land supply, is making full provision for its parish housing numbers set out in Local Plan policy 5 and 20, through Neighbourhood Plans and the Site Allocation DPD, and is under no requirement to meet its Objectively Assessed (housing) Need ahead of completion of the*

Local Plan review in Summer 2019. The proposal is not sustainable development within the meaning of paragraph 14 of the NPPF. As there are no compelling reasons or material considerations indicating otherwise, the proposal should be determined in accordance with the development plan and in accordance with paragraphs 11, 12 and 196 of the NPPF.

It is clear from this that CDC believed it had, and could demonstrate, a five year housing supply of specific deliverable sites for the purposes of Paragraph 47 of the NPPF[63] and that the Paragraph 14 presumption in favour of sustainable development was not engaged.

CDC also included the following 'Informative' on its decision notice;

The Local Planning Authority has acted positively and proactively in determining this application by identifying matters of concern with the proposal and discussing those with the Applicant. However, the issues are so fundamental to the proposal that it has not been possible to negotiate a satisfactory way forward and due to the harm which has been clearly identified within the reason(s) for the refusal, approval has not been possible.

Before we consider the appeal process that followed, culminating in the Court of Appeal decision, it is worth also mentioning two other features of the SPNP which contributed to the policy matrix with which Beechcroft's application failed to comply.

The first is SPNP *Policy 3: The Green Ring*, which states that;

The Neighbourhood Plan proposes the establishment of a Green Ring around the village of Southbourne, as shown on the Policies Map, comprising a variety of green infrastructure assets, including informal open space, allotments, a playing field, a footpath/cycleway network, children's play areas, woodland and land of biodiversity value.

Development proposals that lie within the broad location of the Green Ring will be required to align their public open space requirements with its objectives, so that they contribute to its successful formation and maintenance. Proposals that will lead to the unnecessary loss

---

[63] Paragraphs 14, 47 and 198 of the NPPF 2012 are reflected respectively in Paragraphs 11, 73 and 74, and 12 to14, NPPF 2019.

of Green Ring land or features or that will prejudice the completion of the Green Ring will be resisted.

Policy 3 clearly aims to protect "Green Ring" land – which lies outside the settlement boundary (this is clear from the SPNP Policies Map) – for the provision of "green infrastructure" that is required by the existing settlement of Southbourne and any new development within it. This is quite a novel concept at local level, with a clear rationale in connection with SPNP Policy 1, and akin to Green Belt principles. The Beechcroft application site is within the Green Ring and amounts to "*the unnecessary loss of Green Ring land*". Under this policy too, the outline application was contrary to the SPNP and properly resisted by Southbourne Parish Council ("SPC") and CDC.

The second point of note about the SPNP is a crucial modification made by CDC upon the recommendation of the examiner; the deletion of the following sentence that had been included at the end of the submission draft of SPNP Policy 1 ("Settlement Boundaries");

"[development] *proposals outside the Settlement Boundary will be required to conform to development plan policy in respect of the control of development in the countryside".*

In his examination report the examiner's justification for this recommended deletion – that we shall consider further below – was that;

To the extent that over the life of the Plan proposals might come forward for development outside the settlement boundaries, it would not be appropriate for the Plan to require such proposals to conform to development plan policy in the countryside. That responsibility should be for Chichester District Council to determine through its development plan policies. For this reason I have indicated that if this policy is to be retained, the final sentence of the draft policy should be removed... In the explanatory text, the policy should therefore encourage, rather than direct development, within the established settlements within the parish..."

Given that we are considering this case as a case study for qualifying bodies, we will now look briefly at the events that led to the Court of Appeal decision.

The appeal process

CDC's refusal of the outline application (which SPC had also, naturally, objected to) was appealed by the developer, Beechcroft. The planning appeal was dealt with by a public enquiry later that year and the appeal decision was issued on 2 November 2017, well before the 2018/19 NPPF, and its stricter housing delivery requirements, came into effect.

The appeal inspector identified two main issues for the appeal;

- *the effect of the proposal on the development plan strategy for the location of residential development;* [and],

- *whether the Council is able to demonstrate a five year supply of housing land.*[64]

However, the most critical thing for the appellant to establish first, was the second issue – whether the council had a five year housing supply. If it did not, then according to the NPPF, the development plan policies (of the CLP and SPNP) were not "up-to-date" and the NPPF Paragraph 14 (now Paragraph 11) presumption in favour of sustainable development could be applied. That would invoke consideration of the 'planning balance' of the presumption; whether "*any adverse impacts of* [granting planning permission] *would significantly and demonstrably outweigh the benefits when assessed against the policies in this Framework taken as a whole*".

Notwithstanding CDC's evidence of its five year housing supply sites and the anticipated rate of delivery, the inspector accepted the appellant's projections for some of that delivery being slightly delayed so as to take it beyond the five year period. Consequently the inspector concluded that CDC only had a 4.28 year supply of housing. We consider further below the significance of this in this case, and for neighbourhood planners generally, and the type of evidence on which such crucial judgements rest.

Having established that, then instead of having to show that the proposal was in accordance with the development plan, all the appellant had to do was to convince the inspector that the adverse impacts of the proposed development did not significantly and demonstrably outweigh its benefits.

In the context of this consideration, the inspector found that the application

---

[64] Paragraph 5, Appeal Decision – APP/L3815/W/17/3173380.

did conflict with CLP Policies 2 and 45 and did not accord with the aim of SPNP Policy 1. However, because Policy 1 does not expressly prohibit housing outside of the Southbourne settlement boundary, he concluded that the proposed development was not in conflict with it.

Although the inspector said that *"the proposal would be contrary to the development plan strategy for the location of residential development when considered as a whole"*, that was effectively irrelevant because the lack of a five year housing supply meant that the NPPF presumption in favour of sustainable development was invoked and the 'planning balance' of adverse impacts and benefits had to be considered.

In weighing the planning balance, the inspector considered that because the SPNP had not put a cap on the number of new dwellings in the parish and because, in his view, the proposed development was in proportion to the existing settlement of Southbourne, *"the proposal would not conflict with the policies of the* [SPNP]." It followed that *"the adverse impacts of granting permission would not significantly and demonstrably outweigh the benefits of the proposal* [which therefore] *benefits from the presumption in favour of sustainable development"*.[65] In these views, it should be said, the inspector was completely at odds with the wishes of local people expressed through the SPNP and its planning policies.

Furthermore, in this conclusion the inspector's concerns over conflict with the CLP policies were abandoned. He also ignored not only the very obvious meaning and significance of SPNP Policy 1 but entirely failed to consider SPNP Policy 3 which the development in question is expressly contrary to.

CDC appealed to the High Court where the judge refused to diverge from the reasoning of the inspector, concluding that *"the proposal was "not explicitly contrary to either Policy 1 or* [Policy] *2" of the neighbourhood plan* [and that] *the "amendment" to the neighbourhood plan recommended by the examiner had made it "plain that development outside the settlement boundary and specified areas is a matter for* [the local plan]""*.[66]

Without success in the High Court, CDC took its appeal to the Court of Appeal, its case summed up in the following passage from the leading

---

[65] Paragraphs 51 and 55, Appeal Decision – APP/L3815/W/17/3173380 (at paragraph 26, judgment in *Chichester District Council v SSHLG* [2019] EWCA Civ 1640).

[66] From paragraph 27, judgment in *Chichester District Council v SSHLG* [2019] EWCA Civ 1640.

judgment;

> *The essential argument for the district council ... was that Beechcroft's proposal was plainly in conflict with both the aims and the policies of neighbourhood plan, and the Inspector should have seen that. It was contrary to the objectives and vision of the plan. When the plan was being prepared the site had been rejected as a suitable location for housing development. The proposed development was in conflict with Policy 1 because it was outside the settlement boundary established for Southbourne, and with Policy 2 because it was not on one of the allocated sites and was thus contrary to the parish council's judgment on the suitable locations for new housing. To distinguish as the Inspector did between the aims of the neighbourhood plan and its policies, and to conclude that the proposal was at odds with the former but not in conflict with the latter, was ... irrational and inconsistent with the policy in paragraph 198 of the NPPF' ... [The] alternative argument was that if, on a true reading of the decision letter, the Inspector reached no clear conclusion on the question of conflict with the neighbourhood plan, he erred in failing to do so. The policy in paragraph 198 of the NPPF required him to do it.[67]*

The Court of Appeal thoroughly rejected these arguments in what can only be described as a rather muddled and confusing judgment even in the eyes of planning lawyers, let alone for neighbourhood planners. Whilst it is possible to discern the legal rationale for the Court of Appeal not interfering with the findings of the inspector, it is a questionable logic and certainly one that has little regard for fundamental planning principles. Whilst we deal in more detail with those principles later, the contention here is that even on a strict legalistic analysis the judgment is confused.

Analysis of the Court of Appeal decision

Notwithstanding its various discussions on, and several references to, the statutory presumption in favour of the development plan,[68] the Court of Appeal judgment makes clear that;

> *The dispute in this case, however, is not about the statutory presumption in favour of the development plan, or about the correct*

---

[67] Paragraph 28, judgment in *Chichester District Council v SSHLG* [2019] EWCA Civ 1640.

[68] The presumption at Section 38(6), PCPA cited in paragraphs 31, 32, 34, 51, 52 and 54 of the judgment in *Chichester District Council v SSHLG* [2019] EWCA Civ 1640.

interpretation or lawful application of development plan policy. It is about the meaning of government policy in paragraph 198 of the NPPF and its application by the Inspector in making his decision on Beechcroft's appeal.[69]

Indeed the case before the court did revolve around Paragraph 198, NPPF, but if it was not also about the correct interpretation or lawful application of development plan policy, why was it necessary to repeatedly emphasise that *"None of the Inspector's conclusions betrays any misinterpretation or misapplication of the development plan policies in play"*?[70] It seems that in part, and at least in order to determine the principal issue, the case was very much about the correct interpretation and lawful application of development plan policy.

Before we look in more detail at what was principally in issue – Paragraph 198, NPPF – for completeness let us briefly consider the three presumptions involved and how they were, or at least should have been, considered.

The first, referred to repeatedly in the Court of Appeal judgment, is the statutory presumption at Section 38(6) PCPA that requires planning determinations to *"be made in accordance with the plan unless material considerations indicate otherwise"*. This was not really in issue in this case because even if the proposal had been in accordance with the development plan, which all the decision-makers agreed it was not, there were other material considerations to the determination which were capable of overriding the development plan.

One of those material considerations is the NPPF and, in particular, its presumption in favour of sustainable development – the second relevant presumption. This presumption was engaged due to the lack of a five year housing supply which rendered the development plan "out-of-date" and thereby rebutted the statutory presumption. This invoked the 'planning balance' consideration of adverse impacts weighed against the benefits of the development. Once the inspector had accepted the lack of a five year housing supply, it was this presumption that was most crucial to his decision and in order to help him make the judgement of where the planning balance lay, he was aided by the third presumption.

---

[69] Paragraph 33, judgment in *Chichester District Council v SSHLG* [2019] EWCA Civ 1640.

[70] Paragraph 50, and similarly at paragraph 30 – judgment in *Chichester District Council v SSHLG* [2019] EWCA Civ 1640.

It was the third presumption under Paragraph 198, NPPF – *"where a planning application conflicts with a neighbourhood plan ... planning permission should not normally be granted"* – that was the basis of CDC's appeal. This is not inconsistent with either of the first two presumptions – it merely adds a further layer of detail. In helping him conclude where the balance between adverse impact and benefits lay, the inspector decided that the proposal did not "conflict" with the SPNP policies and, therefore, he was not bound by the Paragraph 198 presumption but was free to grant the planning permission on the basis of the second presumption, the presumption in favour of sustainable development. However, as we shall see, the real question was whether there was a conflict with the SPNP overall, not just with its individual policies.

The inspector's finding that the proposal did not *"conflict with the policies of the* [SPNP]*"* was crucial and was exactly why CDC appealed. If his conclusion on how to apply NPPF Paragraph 198 was incorrect, unreasonable or irrational, that would undermine his conclusion on the presumption in favour of sustainable development which is what enabled him to issue the planning permission.

Precisely what the appeal was about was identified in paragraph 33 of the Court of Appeal judgment; *"It is about the meaning of government policy in paragraph 198 of the NPPF and its application by the inspector in making his decision on Beechcroft's appeal"*.

Paragraph 198 says that; *"Where a planning application conflicts with a neighbourhood plan that has been brought into force, planning permission should not normally be granted."*

Certainly "conflicts" is not a legal or technical term that needs any particular judicial consideration. It is also clear that Paragraph 198 does not refer to neighbourhood plan *policies*, but planning applications that conflict with *"a neighbourhood plan"*.

Furthermore, the issue under Paragraph 198 is not whether there is a conflict with 'the development plan' but specifically with "a neighbourhood plan", and this is very much in the context of other government policy in the NPPF to encourage neighbourhood plans and the makers of neighbourhood plans, qualifying bodies.

It is therefore difficult to understand why the Court of Appeal judgment discusses the statutory presumption (the first of the three referred to above) at such length. Certainly, when considering that presumption, there is plenty of case law to suggest – as the court makes clear[71] – that all elements of the development plan should be considered, but that is not the focus of Paragraph 198.

The main question for the Court of Appeal was actually quite straight-forward.

In deciding whether an application "conflicts with a neighbourhood plan" for the purposes of Paragraph 198, is it the neighbourhood plan as a whole – its aims and policies – that should be considered, or merely the latter? Indeed, this was the question posed by CDC in its appeal.[72]

Having answered that question, the court should then have gone on to consider two further questions. First, did the inspector properly consider whether the Beechcroft proposal "conflicts with" the SPNP? Secondly, did the inspector reach the correct, or at least a reasonable and not irrational conclusion, in answer to that question?

However, nowhere in the Court of Appeal judgment is there a direct answer to the principal question on the interpretation and application of Paragraph 198. The closest it gets is towards the end of the judgment at paragraph 47;

> ... there will sometimes be circumstances in which a [development] proposal ... neither complies with nor offends the terms of any par-ticular policy of the development plan, [but] is nevertheless in conflict with the plan because it is manifestly incompatible with the relevant strategy in it. ... The effect of those policies may be – I stress "may be" – that a proposal they do not explicitly support is also, inevita-bly, contrary to them. Whether this is so will always depend on the particular context, and, critically, the wording of the relevant policies, their objectives, and their supporting text.

Here, the court is clearly saying that a development proposal may be in conflict with the development plan if it is incompatible with the strategy – in other words the aims – of that plan, even if not expressly contrary to its policies.

---

[71] Particularly at paragraph 31, judgment in *Chichester District Council v SSHLG* [2019] EWCA Civ 1640.

[72] At paragraph 28, judgment in *Chichester District Council v SSHLG* [2019] EWCA Civ 1640.

However, this analysis is about how to assess a possible conflict with the development plan, but as the court acknowledged (at paragraph 33) the main issue in this case was about the interpretation of government policy. The court simply failed to determine whether it is just the policies or the policies *and* strategy of 'a neighbourhood plan' that should be considered under Paragraph 198.

However, if a purposive strategy-embracing approach should be applied to a possible conflict with the development plan, there is an even stronger rationale for adopting that approach in the context of a government policy that specifically refers to "a neighbourhood plan" rather than the 'policies' of a neighbourhood plan. This is particularly so when the government policy in question is part of a much wider suite of NPPF policies on planning that together expressly encourage neighbourhood plans and plan-makers.

As a matter of government policy, Paragraph 198 creates a presumption in favour of a neighbourhood plan and the purpose behind it – as evidenced by its policies, vision, aims and overall strategy. For the Court of Appeal to fail to even consider that interpretation of Paragraph 198 or make any finding at all on the correct interpretation of Paragraph 198 renders its decision questionable at best.

Furthermore, the appeal inspector too failed to consider or apply the correct, or even a reasonable, interpretation of Paragraph 198. Even though he said *"the proposal is at odds with the aims of the NP"*,[73] he failed to consider whether that meant it was in conflict with the neighbourhood plan for the purposes of Paragraph 198, and to the extent he did consider that, he concluded erroneously that the proposal did not engage the Paragraph 198 presumption. Surely, therefore, the inspector did err in law in his understanding and application of the policy in paragraph 198, and failed to apply it.[74]

The concluding comments in the judgment are also somewhat confused. The Court of Appeal concluded that;

> ... *even if ... the inspector was at fault in failing to find, under the policy in paragraph 198 of the NPPF, that Beechcroft's proposal was*

---

[73] Paragraph 13, Appeal Decision – APP/L3815/W/17/3173380 (at paragraph 23, judgment in *Chichester District Council v SSHLG* [2019] EWCA Civ 1640).

[74] See paragraph 4, judgment in *Chichester District Council v SSHLG* [2019] EWCA Civ 1640.

> *in conflict with the neighbourhood plan ... the inspector's decision would in those circumstances inevitably have been the same [partly] because the inspector applied the statutory presumption against Beechcroft's proposal; and ... because he recognized that the proposal did not comply with the aims of the neighbourhood plan for the location of new housing, and plainly gave this consideration as much weight as he thought it could reasonably have – and there is no reason to think he would have given it any greater weight if he had accepted, as Mr Lewis submitted, that the proposal was in conflict both with those aims of the plan and with its policies".*

First, it is odd to say that *"the inspector applied the statutory presumption against Beechcroft's proposal"* when he then rebutted the presumption against the development by finding material considerations (the NPPF and housing supply) to support it and grant it planning permission.

Secondly, if the inspector had concluded the proposal was in conflict with the SPNP, then surely there is good reason to think he would have adopted the inference from the Paragraph 198 presumption *"that planning permission should not normally be granted"*. Furthermore, the conflict could have, and a reading of the inspector's decision letter suggests possibly would have, tilted the planning balance against granting permission by weighing the adverse impacts of the proposal more heavily against its benefits.

In short, there is every reason to think that if the inspector had found Beechcroft's planning application to be in conflict with the SPNP, and if he had realised that to be the correct application of Paragraph 198 as he should have, then he would have refused to grant the permission and dismissed the appeal.

One wonders whether, if in those circumstances Beechcroft had appealed the inspector's decision, there would have been the same reluctance by the courts to interfere with it?

In reviewing the assessments made of the SPNP policies themselves, it can certainly be said that the decision of the appeal inspector and the judgments of the High Court and the Court of Appeal put the Beechcroft case that the proposal did not conflict with the SPNP at its very highest. It relied on the very narrow line of reasoning that the SPNP Policy 1 did not expressly prohibit or put any limit on development outside the settlement boundary even though as the Court of Appeal acknowledged[75] the SPNP itself explained the purpose of the policy was *"to protect the essential countryside character of the defined settlement gaps"*.

Even though every planning decision-maker knows the meaning of, and purpose behind, a settlement boundary the reasoning of the Court of Appeal suggests that, to be effective, an NDP settlement boundary policy has to expressly prohibit, limit or put a cap on development outside of the settlement boundary.

In fact, SPNP Policy 1 had contained an appropriate restriction that "[development] *proposals outside the Settlement Boundary will be required to conform to development plan policy in respect of the control of development in the countryside"*.

However, that sentence was struck out by the examiner of the neighbourhood plan on the basis that only CDC could make planning policies for the land outside of the settlement boundary. That is a highly questionable proposition to say the least (and we return to it again below). Subject to general conformity, there is no reason why the SPNP should not have policies that affect the whole of the neighbourhood area, both within and outside of its settlement boundaries and there is no reason not to expressly defer to the local plan policy in order to do so.

Instead of tacitly approving the examiner's rather misplaced interference with the SPNP, the appeal process decision-makers should have considered it, at the very least, as undermining the suggestion that the SPNP had remained silent on development outside of the settlement boundaries. When it was conceived the SPNP was obviously not silent on that issue. The Court of Appeal stressed that "[the SPNP] *says nothing about development outside the settlement boundaries"* and *"no policy in the neighbourhood plan replicates Policy 45"* without any contextual reference to the examiner's unwarranted modification.

Only with rather strained reasoning, and a lack of regard for supporting evidence on the proper construction of SPNP Policy 1, was it possible to find the Beechcroft proposal to be not in conflict with that policy.

However, when considering SPNP Policies 1, 2 and 3 together – and the pattern of future development clearly encouraged by those policies – it

---

[75] See paragraph 19, judgment in *Chichester District Council v SSHLG* [2019] EWCA Civ 1640.

is even more of a stretch to conclude that the proposed development was not in conflict with the neighbourhood plan.

Even on a restricted view of the point of law on which the appeal rested, the Court of Appeal decision is hard to understand. When considering the wider purpose of planning, and the role of neighbourhood plans in particular, the decision really does defy common sense. Following those in *Cherkley Court*, *Welwyn* and *Daw's Hill*, this is another highly questionable Court of Appeal planning decision that indicates an unwillingness to interpret legislation, and attendant government policy, in the context of the intended planning purpose behind it.

At least in *Welwyn* the Supreme Court had the opportunity to put things right and after *Daw's Hill*, secondary legislation was quickly introduced to do so. The damage to the SPNP is unlikely to be undone but at least lessons can be learnt.

Avoiding the Southbourne pitfalls

There is no doubt that the SPC, as the qualifying body for the SPNP, will feel badly let down by the Court of Appeal decision. It is relatively uncommon for an LPA to pursue a legal challenge involving the interpretation of NDP policies all the way to the Court of Appeal, so that CDC had the commitment to do so suggests they – and by association SPC, too – were at least hopeful and quite optimistic about the outcome.

There is also no doubt that the effect of the Court of Appeal decision – that the development of 34 new dwellings on a greenfield site rejected as an allocated site, and outside the settlement boundary yet within the Green Ring, will nonetheless go ahead – flies in the face of the legitimate expectations of all those who prepared and supported the SPNP.

The truth is that relatively few neighbourhood plans are subjected to the scrutiny of the courts. It is also the case that of those NDPs and their policies that are tested in planning appeals, many of them survive such scrutiny with their planning policies upheld against obviously conflicting development proposals, and the appeal dismissed as a consequence.

Nonetheless, the Southbourne case is significant for involving such a recent decision of the Court of Appeal, and gives an indication of what can go wrong where there are any questions about whether to apply the policies of a recently made neighbourhood plan. There are a number of factors – most already considered in this book – that contributed to the

SPNP being undermined in the way that it was, and which are potential pitfalls for every neighbourhood plan.

1. the policies of the local plan

The NPPF makes clear that plans must be positively prepared and "aspirational"[76], and this is often taken to mean drafting planning policies in a permissive way with a minimum of restrictive or prohibiting language. The CLP, adopted in 2015, is a classic example of an NPPF-era local plan that adopts this approach to drafting.

The problem is that because planning is partly about development control or management, a planning policy that cannot say what it really needs to say is prone to losing its effectiveness. Without using restrictive language, it can be difficult in a policy intended to encourage development to certain types of location, that other types of development are inappropriate there. To an extent this is now a widespread problem with current and emerging local plans and is certainly true of the CLP, particularly *Policy 2: Development Strategy and Settlement Hierarchy* and *Policy 45: Development in the Countryside* that were both in play in this case.

This is a problem for qualifying bodies in two respects.

First, the local plan policies do not say what they really mean to say and do not reflect the overall strategy of the local plan as effectively as they should do – for whoever is trying to interpret those policies.

Secondly, and more specifically for qualifying bodies, it makes it more difficult to draft NDP policies that take their lead from the local plan whilst also needing to insert an appropriate level of detail into the policy matrix. SPC was obviously conscious of this when drafting its SPNP policies, particularly its Policy 1.

The CLP seems especially clumsy in identifying the already pressured settlement of Southbourne for the strategic development of 300 new dwellings, and then in a separate policy issuing an indicative housing figure of an additional 50 dwellings for the parish. Obviously this strategy was tested at examination of the CLP but the decision-makers in the appeal process all seemed to take the view that as a strategic hub, there was no reason to limit the number of new dwellings in the Southbourne neighbourhood area.

---

[76] See Paragraphs 16 and 35, NPPF.

A qualifying body should try to anticipate the impact of emerging local plan policies when preparing its neighbourhood plan and if necessary submit representations on relevant local plan consultations.

2. the policies of the neighbourhood plan

A persistent theme of this book is the need to draft NDP policies that work as intended. It is clear the SPNP Policy 1 did not have the intended effect in this case and neither did its Policy 3.

This problem is a recurring one that regularly undermines neighbourhood plans and is exacerbated by the other pitfalls highlighted here. On the one hand NDP policies must be positively drafted and in conformity with the local plan, both in substance and style, and yet any attempt to draft in the appropriate details creatively or innovatively runs the risk of the examiner striking out, in whole or in part, what would otherwise be an effective policy.

SPNP Policy 1 is a case in point in that it attempted, not unreasonably, to defer to the local plan to ensure that only certain types of development could be permitted outside of the settlement boundaries. There were perhaps better and more effective ways of drafting a policy with that effect and, as we have seen, SPNP Policy 1 did not survive with its intended effect intact.

The submission version of Policy 1 was undermined by the examiner and the examiner-modified Policy 1 was undermined by the appeal inspector!

When it comes to drafting its neighbourhood plan policies and whilst the draft plan is going through the examination process, every qualifying body should take independent professional advice.

3. the modification of the neighbourhood plan

There was no need for the examiner to modify the SPNP Policy 1 to the extent that he did. His explanation for modifying – or more accurately his *recommendation* to modify (the decision to do so rested with CDC as the LPA) – the wording of the policy is far from clear or unassailable.

What is not apparent from the references in the Court of Appeal judgment, but emerges from the examination report,[77] is that the examiner's principal concern about Policy 1 was its original title, 'Spatial Strategy'

---

[77] Paragraphs 5.8 and 5.9 and Appendix 1, the examiner's report on the SPNP dated May 2015 .

which he seemed to construe as meaning that the policy was about strategic development.

In fact, there is nothing in the original wording of the Policy 1 that suggests or implies it was attempting to cover strategic development. Furthermore, there is no reason at all why an NDP should not have a spatial strategy for guiding local development in general conformity with strategic objectives within the neighbourhood area. That was the clear purpose and effect of the submission version of Policy 1, which was worded to expressly demonstrate conformity with the CLP.

In any case, if the examiner was irritated by the title of the policy, why did he not simply recommend modification of that, rather than interfere with the wording of the policy itself? He may not have liked the way the policy was drafted, but did he stop to consider whether it offended any of the basic conditions? It appears not. Even if he had, he should have recommended alternative policy wording that would, as far as possible, have served the intended purpose behind it.

Frankly it is difficult to see this modification as anything other than unwarranted interference with the SPNP that had nothing whatsoever to do with the basic conditions. The examiner recommended the modification and CDC, as is normal practice for the LPA in this situation, accepted it and made its decision that the SPNP should proceed to referendum on that basis.

If there is one single factor that contributed more than any other to the Beechcroft appeal succeeding, it is this one. In effect, the examiner's intervention could be said to have ripped the heart out of the SPNP and left it powerless to prevent development completely at odds with the wishes of the people who made it.

4. the lack of formal opportunity to resist a modification
A pattern is emerging here. Each and every one of these pitfalls inevitably leads into the next.

The examiner's unjustified interference with the SPNP could have been prevented if the qualifying body had had a formal opportunity to oppose it. As we have seen, such an opportunity does not exist in most cases in which the examination is held by written representations (as opposed to a hearing) as was the case here.

It may be that SPC was informally consulted by CDC about the proposed changes to Policy 1, but unlikely that it would have been offered any real option to counter those changes. Any resistance to the modification would have had to be agreed and adopted by CDC and that would have led to a more convoluted statutory procedure for finalising the SPNP - something most LPAs are keen to avoid.

This point has been made countless times in the preceding chapters, and this case demonstrates why. The qualifying body, as the NDP plan-making body, should be considered the principal party in the examination process and be fully involved with it. It should certainly have the right of reply to any examiner recommendations both before and after they are considered by the LPA. This need not and should not be an adversarial process, but simply a matter of fully involving the qualifying body in the recommendations and decisions of the examiner and LPA respectively, enabling all three to arrive at mutually acceptable conclusions wherever possible.

If SPC had been properly involved at this stage of the SPNP and aided by sound professional advice and representation along the way, it seems highly unlikely that Policy 1 would have been modified in the way that it was.

5. disregard for certain neighbourhood plan policies
This is another general problem that manifested itself in several ways in this case. Plan-makers and decision-takers will each have their own perspective on a planning policy. A policy considered of principal importance by those who drafted it and brought it into being, may be unfairly subordinated by the decision-taker.

This is an obvious problem for neighbourhood planners as NDP policies are still prone to be disregarded, subordinated or considered of lesser status than local plan policies. The attitude towards the policies of the SPNP of all the decision-makers in this case was arguably less rigorous than it should have been.

Many would say that even if the Beechcroft proposal was not in conflict with Policy 1 of the SPNP, it was certainly contrary to Policy 3 because the site was clearly within the Green Ring zone expressly reserved for green infrastructure. So why was Policy 3 barely referred to in the course of the appeal, and why was it not upheld?

The point here is that when drafting planning policies, it is important to stress the importance of and reasoning behind each one, but also to make clear the obvious connections between any policies that are part of an overall strategy. It may have made a difference in this case if the SPNP had expressly cross-referred Policy 1 and Policy 3, one to the other and vice-versa.

6. the need for a five year supply of housing

This is another major difficulty for neighbourhood planners and again this case demonstrates why. We discuss further in the final chapter why the five year supply as an element of planning policy is so problematic; because it results in many more residential planning permissions but does not in itself achieve its intended aim of increasing the delivery of new homes.

The practical difficulty for qualifying bodies is that local plan and neighbourhood plan housing policies may be declared "out-of-date" at any time if an appeal inspector happens to decide there is not a five year supply.

The all-important statutory presumption in favour of the development plan that the Court of Appeal rightly held so dear in its judgment is completely undermined if the developer can convince an appeal inspector, by any reasoning, that the houses the LPA expects to be built within five years under existing permissions may actually take slightly longer than that to be completed.

If that 'failure', which is often not within the control of the LPA anyway, is established then even the housing policies of a recently adopted local plan are considered "out-of-date" and disregarded because the presumption in favour of the plan is rebutted.

This anomalous situation is made worse by the ease with which a well prepared developer can establish a shortfall in supply by reference to possible delays in other developers completing their developments. In the Southbourne case, CDC genuinely considered that it had a five year supply, and in effect it did – it had recently adopted the CLP including sufficient residential site allocations and permissions, and had a reasonable expectation of their delivery within five years. Beechcroft nonetheless convinced the inspector that varied causes of delay – including other developers' slow negotiations on planning agreements and in discharging planning conditions – meant that a small proportion of the planned for houses *may* not have been completed within five years. Beechcroft's evidence was merely about *estimated* timescales for delivery that cannot be established with any certainty one way or the other.

How could CDC robustly counter such evidence at appeal, let alone have anticipated it when making and adopting the CLP? Even if it had allocated sites and issued planning permissions for twice the number of houses, the appellant could still have found evidence to undermine the estimated timescale for their delivery!

In short, however many houses an LPA plans for, it cannot control or predict when they will be delivered or how a planning inspector may view the five year supply. If the LPA cannot know for sure whether or not it has a five year supply, then neither can a qualifying body. That, in turn, makes it impossible to know if or when neighbourhood plan housing policies may be considered "out-of-date" and at risk of being downgraded as a result.

Such uncertainty inevitably upsets the essence and the efficiency of plan-making. Qualifying bodies must at least be alert to the issue of housing supply and the adverse implications of it.

7. confusing array of planning policies and guidance
There is no doubt that this was another of the problems in the Southbourne case, as it is in many others. It leads to questionable decision-making and inconsistent judicial reasoning.

There are a number of elements in this confusing array, properly considered in the following order; the statutory rules such as the presumption at Section 38(6) PCPA, the statutory development plan comprising the strategic policies and objectives of the local plan and then the policies of the neighbourhood plan if one exists and, finally, the NPPF and PPG which are not part of the statutory development plan but are material considerations.

However, as we have seen it only needs the development plan to be undermined by a rebuttal of the statutory presumption and the material consideration of the NPPF comes into play to turn this whole hierarchy on its head. If the Court of Appeal struggles to clearly explain its reasoning by reference to this policy hierarchy, it is obviously a real challenge for qualifying bodies to properly understand it and make planning policies that withstand its scrutiny.

Furthermore, there are all too many cases in which the court refuses to give any helpful guidance on the meaning of key NPPF terms, simply leaving their meaning to the interpretation of the decision-maker.

To be successful, a legal challenge to a planning permission or an appeal decision must show the decision to be unreasonable or irrational so as to be unlawful. Unless the claim overcomes that hurdle, the court will simply say that it will not impugn the decision of the planning decision-maker, but that judgment – the judgment of the court – is itself subjective. What is unreasonable or irrational in a particular case?

The Southbourne case is a case in point in that in the High Court and Court of Appeal decisions could easily have gone the other way.

Another example is the Guildford Green Belt case[78] (discussed above - *'The big buffer eating into the Green Belt'*, page 175) in which the High Court held that quite normal development pressure for more housing was within the reasonable meaning of "exceptional circumstances" justifying the erosion of the Green Belt. How could any plan-maker possibly foresee that conclusion?

This often confusing and sometimes conflicting array of policies and key terms, such as 'exceptional circumstances' and 'settlement boundary', is inevitably difficult for non-professional plan-makers to navigate, particularly when there is a lack of consistent judicial guidance.

This state of affairs often undermines the purpose behind planning and the legitimate expectations of what planning should achieve. There is little neighbourhood planners can do to change this, other than ensure the careful and purposeful drafting of their NDP policies, but they should at least be forewarned of the potential implications and be aware of the broad policy matrix their neighbourhood plan forms part of.

8. uneven playing field and a 'cultural' mismatch
Whilst it is certainly the case that the courts have upheld some important neighbourhood planning principles, many qualifying bodies do feel pressured by their lower tier planning status and in particular by the over-zealous insistence on ever more residential site allocations and planning permissions. This pressure is compounded by the other issues identified above.

Part of the problem is the intentionally 'junior' status of neighbourhood planning and the fact that, as we have seen, the LPA makes all the formal decisions in the making of an NDP thereby reducing, ultimately, the influence of the qualifying body.

---

[78] *Compton Parish Council & Ors v Guildford Borough Council & Anor* [2019] EWHC 3242 (Admin).

Whilst SPC would no doubt have welcomed CDC's commitment to challenge the permission granted on appeal to Beechcroft, the parish council was nonetheless somewhat sidelined and had no locus, or standing, before the court. For various reasons it will usually be down to the LPA to fight the neighbourhood planners' corner in the courts, but that will only happen if the LPA has supported or based its decision on NDP policies in the first place. In any case, few LPAs show the commitment to do so that CDC did against Beechcroft.

Even in the Southbourne case, the cultural mismatch between local interests and the perceived essential importance of the housebuilders' mission can be discerned. Why was there no careful and holistic assessment, in relation to the area itself and the stated aims of local people, of the practical effects and purposes behind all of the relevant SPNP policies? Why was Policy 3 and its Green Ring principle almost completely ignored? Why was more weight not given to the fact that the SPNP had already allocated sites for the entirety of its housing requirement? And perhaps most significantly of all, why did neither the appeal inspector or the courts appear to recognise that the SPNP does allow for even more housing to come forward within, rather than outside of, its settlement boundaries?

If the competing interests had been equally well represented and balanced evenly against the clear purpose behind the relevant planning policies, these questions would not arise ... and in all likelihood the policies of the SPNP would have been respected and applied in the way that local people expected them to be.

In the final chapter some of these issues, and possible reforms to address them, are discussed further and in a wider context.

Chapter 7: Other Means of Influence

There are several ways in which parish councils, by virtue of being the first tier of local government, have an opportunity to influence planning decisions. These other means of influence have undoubtedly been enhanced and expanded by the localism agenda and the neighbourhood planning regime.

The influence of a parish council with its LPA will inevitably depend to a large extent on the interests and abilities of the individual councillors and officers involved. Some parish councillors are also district councillors on the planning committee of the LPA and they will be ideally placed to get to know the planning officers for the area and to remind or persuade the LPA of the interests of the parish.

A parish councillor or clerk with a good knowledge of planning and who already has a line of communication with LPA officers will obviously exert greater influence. An interest in, and knowledge of, planning can be developed and to an extent comes with being immersed in the subject, something this book is intended to encourage and support. There is no doubt that involvement in neighbourhood planning inevitably also engages interest in the wider planning system and that, in turn, is likely to inform more effective influence on local planning matters.

Neighbourhood plan credibility

This is a term not commonly found elsewhere but is used here to describe the increased recognition and elevated status attributed by the LPA and other decision-makers to a parish council or neighbourhood forum engaged in neighbourhood planning.

There is no doubt that a parish council that has the motivation, organisation and purpose to apply for a neighbourhood area and then embark on producing an NDP will put itself firmly on the radar of the LPA. At the very least the LPA will have to formally respond to, and in most cases grant, the application for area designation. Through the various communications and collaborations that inevitably follow, the parish council should be able to gradually build its influence with its LPA.

Additionally, an ever increasing array of statutory provisions ensures that a parish council with a neighbourhood plan in place or emerging must be recognised by, and has certain opportunities to influence, the LPA on various aspects of the planning regime. Some examples are considered below.

One way in which the credibility of the parish council may be asserted is for it to invoke the general power of competence for itself. It can only do this if it fulfils certain eligibility criteria set out in the implementing legislation; the key to which is having a suitably qualified clerk.[1] The Explanatory Memorandum to that legislation sets out the rationale behind it:

> *The Government's intention in providing eligible Parish Councils with the general power of competence is to better enable them to take on their enhanced role and allow them to do the things they have previously been unable to do under their existing powers.*

Again, it may be said that this is as much about appearances as anything else in that the sort of competencies that may be better enabled by the general power of competence are not precluded by not having it.

In practice, as well as increased credibility and encouragement to be innovative, the advantage of invoking the general power is that it is likely to be the first line of defence against any criticism of a parish council for acting beyond its traditional functions.

Notification of relevant planning applications

It is a long-established requirement that upon request an LPA must notify a parish council of any planning applications within the parish so as to give the parish council the chance to make representations. A neighbourhood forum has the same right in respect of applications in its neighbourhood area.[2]

---

[1] The general power of competence under Section 1, Localism Act 2011 is conferred on parish councils that meet the conditions prescribed under The Parish Councils (General Power of Competence) (Prescribed Conditions) Order 2012; that the council formally resolves that it meets the other conditions of eligibility relating to the proportion of councillors that are members of the council as a result of having been declared elected following an election, as opposed to being co-opted or appointed and to the qualifications of the clerk to the parish council.

[2] Paragraph 8, Schedule 1, Town and Country Planning Act 1990 (as amended).

NPPF

Far more so than in the previous version, the current NPPF expressly recognises the role of neighbourhood plans and provides quite detailed guidance for neighbourhood planners on specific issues, and particularly on *'Delivering a sufficient supply of new homes'.*[3]

As we have seen, under this part of the NPPF at Paragraphs 65 and 66, and at Paragraph 14, the importance of neighbourhood plans and their qualifying bodies in delivering new homes is made clear.

Paragraph 65 requires the LPA to issue a housing requirement figure for each designated neighbourhood area which the NDP must then adopt (as it is unlikely to be susceptible to subsequent challenge). If the LPA cannot issue a housing requirement figure, then upon the request of the qualifying body it must issue an indicative figure[4] from all available evidence, to guide the neighbourhood plan-makers.

Qualifying bodies are also encouraged to identify land for homes by allocating small and medium sites (of less than 1 hectare) in their neighbourhood plans.[5]

Whilst there is no doubt that the prime concern of government expressed through the NPPF is the delivery of new homes, the document also encourages neighbourhood planners in other aspects of planning including; designating land as Local Green Space,[6] making effective use of land[7] and achieving good design.[8]

Increased proportion of CIL

Under the Community Infrastructure Levy ("CIL") Regulations,[9] 25% of the CIL collected in respect of development in the area of a parish council

---

[3]   Chapter 5, NPPF.

[4]   Paragraph 66, NPPF.

[5]   Paragraph 69, NPPF.

[6]   Paragraph 99, NPPF.

[7]   Paragraphs 117 to 120, NPPF.

[8]   Paragraphs 125 to 128, NPPF.

[9]   Regulation 59A, Community Infrastructure Levy (Amendment) Regulations 2013.

with an NDP in place is paid by the collecting LPA to the parish council. Where there is no NDP in place, the neighbourhood portion of the CIL received is 15%.

Brownfield land register notification

Where a parish council or a neighbourhood forum have requested it the LPA must notify that "relevant body" of a proposed entry of land in Part 2 of the brownfield land register.[10] Part 2 of the register lists land that has "*planning permission in principle*".

Local plan representations

Every town and parish council has the opportunity to make representations on local plan consultations held by its LPA.

Provided they are relevant to the consultation any such representations must be considered by the LPA and may prove to be significant when the issues in question are tested at the examination of the local plan. On difficult or contentious issues, well organised submissions by a parish council with valuable local knowledge are likely to be given considerable weight.

It is easy to see why the representations of a neighbourhood plan-making parish council with an already established line of communication with the LPA are likely to be considered more credible and persuasive than those of a local council with no interest in neighbourhood planning.

The process of making a local plan is a long one that takes at least several years to complete and involves several public consultations, usually beginning with identifying and testing the issues and options for the emerging plan.

All parish councils should take the opportunity to make their views known at every stage of the local plan process with carefully considered and, if necessary, detailed and professionally prepared submissions. An existing or emerging neighbourhood plan or even the evidence from neighbourhood plan consultations will also be potentially relevant to the making of a local plan.

---

[10] Regulation 8, The Town and Country Planning (Brownfield Land Register) Regulations 2017.

Anyone who has made representations on local plan consultations, including parish councils, will usually be entitled to appear at a hearing of the local plan examination and to make further submissions, based on their previous representations, to the inspector.[11]

Representations on planning applications

Mention has already been made of the statutory requirement on LPAs to notify a parish council that has requested notification, of every planning application within its parish.

Having been notified of an application, the parish council should then indicate to the LPA whether or not it intends to make representations on it or it may simply submit representations within the 21 day consultation period.

Where a parish council has asked to be notified, as above, of all planning applications, the LPA must not determine an application before receiving the parish council representations or before 21 days has elapsed from the notification unless the parish council indicates it does not want to make representations.[12]

If the parish council makes representations that address material consideration, they must be considered by the LPA and the parish council is, in effect, regarded as a statutory consultee.

Most parish councils do engage in this way on individual planning applications and the LPA's scheme of delegation for planning determinations will set out how those representations will influence the process for determining the application. For example, many schemes of delegation provide that an application will be determined by planning committee where a parish council requests it because its objection remains unresolved.

Here again, parish council representations based on an existing or emerging neighbourhood plan or on evidence from neighbourhood plan consultations will be more credible and persuasive and are more likely to be influential.

---

[11] Section 20(6), Planning and Compulsory Purchase Act 2004.

[12] Regulation 25, The Town and Country Planning (Development Management Procedure) (England) Order 2015.

It is worth making the point that, as with any other representations on a planning application, those made by a parish council should deal only with material considerations and be focussed and objective in their aim. This too is an exercise that often benefits from professional advice and representation.

All too many representations on, and objections to, planning applications include spurious and irrelevant complaints that the planning case officer will be only too pleased to ignore. Under-resourced and overworked planning officers will only want to consider the information that they have to consider when determining an application. Any irrelevant material they will willingly and quite rightly disregard. Most objectors seem to think that if they throw the kitchen sink at it and include any possible grievance, it will add more weight. In most cases, the opposite is true – succinctly focussing on the most powerful points relating to relevant material considerations is likely to produce more credible and persuasive representations.

The starting point for any worthwhile representations is; *'What do we want to achieve from this?'* What is the main objective in making representations – is it to support, or object to, the application? Is it trying to influence some aspect of the proposed development, accepting that it is likely to go ahead in some form?

Such questions need to be carefully considered. It may not be worthwhile seeking the refusal of an application that in all likelihood will be approved. It may be better making reasonable suggestions as to how what is proposed could be improved or made more acceptable.

Remember too that if an application is refused, it may be appealed. Depending on the type of application and the means of appeal, either the original representations on the application will be considered by the appeal inspector or there may be an opportunity to make further submissions to the appeal. The more focussed the representations are, the more persuasive they are likely to be at the appeal too.

Planning enforcement complaints and investigations

Planning enforcement is the other all important element of the planning system on which parish councils can have an obvious influence.

The involvement of parish councils with plan-making and development control decisions is generally well known but the part they can play in effective planning enforcement, the principles of which are considered above in *Chapter 3*, is often overlooked. That influence may be exerted in a number of ways.

A parish council and its members are the eyes and ears of the local community and a vigilant council interested in its local environs will be better placed than anyone to notice apparent breaches of planning.

Many parish councils will want to report any such breaches to the enforcement team of the LPA and that will instigate an enforcement investigation. The parish council should follow up on that and be asked to be kept informed of the outcome of any enforcement investigation.

Due largely to diminishing LPA resources, planning enforcement teams often lack the necessary competence or capacity to pursue enforcement complaints vigorously. Where the breaches in question are considered significant, the parish council should be persistent in its attempts to have those breaches enforced against by robust LPA action.

It is often aggrieved neighbours who feel the adverse effects of planning breaches most acutely and they may well request that the parish council takes up their case on their behalf. Individuals with little expert knowledge of planning enforcement are unlikely to be as effective in requiring a proper enforcement response as the parish council.

Chapter 8: Which Way Next? ... The Future for Neighbourhood Planning

The first thing to say in this concluding chapter is that when reviewing neighbourhood planning to date all the participants, protagonists and interested parties will inevitably have different experiences, and therefore different views, on the extent to which this new regime of localism in planning has been successful or worthwhile.

By definition, localism should reflect different experiences, different views and different aspirations, each relating to the locality from which they originate. In that vein, the purpose of this book is as a general guide to the principles and practice of neighbourhood planning; a branch of localism that is likely to continue to evolve but will only do so with the ever increasing involvement of those with an interest in the area in which they live and, or, work.[1]

Neighbourhood planning ... the story so far

Within a year of the legislative source of neighbourhood plans – the Localism Act – being enacted, the Department for Communities and Local Government ("DCLG") began publishing its regular bulletin, *Notes on Neighbourhood Planning*, now advancing towards its 25th edition. This publication has provided a useful source of general information on the subject and a rolling update on the number of NDPs being made. That number is now approaching 1,000.

In the years since its inception in 2011 the neighbourhood planning regime has of course evolved. The Act that spawned it, a creation of the 2010 coalition government, was heralded by the then planning Secretary of State, Eric Pickles, as an opportunity for local authorities to throw off their traditional public sector shackles and operate more like commercial organisations. This idea was promoted in the very first section of the

---

[1] With that in mind, the author and the publishers invite comment on any part of this book, particularly that which is based on the experience of those working on neighbourhood plans for their area.

Act; the *'Local authority's general power of competence'* which empowers all local authorities, including district and parish councils, simply *"to do anything that individuals generally may do".*[2]

The political motivation for this notion, and for the detailed provisions on neighbourhood planning that followed it, seemed to be to genuinely disseminate responsibility and powers, and some of the associated financial burdens, downwards to lower tiers of the government family and with that, the opportunity for local people too to be more involved in local decision-making in key areas such as planning.

In this spirit of empowerment, the process of neighbourhood planning was intended to be simple, straightforward and free from excessive regulation or interference (even though the primary and secondary legislation introducing it has always been convoluted and that complexity is only getting worse as more secondary legislation is introduced). Indeed, the government guidance initially recommended that the examination of a neighbourhood plan (in contrast to that for a typical local plan) should be 'light-touch'; undoubtedly a worthy objective but, alas, one that quickly proved to be so euphemistic that the ideal of a light-touch was short lived.[3]

Although the prospect of a new local tier of planning that could follow a simple, expedient procedure was always perhaps a little optimistic, the ever increasing complexity of neighbourhood planning is in part a consequence of the shifting political will behind it.

Whilst the provision of locally acceptable housing has always been seen as an obvious benefit of neighbourhood plans, in the early years increasing community engagement appeared to be an end in itself. This was reflected in, and encouraged by, the departmental *Notes on Neighbourhood Planning* bulletin that was published much more regularly until the end

---

[2] As we have seen, the general power of competence under Section 1, Localism Act 2011 is conferred on parish councils that meet the conditions prescribed under The Parish Councils (General Power of Competence) (Prescribed Conditions) Order 2012.

[3] One of the very first NDP examinations (if not the first) – that of the Dawlish NDP in April 2012 – generated a 40-page examiner's report full of technicality and which, in effect, failed that version of the Dawlish NDP and prevented it from going to referendum. The Examiner's Report of May 2012, which seemed to set a precedent for many that followed, could certainly not be said to reflect a light-touch approach.

of 2015 than it has been subsequently.[4]

In May 2015, when the Coalition was dissolved, the milestone of 50[5] NDP referendums had only just been passed and there was widespread concern that the new plans were proving more involved, more time-consuming and more costly – in some cases significantly so – than intended. Neighbourhood plans were simply taking too long to make. The new Conservative government had to have quite a rethink about whether they were worthwhile and cost-effective and, if so, how the still nascent regime could be given fresh impetus.

What emerged from that review was the assertion that more houses tended to be planned for in areas covered by a neighbourhood plan.[6] Consequently, there would be continuing government support and grant funding for them. The emphasis was to change, though, from community engagement being a goal in its own right to it being a necessary means to achieving the primary objective of more housing. Commensurate with that, the DCLG had a name change. and is now the Ministry of Housing, Communities and Local Government.

Whether or not the notion that neighbourhood plans generally result in more housing is accurate, it is nonetheless a convenient one for a Conservative government that will always have to wrestle with a fundamental ideological conflict.

On the one hand, to promise and seek to provide for more new-build housing to alleviate 'the housing crisis' is one of very few politically unassailable policy objectives and certainly one that a Conservative government will always vigorously pursue. However, this inevitably means building on greenfield and often Green Belt land which the traditional

---

[4] Of the 25 or so editions of *Notes on Neighbourhood Planning* to date the first 17 were issued between 2012 and 2015. It was also clear from those earlier editions that the department put the onus on LPAs to encourage the making of NDPs and measured success accordingly, by reference to the number of made NDPs in each LPA area. This seems to be in line with the original political imperative of invigorating local authorities and encouraging community engagement.

[5] A small number given the almost unlimited potential for plans to come forward and the 10,000 or so parish councils in England and Wales. The number of made NDPs subsequently increased exponentially – many of those had of course been in the pipeline for some time previously.

[6] There is no clearly established evidence for this proposition which is therefore questionable – see, for example; https://lichfields.uk/media/4128/local-choices_housing-delivery-through-neighbourhood-plans.pdf.

Tory voters in the shires will always just as inevitably object to.[7]

Offering those who object to large scale housebuilding at least the opportunity of influencing, via neighbourhood plans, where some of that housing should go goes some way to resolving the conflict. Furthermore, given that many of those objectors are likely to be the very same folk who sit on parish councils and NDP working groups, it could be said that encouraging devolved responsibility for more housing via neighbourhood plans is a clever way of passing the political buck on a controversial issue. As we have seen (in *Chapter 6*) devolving responsibility to neighbourhood plans for finding locations for new housing is exactly what the latest NPPF does.

So, nearly ten years after its introduction, has neighbourhood planning been a success? On many levels, the answer is an unequivocal 'yes'.

For a start, in an age of huge development pressures and associated demands on the planning system, neighbourhood planning has survived and is growing. It has been successful simply in the way it has created a local planning regime that genuinely involves, enfranchises and empowers people whose only qualification for it is a commitment to the area they live in. That opportunity has been grasped by many and the 1,000 or so neighbourhood plans made or soon to be made cover a significant area.

Some of those NDPs are works of excellence; well conceived, conscientiously prepared and presented to an excellent standard. Some have attempted local planning policies that are genuinely innovative and which have never been tried at local plan level. Such efforts have been driven by the sheer will of local people to find genuine solutions to very real problems, such as the NDP policies to prevent new dwellings being used as second homes.[8]

For all that, however impressive or innovative a neighbourhood plan may appear and no matter how much it has galvanised the community that created it, the real test is whether it produces the intended outcomes.

---

[7] This inherent conflict was at the heart of the *'Hands Off Our Land'* campaign run by The Telegraph; https://www.telegraph.co.uk/news/earth/hands-off-our-land/.

[8] The St Ives Area Neighbourhood Development Plan 2015 – 2030, discussed at the end of *Chapter 6* is perhaps the best example but there are others that attempted the same thing previously, e.g. The Lynton and Lynmouth Neighbourhood Plan (known as 'The Lyn Plan') 2013 – 2028, and The Roseland Neighbourhood Development Plan ('The Roseland Plan') 2015 – 2030.

Any neighbourhood plan that survives the examination and comes into force intact has achieved a measure of success because its policies will guide development in the area by tending to encourage certain forms of development whilst deterring others, in the way that its makers intended. On that measure alone, the number of plans now in place means this regime has certainly proved to be a successful one. That said, there are a number of NDPs that have been heavily modified – often with key policies deleted or significantly changed – as a result of the examination, and to a degree that is unacceptable to those who made it.

Ultimately, though, the success of any individual neighbourhood plan depends on whether its policies work as intended when interpreted and applied to determine planning applications. It is undoubtedly the case that how NDP policies are applied in practice also depends on how well respected neighbourhood planning is amongst those who make planning determinations (which in most cases will be either LPA planning officers or committee members). Here, there is some way to go and it is maybe too early to say how many plans really achieve what they set out to, or to know whether neighbourhood planning generally is as authoritative as it should be.

Whatever the neighbourhood planning regime has achieved to date, there is no doubt that its future potential is even greater. One thing is for sure – neighbourhood planning is now very much an integral part of the planning system. Exactly what influence this new lower tier of development planning will play in the coming years will depend to an extent on how the wider planning system evolves.

The planning system in 2020 and beyond

So, at the end of the second decade of the 21st Century, what is the state of the UK planning system? An executive summary could read as follows.

Seventy years on, the fundamentals of the regime of town and country planning introduced in 1947 are still firmly in place. Notwithstanding the misapprehensions, or perhaps frustrated aspirations, of some the planning system remains a regulatory system of public administrative law that is still divided into two main functions; forward planning for necessary development, and controlling development to ensure it generally accords with the development plans produced by the forward planning function.

It is testament to the resilience of those fundamentals that the planning system has accommodated such widespread changes; changes in population, in land use and technology, in construction methods and standards, in transport needs, in the character of settlements of all sizes and in many other cultural aspects. The planning system guides, reacts to and arbitrates on proposals for development; it does not generate, initiate or in any meaningful sense even facilitate development. Developers do that.

Of course, there have been numerous changes within the overall structure, including those to permitted development rights and use classes, to the law on planning enforcement, and to the constantly changing procedures for the making and testing of development plans. There are ongoing changes to the structure of local government with unitary authorities subsuming several district councils in many areas. There is now a separate planning process[9] for, and a government-appointed commission for considering and promoting, national infrastructure projects. There has also been a huge increase in the number of substantive issues that planning determinations must take into account, from flood risk to affordable housing and much more besides. But the core functions of the regulatory system itself have actually changed very little.

One of the most notable changes to those functions is a change of emphasis – a cultural change – that the planning system should simply allow for more development. This change has of course been brought about by the widely perceived increased need for new development of all types. There is no doubt that a buoyant construction industry reflects and helps to maintain, in the short term at least, a buoyant economy.

The main features of this cultural change in planning are the presumption in favour of sustainable development and the National Planning Policy Framework, the current manifestation of national planning policy. The NPPF and its attendant Planning Practice Guidance are produced by, and can therefore be quickly changed by, government ministers acting under the executive power of the government, the PPG particularly so – as it is only published online it can be, and is, updated at a stroke with no recourse at all to Parliament. Most MPs probably don't know what PPG even stands for!

This is significant because whilst we still have what is known as a plan-led system, the workings of which are enshrined in legislation and the

---

[9]   Under the Planning Act 2008.

primacy of the development plan,[10] the making and interpretation of the statutory development plan (which as we have seen includes local plans and NDPs but not the NPPF) is again, and arguably more than ever, subject to ministerial diktat – something localism was initially intended to move away from. There is no doubt that a plan-led system subject to the overarching control of ministers rather than Parliament is somewhat of an anomaly. It is also undoubtedly the case that the 2018 NPPF issued by the Conservative government is far more prescriptive than the original 2012 version introduced by the Coalition, the stated aim of which was to *reduce* the prescriptiveness of national planning policy.

There are many very good reasons to move away from the centralist approach of over prescriptive national policies which have character-ised the planning system since its inception. Whilst the structure of the system itself is essentially sound, some of the outcomes from it have been disastrous; the result of poor judgement applied by national planning guidance that has little regard for the distinctiveness of different parts of the country or the people who live or work in those very different areas.

A good example of such a failure and of a disastrous national planning policy[11] that promoted it, is the phenomenon of the out-of-town retail park. These soulless, poorly designed places are about the most unsus-tainable and abject forms of development imaginable that only really work for the corporate retailers and fast food outlets that typically occupy them. Now, though, these out of town developments increasingly include leisure attractions – cinemas, gyms, hotels and nightclubs – in their offer-ing, further reducing the vibrancy of town centres at all times of the day. They are the leading cause of high street decline and the demise of the various community benefits associated with town centres – the internet and volume online shopping came some years later. Retail parks obviously encourage increased car use, and goods delivered to them by road haulage as they are typically located far from any rail freight depot.

The main driver for out-of-town retail parks was not a planning related one at all – it was simply to create more competition in the retail sector. The problems with these developments was quite quickly realised and although subsequent revisions to national policy have tried to put a brake on them in order to reinvigorate the high street, the damage has long since been done and the trend for out-of-town retailing, now firmly

---

[10] By virtue of Section 38(6) of the Planning and Compulsory Purchase Act 2004.

[11] Planning Policy Guidance – PPG 6: Major Retail Development January 1988.

established, is impossible to control. Even now proposals for such development only have to pass a weak sequential test[12] that developers in the sector are well used to overcoming. In short, out-of-town retail and leisure parks – the epitome of unsustainable development – are the new town centres.

So, there is inevitably an inherent tension between the centralist top-down guidance of the NPPF and the bottom-up plan-making of localism and neighbourhood planning. This is one of many rather nuanced contradictions inherent in today's planning system that will continue to test that system over the coming years.

Others, some of which this book has already touched on, include the misconceptions about the real housing crisis; a significant shortfall in the amount of the right type of affordable residential accommodation where it is needed. The solution to this is complicated and multi-faceted but essentially involves different types of housing provision by various sectors focussed on areas where there is a proven need, be it beds in care homes or affordable starter homes for young families.[13]

Government continues to take a far too generalised approach to the requirement for housing with no genuine attempt to understand specific evidence of where real need lies, even though that evidence is readily accessible and easy to analyse.[14] The crisis will not be solved by over-prescriptive policies to generate planning permissions for 300,000 homes a year that developers will only build if the economic conditions are right. Trying to force the planning system to provide for this arbitrary target will inevitably compromise the most important functions of development

---

[12] Paragraphs 86 to 90, NPPF.

[13] It is simply not credible to assert there is a general shortage of bricks and mortar caused by a constipated planning system when there are hundreds of thousands of unimplemented residential planning permissions, hundreds of thousands of empty homes and commercial buildings ripe for easy conversion to habitable condition, over a million unoccupied bedrooms in underoccupied houses and many thousands of newly built dwellings in our main cities. These newly built city dwellings lie completely empty because they are bought by foreign – 'buy to leave' – investors, not to live in, but as tax-free investments whilst effectively pushing whole families and communities out of the area they call home – that is a housing crisis – see https://www.standard.co.uk/news/london/scandal-of-the-buy-to-leave-investors-who-keep-flats-empty-8702570.html.

[14] The housing waiting lists held by every Housing Authority in the country are a good place to start – the Housing Authority and the LPA are usually one and the same council.

planning; placemaking and the provision of all the necessary infrastructure and amenities that are essential to maintaining a decent quality of life for the occupiers of new – and existing – dwellings.

The government's annual target for new homes and the stringent policies in place to pursue it also fail to have due regard to the increasing problems of flood risk,[15] the need for more efficient and sustainable modes of everyday transport and of course, climate change and the various other problems that will cause. The future planning system will have to address all these issues – and much sooner than most politicians realise.

Planning also has an obvious role to play in a whole range of social issues that are not directly related to climate change, including mental and physical health, education and poverty. The layout and density of development, the retention of trees and green space and the proximity of services and amenities all have a huge impact on human health and wellbeing and positive social interaction. Whilst LPAs and other public bodies already have a whole range of responsibilities and powers in relation to these matters, there a few imperatives for them to be taken seriously and looked at holistically when planning for future development. Planning policies often pay lip service to these issues but if considered inconvenient or uneconomic, developers will simply ride roughshod over them. Planning conditions all too often seek merely to impose token mitigation and even then, they often lack bite and are rarely enforced.

The dominant and overarching government-made planning policies of the NPPF and PPG, such as the presumption in favour of sustainable development and the Housing Delivery Test, trump what are currently considered to be secondary issues such as those referred to above. That seems likely to change. Those campaigning for a better environment to live and work in, will increase in number and become mainstream. It is no longer credible to pretend that protests against climate change are on the fringe and have no real relevance to planning when every year more and more people have their homes and livelihoods ruined by floodwater (and other environmental disasters which are increasing in frequency due to the changing climate). The secondary issues of today will be the principal and overriding concerns of tomorrow and the planning system will have to address them.

---

[15] Thousands more new homes are planned in high-risk floodplains; https://www.telegraph.co.uk/news/2019/11/15/uk-weather-ten-thousand-homes-planned-high-risk-flood-plains/.

Returning to the structure of the planning system and its core functions, the most significant change to that – in recent years anyway – has undoubtedly been the introduction of neighbourhood planning. It is maybe to be expected that a book on neighbourhood planning would make that claim. However, the reality is that previously the makers of all statutory development plans had been local authorities (whether county, district, city or unitary council) and their employed officers, and to all intents and purposes the functions of plan-making and decision-taking (planning determinations) were undertaken by the same authority.[16]

Introducing a new lower tier of the statutory development plan and conferring upon parish councils new powers to require the LPA to bring these plans into effect was indeed a radical departure. A particularly innovative feature was to enable the formation of a neighbourhood forum for the purposes of designating a neighbourhood area and making a neighbourhood plan in unparished areas. There is also scope for making a business neighbourhood plan to cover an area wholly or predominantly used for business.

This regime allows the potential for universal coverage of neighbourhood plans; plans that can be conceived, prepared, made and monitored by local communities of all shapes and sizes wherever they are in England and Wales and whatever their ambitions and aspirations for their area may be.

So, two decades into the 21st Century the planning system is still in pretty good shape with resilient fundamentals that allow infinite adjustments to the substantive and procedural details of that system. Currently, it is suffering from overzealous government interference but that is maybe just a phase and on the plus side the brave new world of neighbourhood planning offers the glimpse of a brighter future.

As the preceding chapters have hopefully demonstrated there is genuine scope within the neighbourhood planning regime for local people to achieve important things for their communities. Huge potential in fact. Now, in the last part of this concluding chapter we consider – or perhaps review (as we have touched on some of these things already) – to what extent that potential has been fulfilled thus far and in what respects the

---

[16] There were higher tiers of the development plan previously. The statutory county-level structure plans were abolished by the Planning and Compulsory Purchase Act 2004, and replaced with non-statutory regional spatial strategies produced by regional development agencies; these too were abolished in 2011 to make way for a new lower tier – the Neighbourhood Development Plan.

process of neighbourhood planning falls short and could be improved. Finally, we shall consider some ideas as to how more of that potential could be fulfilled.

Neighbourhood planning into the future

Difficulties and suggested reforms

The resurgence of centralism

We have reviewed the story so far in general terms but before considering the future potential of neighbourhood planning it is worth considering some of the impediments to progress and how they may be alleviated.

We cannot avoid the profound dichotomy of over-prescriptive national policies that militate against the fundamental ethos of 'bottom-up' neighbourhood planning. This problem has worsened significantly with the introduction of the 2018/19 NPPF as a result of its far more prescriptive policies on housing and, in particular, housing delivery. This policy position represents a marked change of emphasis and an attempt to force some of the responsibility for housing *delivery* – rather than merely *planning* for more housing – on plan-makers, including the volunteers who produce neighbourhood plans, who are powerless to affect it (housing delivery that is).

Few people become involved in producing a neighbourhood plan because they want to see new-build open-market housing on a scale the government is insisting on. Everyone is a NIMBY (not-in-my-back-yard). Any sane individual, whoever they are, will always object to development that they consider will adversely affect them, the area they live in or the value of their property. Those with a particular interest in and commitment to their area may be persuaded to engage with neighbourhood planning in order to guard against inappropriate and overbearing development and, instead, to plan for and promote well conceived development for which there is an established need.

The housing policies of the NPPF fail to reflect that balance, and that is likely to lead to one or more of the following consequences.

First, and whatever their substantive merits may be, the formula for assessing local housing need, the Housing Delivery Test and all the attendant national policies and guidance are far too complex. Whether or not they prove to be unworkable remains to be seen but it is very obvious to all concerned that this policy package is highly technical and places a significant additional burden on LPA officers and neighbourhood plan makers. In many cases that will mean a greater strain on the process of producing an NDP and on the LPA resources for supporting it, and that in turn is likely to deter some from embarking on, or completing, that process.

Secondly, these convoluted national policies are likely to lead to more legal challenges against NDPs by developers maintaining there has been a failure of the Housing Delivery Test. This is the last thing qualifying bodies need and is another obvious deterrent to making a neighbourhood plan – a plan that is at risk of being undermined by a litigious developer.

Thirdly, this national policy package may, via a process of attrition, achieve its intended objective of hundreds of thousands of planning permissions for new houses – some on greenfield and Green Belt sites – contrary to the wishes of local people. Developers will have even more choice over which planning permissions to build out and some prospective neighbourhood planners may question whether their project is worthwhile. Others will be galvanised into producing an NDP that at least attempts to guide development in accordance with local aspirations as opposed to central government housing targets.

It is to be hoped that the policy balance will swing back to encouraging neighbourhood plan making as an end in itself – one that produces genuinely sustainable development for which there is local need and approval. There is also no doubt that genuinely and effectively empowered neighbourhood plans and processes, with less overbearing centralist constraint, will result in plans and planning decisions being made more quickly – the very thing the politicians say they would like to see.

The difficulties of getting started ... and maintaining momentum

One of the typical difficulties for an NDP group, having decided to go ahead with a neighbourhood plan, is getting started with it and then identifying the main issues to be covered. During the early stages of a plan, real progress can be elusive and there may be several periods of hiatus that sometimes result in the initial interest and momentum being lost completely. These difficulties are almost inevitable given that qualifying bodies and NDP steering groups are not comprised of paid planning officers, but volunteers often with no planning expertise at all.

These problems are not helped by the fact that the detailed rules and procedures, most of which in themselves are relatively straightforward, are 'hidden' in an excessively convoluted array of legislation. Yes, there is a high volume of general online guidance provided by Locality and others and this will be useful for some but that guidance is not usually able to address specific issues or queries relating to particular local circumstances. This is the kind of support that LPAs are supposed to provide but LPA support for neighbourhood plans is variable at best and rarely as attentive as it needs to be.

The problem of the regulatory maze could be eased by consolidating the neighbourhood planning legislation into a single, principal Act of Parliament, and significantly better resourced LPAs would no doubt provide more reliable and bespoke support to those who need it. However, neither is likely. The truth is that for many qualifying bodies aiming to produce an *effective* NDP, engaging suitably qualified professional advisers is essential.

Obvious flaws in the legislative process and possible reforms

There are two very real problems for qualifying bodies inherent in the NDP plan-making process.

The first is that not infrequently an examiner is persuaded by a developer to significantly modify an NDP based on the merits of a site or sites rejected by local people in consultations and as a result not favoured in the plan.

However, the only purpose of an NDP examination is for checking that the plan complies with the basic conditions (see *Chapters 4* and *5*) and certain other basic administrative requirements. It is not supposed to be a forum for reviewing the content of the plan unless it falls foul of one of the basic conditions.

However, professional advisers engaged by developers can easily find arguments to persuade an examiner that the basic conditions are invoked even when in reality their site has simply been discounted on its planning merits – something the examination should not interfere with.

Part of the problem is that the first of the basic conditions is whether it is "*appropriate*" to make the plan, "*having regard to national policies and advice contained in guidance issued by the Secretary of State"*.[17] It is all too easy for a developer to raise at least an argument that a particular NDP policy is inconsistent in some way with an element of the NPPF or PPG and that inevitably turns into a consideration – by the examiner – of why the developer's site was discounted; a matter that should be decided by local people via public consultation.

What is somewhat anomalous about this situation is that by the time an NDP reaches the examination stage it should already have been signed off by the LPA, pursuant to its statutory duty to assist, as being consistent with an overarching local plan – that has been through its own examination to test its compliance with national policies – and as compliant with the basic conditions.

There must be a point in the NDP process, when the qualifying body is still meaningfully involved, at which it can be confident that the substance of its NDP is fully compliant with the basic conditions, or at least that it should not be subject to substantive changes or deletions instigated by third parties who have already had ample opportunity to make their case.

To avoid such unnecessary and potentially disruptive interference with an NDP at the examination stage, the legislation should be amended to ensure that the examination is simply the final administrative check it was always intended to be (hence the term light-touch that was originally used to describe it). Only in clearly prescribed circumstances should individual NDP policies and site allocations that have already survived the scrutiny of the LPA be reconsidered at the examination.

Secondly, and in any case, the related issue of the lack of the qualifying body's involvement in the examination process (see *Chapter 5 – Potential pitfalls with Regulation 16 and the examination process*) should certainly be addressed. Although this point has been made emphatically earlier in the book, it is difficult to overemphasise. It really makes no sense that a neighbourhood plan – initiated and produced entirely by the qualifying body and the volunteers supporting it – is at its most critical juncture subject to third party objections and the examiner's recommendations to which in most cases (that is, unless there is a hearing) the qualifying body has no right of reply. This also deprives the qualifying body of the right to make amendments to the plan in the light of any objections or modifications recommended by the examiner.

---

[17] Paragraph 8, Schedule 4B, TCPA.

The LPA may work collaboratively with the qualifying body at this stage and some do, but many do not and there is nothing to compel them to. We must not forget that whilst the LPA has a financial interest (government grants for every NDP made) in getting a neighbourhood plan through the examination, it will not necessarily support or agree with the content of the plan. Even if LPA planning officers are supportive of the plan submitted for examination, LPA council members may have different motives for supporting third party objections or examiner recommendations that may alter the draft plan submitted by the qualifying body.

For various reasons the LPA will often want certain development proposals – particularly for housing which the LPA is under ever increasing pressure to deliver – provided for as easily and quickly as possible. The LPA therefore has a real incentive to work with developers on such proposals, even if they conflict with the wishes of local people expressed through a draft neighbourhood plan. The LPA also has a working relationship with the NDP examiner that the qualifying body is often excluded from.

The input of developers with an interest in the plan is invited at the examination but that of the qualifying body is not. This allows, if not encourages, the LPA and the examiner to make their examination deliberations without involving the qualifying body and therefore based on a very one-sided argument. (This alone is a very good reason for NDP plan-makers to engage their own professional advice.)

This anomaly is simple to resolve. The qualifying body should have the right to make representations to the examination pursuant to the Regulation 16 publicity and then be allowed to make further comments in response to any third party representations, prior to the examination itself. Simple amendments to the statutory procedure would achieve this and indeed the power to make regulations to this effect already exists under the primary legislation.[18]

Furthermore, the qualifying body should as a matter of course in every case have the opportunity to make representations to the LPA in response to any modifications proposed by the examiner,[19] before the LPA makes its decision on whether or not the NDP should proceed to referendum. The LPA should be under a duty to at least consider, and respond with

---

[18] Paragraph 11, Schedule 4B, TCPA.

[19] Currently under Paragraph 13, Schedule 4B, TCPA, the qualifying body only has an opportunity to make representations on the invitation of the LPA where the latter intends not to follow the examiner's recommendations.

reasons to, any such representations from the qualifying body before deciding whether to hold a referendum.

These proposed reforms are relatively minor but could have a significant effect by giving the qualifying body the right to be fully involved in the due process of its own neighbourhood plan.

Consideration of these issues and possible reforms to address them begs the question of whether more radical changes to the process could be considered. For example, could the current examination be done away with altogether?

It was entirely logical for the innovative and newly introduced neighbour-hood development plans to be subject to a much simpler version of the procedural tool already used to see local plans through to adoption – an examination. The more involved and far-reaching local plan needs an examination – the scrutiny of an inspector appointed by the Secretary of State over the development plan prepared by an LPA. However, it is arguable that this vital step in the due process of a local plan is not really necessary for an NDP.

This is particularly so given that an NDP is overseen and ultimately made by the LPA acting in the capacity of a scrutinising authority. It would make some sense for the NDP examination to be abolished and to impose greater responsibility on the LPA by reinforcing its existing statutory duty to assist with a neighbourhood plan from start to finish.

The qualifying body and its NDP would still be – as now – ultimately in the hands of the LPA which has the responsibility for bringing the plan into force, but if at the final checking stage the LPA refused to progress the NDP in accordance with the wishes or intentions of the qualifying body, the latter could have a right of referral to the Secretary of State. An inspector – or examiner – would then be appointed to conduct an examination only on the issues of disagreement between the LPA and the qualifying body.

Such reform – that would provide for an examination only in a few cases where necessary – would engender a far more purposeful and collabora-tive approach between the LPA and the qualifying body and would make the statutory process more efficient, less costly and more predictable for all concerned.

Another procedural simplification that could be assimilated into the aforementioned proposals or work as a separate reform is the merging of Regulation 14 pre-submission consultation and publicity and Regulation 16 publicity (which is also a consultation inviting third party representations) into a single exercise. This would allow a more straightforward, collaborative and purposeful procedure via which the qualifying body, the LPA, the consultation bodies and third party interests would all have their respective inputs at the same time, allowing more transparency and predictability than at present.

Unleashing future potential!

Entrench and consolidate

If the fundamentals are right and if the due process of an emerging NDP, particularly in respect of the involvement of the qualifying body, is improved and made more efficient then there is real potential for neighbourhood planning to evolve significantly and to make the planning system more purposeful, responsive and efficient.

However, before that potential can be unlocked, neighbourhood planning must continue to embed and become entrenched. Part of this process should involve LPAs taking a more consistent approach to their statutory duty to support the making of neighbourhood plans and, generally, to take them more seriously. Decision-takers too, must routinely observe the detailed requirements and constraints that, increasingly, only NDPs impose on proposed development.

Culture change

There is a pressing need to restore the founding ethos of localism if neighbourhood planning is to continue to flourish. It is clear that all NDPs must be regularly reviewed; this means at least every five years if not more frequently. Almost as soon as one review is successfully complete work needs to start on the next. Many neighbourhood plans now in force are already due, or overdue, a review which in some cases will not even have been thought about. This will beg the question of many – is it worth the considerable effort required if the results of that effort are so quickly overridden, superseded or otherwise rendered ineffective by the NPPF and its swingeing approach to housing delivery?

Genuine consolidation of the neighbourhood planning regime will need a background of less central government interference and a loosening of over-prescriptive national policies, especially those on housing and housing delivery. The empowerment of local people to influence develop-ment in their area must again be the principal and overriding objective if positive and effective neighbourhood plans are to grow in number. It will be ever more difficult to convince volunteers to show the commitment necessary to make an NDP if, on the issues of most importance to them, their hands are tied.

The full potential of neighbourhood plans will not be realised if they are seen only as a means of defending an area against unwanted devel-opment (simply by directing it to the least inappropriate locations); a necessary imperative certainly, and one that will surely galvanise many into action, but it will not encourage positive place making and the build-ing of resilient, balanced communities that set, and strive to fulfil, their own objectives. This was undoubtedly one of the founding tenets of neighbourhood planning under the Localism Act.

Pervading that legislation was an unusually optimistic implication that local authorities, parish councils, neighbourhood forums and the commu-nities they serve could all take advantage of the greater responsibilities devolved to them by picking up the baton and running further than expected with it; by using their new powers to push the boundaries of what localism in practice actually means.

This is not an unrealistic ideal but it does require a significant culture change; a breaking out from the ingrained inertia and unambitious, insti-tutionalised thinking that so much of our local government and associated NGOs are mired in. Arguably, this change needs to happen anyway.

National politicians, particularly those in government, generally have very little interest in localism because it is seen as too parochial. Of far more interest to them is sorting out international trade deals that may hold the promise of a boost to the UK economy and increased economic growth. Even purely in planning terms, government ministers get far more exer-cised about flagship infrastructure projects of dubious economic merit or public benefit. Yet fluctuating economic fortunes are not the cause of the most endemic and difficult to solve national issues, and neither is economic growth in itself a solution to them. In fact, it usually has the opposite effect.

National issues that the politicians are duty bound to take an interest in but often fail to grasp are an aggregation of problems that arise locally. We are talking here about everything from social deprivation to climate change, from species extinction to knife crime, from care of the elderly to flooding, from urban pollution to childhood obesity, from a lack of quality jobs to unsafe roads.

When considered from a top-down national perspective, whether by politicians or media 'experts', these issues seem impenetrable but at local level they are often susceptible to relatively simple solutions. Many if not most of these issues, and the solutions to them, are closely related to the environment we live in, and therefore, to planning. So, it is not straying into the realms of political philosophy or idealism to suggest that the achievements of duly incentivised and empowered local communities could help to solve some of the fundamental issues in our society.

Far from being unrealistic, this is what localism is all about and exactly what the whole raft of neighbourhood planning and related legislation under the Localism Act set out to achieve. Why else is that legislation predicated on the pragmatic yet all-embracing principle of the general power of competence that encourages and, in case of doubt, enables local authorities including town and parish councils "*to do anything that individuals* [or for that matter other organisations] *generally may do*"?

The general power of competence is in effect saying to all local authorities, go out there and do it, make things happen, facilitate solutions rather than administrative obstacles ... and don't sit on your hands and make excuses about jurisdiction or typical local authority functions. If the general power of competence is not saying that, then what is it saying? What is its purpose and what was the thinking behind it?

Remember too that in order to make sure the neighbourhood plan making powers could have universal effect – that is, in unparished areas as well as in parishes – an entirely new type of statutory body was created, the neighbourhood forum. It would have been far simpler and more in keeping with convention if neighbourhood planning had been made the sole preserve of existing town and parish councils, already well established members of the government family. Instead, anyone in an unparished area motivated to do so by an interest in that area, can get together with like-minded individuals and form a neighbourhood forum. Furthermore, the law formally recognises that group and confers upon it all the essential plan-making powers of a parish council.

There are many planning professionals including some lawyers and judges who still fail to fully grasp the extent of the neighbourhood planning legislation and the potential it was undoubtedly intended to introduce. Many regard it simply as a political expedient to replace one tier of the planning system that for several, essentially political, reasons had fallen out of favour – regional planning (that itself had superseded county structure plans) – with another; a new bottom tier more easily controlled by ministers. And there's the rub. There is of course something in that narrow view and yes, as we have seen, neighbourhood planning is very much subject to government-made planning policies and guidance. But that in no way undermines or contradicts the assertion that the vision behind localism and the statutory framework itself offers far greater potential – a potential that can probably only be realised by a culture change and a fresh approach.

New ways of doing things

So, if a much needed change in the culture of town and country planning and taking a more holistic view represent new ways of *thinking* about things, we also need to find new ways of *doing* things; ways of bringing about a more enlightened focus and of energising the process of neighbourhood planning and the people involved with it.

There must be greater incentives to encourage a more purposeful approach to plan-making and better and more innovative outcomes from it.

Such incentives could include competitions with bonus government grants available for NDPs that exhibit an innovative approach of wider application to a particular problem or issue, or for projects shown to bring special or pronounced community benefits that come to fruition through neighbourhood planning, whether via an NDP, an NDO or a CRBO.

Any new way of doing things that involves and enfranchises younger plan-makers should be commended and encouraged. On the one hand it may be seen as inevitable – due to the level of volunteer input currently required – that neighbourhood plan-making is usually led by retirees.

However, dynamism and innovation are more likely to come from younger generations, from those with a real interest in what the world will look like for their children. By definition, planning – and no less neighbourhood planning – is something undertaken now to influence the future. More folk with a pressing interest in the future must somehow be encouraged to become involved.

This may well involve additional funding for qualifying bodies to directly employ a neighbourhood plan facilitator or a specialist planning officer, expert in neighbourhood planning and with the primary responsibility of helping the qualifying body to efficiently produce its plan. This would not offend the principle of community-led planning as the facilitator's role would be simply that. (Most NDPs are already subject to the direct professional input of a parish council employee, the parish clerk. However, the responsibilities of the clerk cover all parish functions and they are not usually planning professionals or experts.)

In its outcomes too, neighbourhood planning could and should aim to be bolder. As we have seen, the planning system is essentially regulatory and does not generally facilitate development. However, some of the particular planning powers devolved under localism do, to an extent, cross that boundary. CRBOs and the provisions on listing of community assets are examples of powers for local people to do more than merely plan for development that others will build.

One area that has real untapped potential is what may best be described as stakeholder investment. What should prevent any organisation from sponsoring or supporting a particular neighbourhood plan, a number of NDPs or neighbourhood planning generally?

As a formal, statute-based regime driven by ideas and the opportunity of putting those ideas into practice, neighbourhood planning is a perfect and easily accessible platform for any organisation from any sector to influence and achieve things at a local level and in so doing become a stakeholder in a neighbourhood plan or plans. Given the amount of money that most businesses, large charities and NGOs spend on publicity and marketing of one kind or another – often with less than convincing results – the opportunity for such direct involvement with, and feedback from, the public at large could be significant.

The stakeholder could provide as much or as little support, whether in the form of expert input or financial assistance, as they and the qualifying body see fit and agree to.

Whether it be an environmental charity trying to introduce universally an element of policy into all NDPs, a local developer trying to promote and have allocated in an NDP one of its sites or simply a philanthropic local resident wanting to make a donation towards the costs involved, the only caveat should be absolute transparency and openness.

Transparency and integrity could be enshrined in and guaranteed by a stakeholder agreement under which the stakeholder and the qualifying body would need to publish the exact terms of any such stakeholder investment and their agreement to facilitate it. Those terms would need to be clear about what the stakeholder and the qualifying body expect to gain from the arrangement and how each intends to achieve that. The stakeholder would fully declare its interests in the neighbourhood area.

With such information made public, all NDP consultations and decision-making would be made in full knowledge of it and against that background. Ultimately of course, so would the public vote at the NDP referendum, which would be the final audit of any such arrangement. In reality, qualifying bodies would in most cases be able to anticipate dubious motives or unpopular investments and refuse to agree to them in the first place, and it would be entirely within their power to do that.

There is also no reason why there should be any limit on the number of different stakeholder investments into any one plan. A new element could be introduced into the statutory process for NDPs and NDP reviews – a time period within which formal third party interest is invited. During that period potential stakeholders could make their pitch to the qualifying body, that would then be required to consider it, and in certain circumstances consult on it, before making a decision on whether or not to accept the investment proposal and if so on what terms.

The type of stakeholder or investments permitted need not be constrained by legislation but new regulations would be needed to govern the process for administering them. That process could adopt the same pattern as the existing statutory procedure and need be no more complicated, ideally far less so. Implicit in any such scheme would be that the stakeholder has no guarantee of any particular outcome or benefit from the NDP. There would be no recourse for a disgruntled stakeholder except, perhaps, for any breach of the stakeholder agreement.

In short, governed by a simple set of procedural regulations, potential stakeholders could decide whether or not, and if so on what terms, to invest in a particular NDP or NDO.

In principle, the concept of stakeholder investment is not dissimilar to a *Planning Performance Agreement* ("PPA"),[20] whereby the developer pays the LPA for what is in essence a bespoke planning determination service, the key elements of which – but not of course the final outcome – are agreed between the parties in advance. What the planning applicant gets

---

[20] See Paragraph 016, PPG on *'Before submitting an application'*.

from a PPA is a direct line to, and therefore inevitably greater account-ability from, the planning officer dealing with their application; in other words, the decision-taker. In essence the developer achieves a stake in the process and although that does not guarantee the desired outcome, it of course makes it more likely. That greater chance of success is what any stakeholder seeks to establish.

Just so with a stakeholder investing in neighbourhood planning. What stakeholder investment could mean is that a lot more organisations with an interest in, or that should have an interest in, the process get involved at an early stage and maintain that involvement throughout. By invest-ing in the process rather than merely making representations on it, the stakeholder will be demonstrating a level of commitment in the hope of attracting a reciprocal response from local people. That may result in a significant influence on the NDP or individual policies within it but only, of course, if the stakeholder's pitch is sufficiently popular.

Neighbourhood plans involving several stakeholders could gain the ben-efit of multiple professional inputs working together to collaboratively resolve issues as they arise, rather than litigating them after the event when the qualifying body has no opportunity of addressing them.

The resulting NDP will inevitably be a better resolved, more purposeful document that fairly reflects some important third party interests as well as, and still most importantly of all, those of local people. More gener-ally this approach will almost certainly lead to the genuine testing and cross-fertilisation of ideas and outcomes.

The way that this could work for national companies, charities and NGOs is that they could submit their own standardised stakeholder proposal, with any appropriate variations, to all qualifying bodies seeking the inclu-sion of certain specialist elements into relevant NDP planning policies. In selected cases where the interests of the organisation are a particular priority, it may be willing to second a relevant expert or officer to advise and support the qualifying body in pursuance of the agreed objectives.

This type of strategy could be of particular benefit to the ever increasing number of environmental charities, NGOs and campaign groups, many of which seem to recognise the potential importance of neighbourhood planning but nonetheless concentrate their efforts on lobbying central government. Whilst this may be understandable it generally has only a modest success rate, at least in terms of tangible achievements. Strategies focussed on trying to achieve specific objectives from the bottom up

– and then using exemplars to promote the cause – could prove much more successful.

There is nothing preventing such organisations, indeed any organisation, from pursuing a stakeholder investment approach with any NDP or qualifying body right now. There is nothing in the existing legislation that prevents that; actually, far from it – it is exactly the sort of approach that the general power of competence was introduced to encourage. The only constraints are that any such activity should be lawful (so it must of course avoid the commission of an offence under the Bribery Act) and transparent. In considering the question as to why the general power is not more freely and enterprisingly invoked, we must conclude that the necessary attendant culture change has yet to happen.

So, although the environmental charities and NGOs could even now make bespoke approaches to NDP qualifying bodies, they tend to prefer lobbying strategies aimed at politicians and civil servants. Position statements of that type may be of interest to NDP plan-makers who take the trouble to look for them but there is nonetheless little a qualifying body can do about an approach aimed over their heads at the upper tiers of government. The problem for the lobbying organisations is that such shots score few hits; their narrow focus is easily avoided by the upper echelons and all too often finds deaf ears and closed minds. They may be better gaining wider support for their objectives first through more easily accessible local channels such as, yes indeed, neighbourhood planning!

In advance of the 2019 General Election for example, Sustrans, the UK walking and cycling charity, launched its manifesto[21] which set out *"five main asks"* of an incoming government, one of which is to *"commit to a 20-minute neighbourhood planning principle for all cities and towns."* According to the manifesto this principle should be underpinned by a policy in the NPPF, and in part facilitated by LPAs compulsorily purchasing proximate brownfield sites and by a new Transforming Places Fund to support appropriate schemes.

Sustrans is a well known and well resourced national charity that has already done great things, such as creating and promoting the National Cycle Network. Its proposed '20-minute principle' is an excellent one that if universally and wholeheartedly adopted would be truly transformative

---

[21] 'Sustrans' Manifesto for UK Government'; https://www.sustrans.org.uk/ our-blog/news/2019/november/sustrans-election-manifesto-calls-for-20-minute-neighbourhood-planning-reform-to-cut-carbon-emissions/.

in all the ways the charity says it would, and probably more besides. It is clearly and coherently presented in an impressive, professionally produced document.

However, even if the recommended new NPPF policy materialised, several questions would remain. Would that policy be forceful enough to impose the principle effectively at neighbourhood plan level and, even if it did that, would the NDP policies be routinely and rigorously observed? Affirmative answers to these questions would mark a real achievement indeed but, it has to be said, they look unlikely to be forthcoming.

The kind of measures promoted by Sustrans would arguably be more likely to come into practice and, once a reality, more likely to achieve the intended aims, if they were introduced via individual neighbourhood plans and could therefore take account of particular local circumstances. Would not that in itself – regard for local circumstances – make the proposed measures even more credible and likely to be successful?

Surely it would, for a number of reasons. The first is that the workability and likely success of specific local measures can be more reliably assessed and predicted.

Secondly, any obstacles to implementation can be anticipated and resolved more efficiently locally.

Thirdly, the benefits of such measures can be promoted to, and gain the support of, local people who would have a vested interest in them. If the measures are seen to work in one locality, it becomes easier to campaign for them across a wider area.

It must be worth environmental organisations and others at least considering investing their message and proposed reforms at the heart of the neighbourhood planning system by becoming involved in and assisting with individual plans, bespoke NDP policies and specific sites.

Perhaps a new statutory framework to provide for and facilitate more targeted stakeholder investment would encourage just that as well as the inevitable culture change that would need to form a part of it.

Wider public interest and support

Coupled with the reforms proposed above and as part of the changes required for the full potential of neighbourhood planning to be realised, wider public interest and support is needed. Public participation in plan-making and even in the turn out for NDP referendums is currently variable at best and often really quite low.

So greater public interest and support would be a catalyst *for* the changes needed but it would also be a likely outcome *of* those changes. Certainly, stakeholder investment is likely to generate more interest from the public, whilst at the same time the potential for a wider audience will attract more stakeholder interest. The two would be mutually supportive. Whilst a wholesale rebranding may not be needed, the 'marketing' of the neighbourhood planning regime would undoubtedly benefit from a freshen up to usher in any substantive changes.

Planning is the answer

Attractive, well planned settlements that enable people to easily and safely access all of their day-to-day work, retail and leisure needs by walking, cycling and public transport are at least part of the solution to many social ills and impending national crises. Add in efficient and purposeful land use and carefully considered environmental protection, both key components of planning, and almost all society's problems are directly or indirectly covered by this subject area. For 'planning', read 'neighbourhood planning' and – via a statutory framework and due process – powers of governance are devolved to local people to directly affect all aspects of their lives.

Not infrequently during national elections and referendums do we hear the term 'grass roots politics' applied to various campaign groups with an interest in the outcome. Neighbourhood planning is grass roots politics in action – communities not merely agitated to influence their future but *empowered* to do so. Neighbourhood planning is a genuinely radical innovation for the planning system; it offers the potential to deal with issues that our politicians fail to grasp and to facilitate a wide range of practical achievements.

Postscript

Even if nothing of any significance had happened during its 12 months, the Year '2020' was always going to be symbolic at least.

Those looking for signs that the year was going to be ominous rather than merely symbolic noted that the UK was emerging from one of its wettest winters on record and parts of the country had suffered catastrophic floods, whilst on the other side of the planet Australia's wildfires were the worst ever and completely out of control. To many, these signs of increasingly rapid climate change appeared prescient and apocalyptic.

At around the same time – in the first three of months of 2020 – four documents were published by the government which all have obvious significance for the future of our environment here in the UK. For the purposes of our brief consideration here, they can be paired up as follows;

- the 'Oakervee Review' of HS2 (February 2020) and the 'Decarbonising Transport' Policy Paper published by the Department for Transport ("DfT") (March 2020);

- the 'Living with Beauty' report of the Building Better Building Beautiful Commission ("BBBBC") (January 2020) and the 'Planning for the Future' Policy Paper published by MHCLG (March 2020).

So when there are now more immediate concerns for everyone living in the UK and beyond, of what relevance are these pre-corona government publications?

The answer is that they go to the essence of the two central themes of this book, 'planning' and 'localism' – or more accurately 'the potential influence of localism under a resurgent centralism'. In fact, the mere publication of these, in some respects conflicting, reports highlights the significance and intensity of the localism/centralism dichotomy. They also pose questions that they could not have anticipated even when they were published; to what extent will their conclusions or even the issues they cover still be relevant in the post-2020 world rather than the pre-2020 world that spawned them? Finally, three of them at least have direct relevance for neighbourhood planning.

However, the one maybe not directly relevant – the Oakervee Review – does have very real implications for neighbourhood planners in the future because, as the report acknowledges, HS2 is supposed to be part of a massive strategic project to rebalance the economy and redistribute more housing and commercial activity to the Midlands and the north of the country. That would obviously involve the planning of local develop-ment through neighbourhood plans. Oakervee makes clear that HS2 is only worthwhile if that strategy is followed through but indicates there is currently little sign of that happening.

In fact, anyone reading the Oakervee Review will appreciate its findings – that it was given only an incredibly short time of a couple of months to produce – are marginal to say the least. The conclusion that HS2 should go ahead is subject to a multitude of conditions and caveats and even the principal justifications for that conclusion are secondary at best; the need for greater capacity and reliability on the rail network, the lack of an alternative solution already at the post-planning stage and, thirdly, that to abandon the project now would damage *"the fragile UK construction industry and confidence in UK infrastructure planning"*.[22] What a sorry state of affairs. The solution fails even to address the main problem. How will HS2 rectify under-capacity and abysmal reliability in the many parts of the country beyond its reach? This is centralism writ large – however ill-conceived and lacking in objective justification this government vanity project may be, and notwithstanding the huge cost and environmental degradation – let's crack on regardless!

By contrast, the 'Decarbonising Transport' Policy Paper informs us that;

> *Climate change is the most pressing environmental challenge of our time. There is overwhelming scientific evidence that we need to take action, and doing so is a clear priority for the Government ... [so] ...*

> *In the coming months we will work with you to develop the plan, with a vision for how a net zero transport system will benefit us all* [including]:

>> *Public transport and active travel will be the natural first choice for our daily activities. We will use our cars less and be able to rely on a convenient, cost-effective and coherent public transport net-work* [and] ...

---

[22] Paragraph 3.1, Oakervee Review - https://assets.publishing.service.gov.uk/government/uploads/system/uploads/attachment_data/file/870092/oakervee-review.pdf.

> *Clean, place-based solutions will meet the needs of local people.*
> *Changes and leadership at a local level will make an important*
> *contribution to reducing national GHG emissions.*[23]

It remains to be seen whether or not the government will succeed in, or even get close to, these objectives but the vision is there, at least from the DfT and the Secretary of State for Transport.

This DfT publication is a comprehensive, detailed and well evidenced report that addresses the carbon emissions and decarbonisation of all modes of passenger and goods transport in the UK, with clear policy proposals for meeting emissions targets in order to combat climate change. It seeks to promote public transport and details current work and planned projects in sections on buses and coaches and on passenger rail (yet contains not a single reference to 'HS2').

Also encouraging and of obvious relevance to planning, is the report of the BBBBC, an independent body set up to advise government on how to promote and increase the use of high quality design through the planning system.

The executive summary of the 'Living with Beauty' report[24] includes the following mission statement;

> *We advocate an integrated approach, in which all matters relevant*
> *to placemaking are considered from the outset and subjected to a*
> *democratic or co-design process. And we advocate raising the profile*
> *and role of planning both in political discussions and in the wider*
> *debate concerning how we wish to live and what kind of a country*
> *we want to pass on.*
>
> *Our proposals aim for long-term investment in which the values*
> *that matter to people – beauty, community, history, landscape – are*
> *safeguarded. Hence places, not units; high streets, not glass bottles;*
> *local design codes, not faceless architecture that could be anywhere.*
> *We argue for a stronger and more predictable planning system, for*
> *greater democratic involvement in planning decisions, and for a*

---

[23] Minsterial Foreword, page 3, Decarbonising Transport Policy Paper https://assets. publishing.service.gov.uk/government/uploads/system/uploads/attachment_data/ file/878642/decarbonising-transport-setting-the-challenge.pdf.

[24] https://assets.publishing.service.gov.uk/government/uploads/system/uploads/ attachment_data/file/861832/Living_with_beauty_BBBBC_report.pdf.

new model of long-term stewardship as the precondition for large developments. We advocate a radical programme for the greening of our towns and cities, for achieving environmental targets, and for regenerating abandoned places. The emerging environmental goals – durability, adaptability, biodiversity – are continuous with the pursuit of beauty, and the advocacy of beauty is the clearest and most efficient way forward for the planning system as a whole.

The report makes detailed recommendations across the following subject areas;

1.   *Planning: create a predictable level playing field*

2.   *Communities: bring the democracy forward*

3.   *Stewardship: incentivise responsibility to the future*

4.   *Regeneration: end the scandal of left behind place*

5.   *Neighbourhoods: create places not just houses*

6.   *Nature: re-green our towns and cities*

7.   *Education: promote a wider understanding of placemaking*

8.   *Management: value planning, count happiness, procure properly*

The central theme of these policy proposals is that people value beauty in their environment and achieving that – through placemaking – brings significant benefits in public health and wellbeing. The planning system needs recalibrating with a focus on placemaking, by imposing higher standards – and where necessary effective enforcement – to achieve higher quality development. Public engagement and community empowerment are also fundamental to placemaking and no longer should we accept the poor quality, dysfunctional development that results from false economy and low levels of investment.

Last and probably also least in this quartet of government publications is the rather tired offering from MHCLG. In contrast to the much needed purpose and focus of 'Living with Beauty' and 'Decarbonising Transport', the 'Planning for the Future' Policy Paper[25] – a direct counterpart to the DfT document – is devoid of inspiration or genuinely new ideas. Instead it merely repeats the same old rhetoric in pursuance of the centralist 'more housing at any cost' dogma and regurgitates old ideas that have already proved to be abject failures the first time round, whilst the means of achieving its more credible objectives are already in place.

Although only a policy paper with more detailed proposals to follow, 'Planning for the Future' makes reference to the 'Living with Beauty' report but ignores its proposals. The stated aims of 'Planning for the Future' are inherently contradictory and its rhetoric misleading;

> *Technology, the way we work and live and our understanding of the value of the environment have been transformed since the Town and Country Planning Act of 1947. The planning process has failed to keep pace. It is now complex, out-of-date and fails to deliver enough homes where they are needed. We will act to change this.*

This is an astonishing admission by the planning minister, Robert Jenrick, the Secretary of State for Housing, Communities and Local Government to give him his full title. If indeed *"the planning process has failed to keep pace"* as he maintains, the blame for that must be laid at the door of the government in power – and which has legislated over the planning process – for the last ten years; the government in which Mr Jenrick is a minister! This is particularly so given that it was one of Mr Jenrick's predecessors who first introduced the NPPF in 2012 and another who revised it in 2018/19; in both cases with the intention of securing for ministers even greater control of the planning process. How many terms in office, one may ask, does Mr Jenrick reckon his government will need to change the planning process to suit its requirements? The *"we will act to change this"* rhetoric has been heard many times before and is now hollow indeed.

In fact, the planning process has *constantly* evolved through numerous, and many recent, pieces of primary and secondary legislation since the original Act of 1947; not only keeping pace with technology but providing hundreds of thousands of planning permissions for new housing – many more than developers are able to build out.

Far from failing to deliver enough homes, in the last two years the planning process has issued tens of thousands *more* residential planning permissions

---

[25] https://assets.publishing.service.gov.uk/government/uploads/system/uploads/attachment_data/file/872091/Planning_for_the_Future.pdf.

than even the government's annual target of 300,000, and as we also know, delivery is in the hands of developers not the planning system.

Ironically, as well as the important issues the planning process simply must tackle, it is the spurious measures the government imposes that become obstacles and increase the complexity it complains about. The misconceived Housing Delivery Test (discussed above in *Chapter 6*) is an example of this, yet 'Planning for the Future' proposes increasing the HDT threshold to 75% – more pressure on LPAs to issue planning permissions that developers will simply not build out at the rate expected of them. The response to that, according to this flawed logic, is to plan for *even more* residential planning permissions.

Ironically too, the mechanisms are already in place to plan for and manage the development of "*affordable, green and beautiful homes for everyone*". Mentioned in the policy paper but a recommendation of the BBBBC, these ideals are thwarted by the pressure to grant ever more residential permissions that inevitably undermines the quality of consequent development. This constant pressure for more and more houses to be delivered ever more rapidly also undermines placemaking via neighbourhood plans and community empowerment. This is exactly what happened in the Southbourne case, discussed at length at the end of *Chapter 6*, and is directly contrary to the proposals of the 'Living with Beauty' report.

Furthermore, the 'quantity over quality' problem identified in 'Living with Beauty' will only be made worse by rewarding LPAs for the number of new residential permissions they issue, rather than the quality of the development resulting from those permissions, yet that is exactly what is proposed via a 'reformed' New Homes Bonus.

The planning policy paper also proposes new permitted development rights to allow extension of existing residential blocks by up to two storeys and to allow vacant commercial buildings, industrial buildings and residential blocks to be demolished and replaced with completely new residential development without the need for a planning application. In all our major cities there is already an abundance of blocks of flats – sorry, apartments – many of which lie empty having been sold to wealthy foreign investors who have no intention of living there; the 'buy to leave' brigade.

This proposal is also highly questionable in view of other policy imperatives such as the re-use of existing buildings, regenerating high streets and, of course, climate change, not to mention improving the quality of development.

Relatively recently introduced permitted development rights[26] that allow residential conversions from agricultural, storage, retail and office buildings have resulted in many poor quality conversions and substandard dwellings. To now extend permitted development to include large scale demolition and rebuilding on what will generally be important urban sites with significant potential for carefully planned new development, is out of touch and ill-conceived. It would significantly reduce the scrutiny of the development control function – which is, of course, the main point of the proposals – and in so doing circumvent the influence of neighbourhood plans and the communities they serve.

'Planning for the Future' does nothing to advance localism or neighbourhood planning. To make matters worse Mr Jenrick has threatened "*the ruination of the countryside*" unless local people "*allow*" ever more housing to be built in and around where they live.[27] As we have seen throughout this book there are already plenty of measures in the NPPF alone to ensure neighbourhood planners pursue the government's housing agenda. The much needed reform of fundamental planning principles urged by the BBBBC requires a more enlightened approach than the one outlined in this MHCLG paper.

So, just before this book goes to print in May 2020, we now know for sure that this year will be more than symbolic and ominous but era-defining and game-changing. We know the post-2020 world will be very different, but currently have no idea of the full extent of how society in the UK and worldwide will change.

Yet, as ever, the answer lies – at least partly – in planning. Whilst the impending catastrophe that is climate change has, for now, been put on hold by the immediate crisis of coronavirus, there has been prompt recourse to, and implications for, the planning system.

Two statutory instruments have introduced new permitted development rights. The first[28] temporarily modifies the planning use class of pubs, restaurants and cafés to enable them to provide takeaways during the

---

[26] Under Part 3, Schedule 2, GPDO.

[27] https://www.telegraph.co.uk/politics/2020/03/12/homeownersmust-allow-build-ing-near-risk-ruination-countryside/.

[28] The Town and Country Planning (General Permitted Development) (England) (Amendment) Order 2020.

coronavirus lockdown. A few days later further legislation[29] was rushed through to enable local authorities and health service bodies to construct field hospitals and associated development "*for the purposes of preventing an emergency, reducing, controlling or mitigating the effects of an emergency or taking other action in connection with an emergency*".

To facilitate continued working through the lockdown, other secondary legislation[30] enables LPAs to be flexible in their administration of meetings – now all by online video – and consultations, including all those relating to planning. New regulations[31] have deferred all local elections and neighbourhood plan referendums until at least May 2021.

These provisions and the lockdown generally will effectively suspend most neighbourhood planning activity and will certainly interfere with the administration of the formal stages of the plan-making process from Regulation 14 onwards. There is more fine-tuning of the planning system in the pipeline, such as extending various planning timescales and deadlines that would otherwise expire during lockdown, including the time period for implementing a planning permission and periods for invoking certain permitted development rights.

All of these changes have emanated from, or in consultation with, the government department whose Secretary of State maintains the planning system is too slow to react to change and fails "to keep pace". The current crisis has shown very clearly that when it needs and wants to – particularly in times of national emergency or when there is broad political consensus for it – the government can act very quickly indeed to change the law of the land.

The most recent amendments to the GPDO, for example, were laid before Parliament on 8 April 2020 and came into force "*at 10am on 9 April 2020*".[32] Not bad for a sluggish planning system that fails to keep pace!

---

[29] The Town and Country Planning (General Permitted Development) (Coronavirus) (England) (Amendment) Order 2020.

[30] The Local Authorities and Police and Crime Panels (Coronavirus) (Flexibility of Local Authority and Police and Crime Panel Meetings) (England and Wales) Regulations 2020.

[31] The Local Government and Police and Crime Commissioner (Coronavirus) (Postponement of Elections and Referendums) (England and Wales) Regulations 2020.

[32] The Town and Country Planning (General Permitted Development) (Coronavirus) (England) (Amendment) Order 2020.

Another fundamental truth emerges from the corona crisis which is that whilst government, and only government, can change the law, most of the initiatives and actions necessary to keep communities functioning during the lockdown have been undertaken by communities themselves, by local people who know what is needed and where it is needed – people with the local knowledge and motivation that national politicians cannot possess and usually have little interest in; that is localism.

Whilst the full effect of post-2020 changes are impossible to predict, many immediate consequences of the lockdown are likely to have lasting effect. Some sectors, including high street retail and business air travel, will contract. With many employers and employees realising the benefits of home working, the technology-led revolution in working arrangements that was initially predicted 20 years ago may at last become a reality. That would transform the amount, and the means by which, we travel for work – and how we use existing office space.

These and other changes in the way we live day-to-day will have a significant impact on the three objectives of sustainable development under the NPPF – economic, social and environmental – which in turn will have significant implications for new development and how we plan for it.

The bigger picture is that the far more serious crisis of climate change remains, and with an increasing realisation that it can be abated by reduced human activity and consumption, new practices and more effective policies to slow the rate of climate change may come about more quickly than they otherwise would. Recognising such imperatives may be the key to business innovation and future economic growth.

The DfT's 'Decarbonising Transport' projections and the 'Living with Beauty' proposals are not only well future-proofed against a post-corona view of the world but arguably have even greater urgency in light of it. The same cannot be said for the Oakervee Review. In a world of dramatically reduced business travel, if and when HS2 is eventually built, what will the advantages of reducing the London to Birmingham journey time by a few minutes really be, and will they be worth the monumental cost?

As for the 'Planning for the Future' proposals, they too will need a rethink and hopefully that will emerge from consultation. Of course, there should be redevelopment of brownfield land in existing settlements but to a large extent measures to achieve that already exist. The proposed permitted development rights for the wholesale demolition and rebuilding of existing blocks will only hasten the demise of the high street and the business zones that typically emanate from it. It's all very well simply replacing all other planning uses with housing, but not if there are fewer local jobs, shops and services available for an ever increasing number of residents. Where *will* the jobs for those folk be? How will the sense of community and place be achieved if the economic and cultural heart of the settlement has been stripped out?

Answers to these questions will need an even sharper focus after the economic shutdown of 2020. The solutions do not lie in permitted development that undermines the proper scrutiny of plan-making and development control. There may well be a need to reconsider the role of the high street but as the BBBBC rightly says, that is a function of place-making. Exactly how it is done should vary from place to place through the process of neighbourhood planning and community empowerment, by exerting a purposeful influence based on local knowledge and aspira-tions. It cannot be achieved by ubiquitous permitted development rights.

More broadly, rather than seeking to encourage development with the minimum of quality control via procedural but highly technical shortcuts that actually *increase* complexity, would it not be better to facilitate the energy efficient redevelopment and refurbishment of existing buildings for planning uses for which there is a proven need? This could be relatively easily achieved under the current system, with properly resourced and incentivised LPA planning officers and neighbourhood planners using existing measures such as planning obligations and conditions to secure good design, trees and open spaces and green travel plans.

Implicit in any notion of planning for the future must be a consistent and joined up central government approach to policy making. Different departments such as MHCLG and DfT, and those advising them, must be on the same page and should issue policy statements that are integrated and complimentary.

Amidst the inevitable post-corona public funding crisis it may also be worth remembering one of the founding tenets of the general power of competence and of neighbourhood planning; to relieve the public purse of some of the financial burden of plan-making by empowering parish councils and their volunteers to take on that responsibility at the local level.

Planning is the answer and the answer is in planning ... but perhaps the *real* power for change lies in neighbourhood planning.

Glossary of terms

Word, phrase or acronym	Definition
Affordability adjustment factor	This is an element in the standard method set out in the PPG for calculating the 'minimum annual local housing need figure'; the affordability adjustment factor is applied to the average annual projected household growth figure to take account of the affordability of the area in question.
Annual Position Statement ("APS")	A means by which an LPA can demonstrate a five year supply of deliverable housing sites – see Paragraph 74, NPPF.
AONB	Area of Outstanding Natural Beauty.
Area Action Plan ("AAP")	An optional Development Plan Document ("DPD") providing planning policies or guidance for a particular location or area.
Article 4 Direction	A direction made by the Secretary of State or an LPA, under Article 4 of the GPDO, to withdraw specified permitted development rights across a defined area.
Asset of Community Value ("ACV")	Land or buildings nominated by a local voluntary or community group and included on the LPA List of Assets of Community Value – see Part 5, Chapter 3, Localism Act 2011.
Basic conditions	The conditions of a Neighbourhood Development Order set out in Paragraph 8(2), Schedule 4B, TCPA as applied to neighbourhood plans by Section 38A, PCPA.

Word, phrase or acronym	Definition
Basic conditions statement	A statement submitted by the qualifying body with its neighbourhood development plan (NDP) or Order (NDO) to demonstrate compliance with the basic conditions.
Breach of condition notice	Notice served by the LPA under Section 187A(2) TCPA requiring the breach of a planning condition to be remedied.
Brownfield land register notification	Notification to a parish council or neighbourhood forum under Regulation 8, The Town and Country Planning (Brownfield Land Register) Regulations 2017.
'Buffer' of deliverable sites	As set out in, and defined by, Paragraph 73, NPPF.
Business neighbourhood area	A designated 'neighbourhood area' occupied wholly or predominantly by businesses.
Certificate of Lawfulness of Existing Use or Development ("CLEUD")	A certificate of lawfulness issued by the LPA under Section 191, TCPA.
Certificate of Lawfulness of Proposed Use or Development ("CLOPUD")	A certificate of lawfulness issued by the LPA under Section 192, TCPA.
Certificates of lawfulness	CLEUD or CLOPUD.
CJEU	Court of Justice of the European Union.
Community asset	An Asset of Community Value ("ACV").

Word, phrase or acronym	Definition
Community Infrastructure Levy ("CIL")	A levy charged by the LPA on new development in their area, to fund necessary infrastructure – pursuant to the Planning Act 2008 and the Community Infrastructure Levy Regulations 2010 (as amended).
Community Interest Group ("CIG")	A group as defined by Regulation 12, The Assets of Community Value (England) Regulations 2012 for the purposes of bidding for or purchasing an ACV pursuant to Section 95, Localism Act 2011.
Community nomination	Nomination of an ACV made by an appropriate body under Section 89(2), Localism Act 2011.
Community organisation	A body corporate that must meet the conditions set out in Paragraph 3, Schedule 4C, TCPA and Regulation 13, Neighbourhood Planning (General) Regulations 2012 (as amended by the 2016 Regulations) – for the purposes of a CRBO.
Community Right to Build Order ("CRBO")	A form of development order granted to a community organisation under Schedule 4C, TCPA.
Completion notices	Notice served by the LPA under Section 94 TCPA requiring development to be completed in accordance with a planning permission.
Conservation area	An area designated by the LPA for its special architectural and historical interest.

Word, phrase or acronym	Definition
Consultation statement	A statement submitted by the qualifying body detailing the public consultations undertaken on its neighbourhood development plan (NDP) or Order (NDO).
Development control	The term used – as a precursor to 'development management' – to describe the planning authority function of controlling or managing development.
Development management	The term used – as a successor to 'development control' – to describe the planning authority function of controlling or managing development.
Development plan	Plan formally adopted in accordance with the relevant legislation containing planning policies by reference to which planning determinations are made; the development plan comprises the local plan for each LPA area and where one has been made, a neighbourhood plan.
DCLG	Department for Communities and Local Government (now Ministry of Housing, Communities and Local Government).
DMPO	The Town And Country Planning (Development Management Procedure) (England) Order 2015.
Discontinuance notice	Notice served by the LPA under Section 102, TCPA requiring discontinuance or use of, or works to, buildings.
Enforcement notice	Notice served by the LPA under Section 172, TCPA requiring breach of planning to be remedied or to cease.

Word, phrase or acronym	Definition
Examination	The scrutiny and testing of an NDP by a Planning Inspector appointed by the Secretary of State – see Paragraph 8, Schedule 4B, TCPA.
General conformity	The principle – and one of the basic conditions – that an NDP must be in general conformity with the strategic objectives of the local plan.
GDPR	General Data Protection Regulation.
GPDO	Town and Country Planning (General Permitted Development) Order 2015.
Grampian condition	A condition imposed on a planning permission that makes the development conditional upon other works outside of the application site and therefore not within the control of the developer being undertaken first – a common example is off-site highways works. The term derives from the case of *Grampian Regional Council v City of Aberdeen District Council* (1984) 47 P. & C. R. 633.
Household growth projections	Data produced by the Office for National Statistics based on projected changes in UK population.
Housing delivery test	The annual measurement of housing delivery for each LPA area – see the Housing Delivery Test Measurement Rule Book, July 2018 published by MHCLG and Paragraphs 73 to 75, NPPF.
ICO	Information Commissioner's Office.

Word, phrase or acronym	Definition
Injunction	Judicial order either restraining a person from, or compelling them to carry out, a certain action or behaviour.
Issues and options	Refers to the issues and the possible options arising from them that need to be considered as part of the plan-making process. An Issues and Options Consultation is often the first public consultation stage of any NDP or local plan.
Judicial review	A procedure by which a court, on the application of an aggrieved party, can review an administrative decision or action by a public body and make a declaration, order or award in response to the application.
Listed buildings	Buildings or structures listed for their historic or architectural interest under the Planning (Listed Buildings and Conservation Areas) Act 1990.
Listed buildings enforcement notice	Notice served by the LPA under Section 38, Planning (Listed Buildings and Conservation Areas) Act 1990 requiring unauthorised works to a listed building to be removed or remedied.
Local Development Framework ("LDF")	The suite of documents that comprises all of an LPA's local development documents including its Development Plan Documents, any Supplementary Planning Guidance and other attendant documents.
Local Housing Need ("LHN")	A figure, usually expressed as an annual requirement, of the number of new dwellings needed in a particular area calculated in accordance with the standard method set out in the PPG.

Word, phrase or acronym	Definition
Local plan	The development plan – a part of the Statutory Development Plan – that every LPA is under a statutory duty to produce for its area.
LPA	Local planning authority.
Making of a neighbourhood plan	The coming into force of a plan – equivalent to the 'adoption' of a local plan.
Material change of use	A change of use that constitutes 'development' within the meaning of Section 55(1), TCPA.
Material start	A building or engineering operation that is sufficient to implement a planning permission.
MHCLG	Ministry of Housing, Communities and Local Government.
National Planning Policy Framework ("NPPF")	National planning 'policies' made by government to guide plan-makers and, in the absence of an up-to-date local plan, decision-takers.
Neighbourhood area	The area designated by the LPA, upon the application of the qualifying body, as the area to be covered by a neighbourhood plan.
Neighbourhood Development Order ("NDO")	An order issued by the LPA granting planning permission for a particular type of development in a particular area.
Neighbourhood Development Plan ("NDP")	A plan containing local planning policies for a particular area known as the neighbourhood area.

Word, phrase or acronym	Definition
Neighbourhood forum	The neighbourhood plan-making body in an unparished area.
Objectively Assessed Housing Need ("OAN")	Housing need calculated in accordance with the standard methodology as set out in the PPG.
Occupancy conditions	Planning conditions to limit or restrict occupancy of the planning unit or a dwelling within the planning unit.
ONS	Office for National Statistics.
Operational development	A term to describe the carrying out of building, engineering, mining or other operations in, on, over or under land – one limb of the Section 55(1), TCPA definition of 'development'.
PCPA	Planning and Compulsory Purchase Act 2004
Permitted development	The various types of development prescribed in the General Permitted Development Order 2015 (as amended) as not requiring planning permission.
Planning appeal	Generally used to describe an appeal against the refusal of planning permission but may be an appeal against a planning condition or against an enforcement notice.
Planning conditions	Conditions attached to a planning permission.

Word, phrase or acronym	Definition
Planning Contravention Notice ("PCN")	A notice served by the LPA to notify an owner or occupier of land of possible breaches of planning and to request relevant information in relation to the breaches alleged.
Planning Enforcement Order ("PEO")	An order applied for by the LPA and issued by the Magistrates Court in cases of concealed breaches of planning pursuant to Section 171BB, TCPA.
Planning harm	Term used in the enforcement context to describe unauthorised development or a breach of planning that causes a significant adverse impact.
Planning obligations	Legal obligations on a developer pursuant to Section 106, TCPA – the term may be used to describe a Section 106 agreement or undertaking or the individual obligations under it.
Planning Practice Guidance ("PPG")	Online national planning guidance published by the government.
Pre-commencement conditions	Planning conditions that must be discharged prior to any development commencing pursuant to a planning permission.
Qualifying body	The makers of a neighbourhood plan – a town or parish council or, in an unparished area, a neighbourhood forum.
Referendum	The vote of local residents – and in the case of a business neighbourhood plan, local businesses – that determines whether a neighbourhood plan will come into force.

Word, phrase or acronym	Definition
Revocation and Modification Orders	Orders issued by the LPA under Section 97, TCPA to either revoke or modify a planning permission.
Screening report	A report issued by the appropriate authority to explain whether, and if so why, a particular project should be subject to a full environmental assessment.
Section 106 agreement	An agreement made pursuant to Section 106, TCPA to secure planning obligations or planning gain from a developer.
Section 215 notice	Notice served by the LPA under Section 215, TCPA requiring land to be cleared or tidied in the interests of the amenity of the area.
Special Area of Conservation ("SAC")	A site designated, and defined, under the European Union Habitats Directive (92/43/EEC), also known as the Directive on the Conservation of Natural Habitats and of Wild Fauna and Flora.
Spot listing	The process for listing a building (as a Listed Building) on an individual basis – often in response to a third-party request – rather than a formal review of buildings in an area.
SSSI	Site of Special Scientific Interest.
Statutory development plan	That part of the development plan that has statutory effect, namely a local plan and, if in force for the area in question, a neighbourhood plan.
Steering group	A group of individuals appointed by the qualifying body to steer, organise and manage the neighbourhood plan process.

Word, phrase or acronym	Definition
Stop notice	Notice served by the LPA under Section 183, TCPA requiring activities considered to be in breach of planning to cease within a (short) specified time period.
Strategic Environmental Assessment ("SEA")	The environmental assessment of policy, plan and programme making.
Strategic planning policy	A planning policy in a local plan dealing with strategic matters and strictly, therefore, beyond the scope of neighbourhood plan policies.
Supplementary Planning Document ("SPD")	Non-statutory document produced by the LPA to accompany a local plan and provide detailed guidance on how its policies or proposals will be implemented.
Sustainability Appraisal ("SA")	A comparative assessment of different development options against sustainability objectives.
Sustainable development	According to the classic definition – and cited at Paragraph 7, NPPF – this is "development that meets the needs of the present without compromising the ability of future generations to meet their own needs".
TCPA	Town and Country Planning Act 1990.
Temporary stop notice	Notice served by the LPA under Section 171E, TCPA requiring activities considered to be in breach of planning to cease immediately.

Word, phrase or acronym	Definition
Time-limiting condition	Planning condition limiting the time within which a planning permission must be implemented. The standard time limit is three years from the date the permission is issued.
Tree Preservation Order ("TPO")	Order issued by the LPA to protect a specified tree or trees by making it necessary to apply for consent for any works to the tree(s) in question.
UCO	Town and Country Planning (Use Classes) Order 1987.
Unilateral undertaking	An undertaking given unilaterally by a developer, pursuant to Section 106, TCPA to fulfil, upon the grant of a planning permission, planning obligations in relation to the proposed development.
Welwyn principle	A wider common law principle that 'no person shall benefit from their own deceit' applied to planning and planning enforcement in the case of *SoS for Communities and Local Government & Anor v Welwyn Hatfield BC* [2011] UKSC 15.
Windfall allowance	When predicting the housing supply during the period of a development plan, an allowance made for housing sites that come forward from ad hoc planning applications.

Index